AN
A–Z
OF
RACING
ANECDOTE

AN
A–Z
OF
RACING
ANECDOTE

PETER LONG

Copyright © 2011 Peter Long

The moral right of the author has been asserted.

Apart from any fair dealing for the purposes of research or private study, or criticism or review, as permitted under the Copyright, Designs and Patents Act 1988, this publication may only be reproduced, stored or transmitted, in any form or by any means, with the prior permission in writing of the publishers, or in the case of reprographic reproduction in accordance with the terms of licences issued by the Copyright Licensing Agency. Enquiries concerning reproduction outside those terms should be sent to the publishers.

Matador
5 Weir Road
Kibworth Beauchamp
Leicester LE8 0LQ, UK
Tel: 0116 279 2299
Email: books@troubador.co.uk
Web: www.troubador.co.uk/matador

ISBN 978 1848764 330

British Library Cataloguing in Publication Data.
A catalogue record for this book is available from the British Library.

Printed in the UK by TJ International, Padstow, Cornwall

Matador is an imprint of Troubador Publishing Ltd

*To Victoria, Lisa and Gratian for their help in various ways
to get this book published*

ACKNOWLEDGEMENTS

Every effort has been made to obtain permission to reproduce extracts from various books, journals and magazines, and every effort has been made to trace copyright holders of the material quoted, but in some cases, where this has not been possible, care has been taken both to keep to the sense intended and not to put another meaning on it. Exerpts from *Horsetrader* (Robert Sangster's biography of Nick and Patrick Robinson) have been reprinted by kind permission of HarperCollins Publishers Ltd © 1993 P. and N. Robinson. Patrick is the author of six previous books (three on horseracing) and Nick published the bloodstock magazine *International Pacemaker* from 1973 to 1988.

In addition I would like to thank Gratian Dimech, my stepson, who has been particularly busy of late, running his very successful video company, but has still found time to teach his 'wicked stepfather' about computers (after all, when I was at school we didn't even have calculators). Thanks also to Jeremy Thompson, MD of Troubador Publishing, for his unstinting efforts on my behalf; and Robert Forsyth of Chevron Publishing, who specialises in 'Ship' not 'Horse' books.

Last but not least, I would like to thank my wife, Victoria, who one weekend, when I was contemplating a more or less idle retirement, pointed out that I still had an unpublished book somewhere among my files this last 15 years. Certainly, without her encouragement, there it would have remained, never to be updated or compiled.

Peter Long
April 2011

PREFACE

Some of you will undoubtedly wonder why a particular 'turfite' has not been included here. Maybe it is because he or she has neither made a memorable quote nor did anything worthy of inclusion in these pages. Perhaps I could neither find anything of an anecdotal nature, or perhaps he didn't gamble heavily enough, nor take the lead in some fraud – to summarize – perhaps he/she did nothing to amuse the reader. I decided it is not enough to have won one or more classic races, or to have owned a famous racehorse. After all, there are such things as encyclopedias (for those of you who are purely looking for facts).Not to mention Google.

There are doubtless others of you who wonder why I have not included extracts from a lot of recently published material, such as *Lucky Break*, the autobiography of Paul Nicholls, the N.H. trainer, Mark Thiston's biography of Northern Dancer, the most prepotent sire of recent years, *Fallon*, the biography of the jockey, and Richard Dunwoody's book *Method in My Madness* – a book which he may have only had published in 2009 but, as he said himself, he had already been 10 years out of the saddle by then. The others, good as they may be, I didn't have time to evaluate this time round. Next time (if there is one), I promise.

A

AGA KHAN III   d. 1957

He built up one of the greatest studs between the wars convinced of the primacy of speed, with George Lambton doing the buying. "Breeding for speed has made the British thoroughbred, and the ultimate remedy must be more and more speed," was his maxim. His most exciting acquisition, a spotted grey filly who inherited the brilliant speed of both her parents, The Tetrarch and Lady Josephine, went for a near record 9100gns, and had already won that in stake money by Goodwood in 1923. Her name was Mumtaz Mahal, although to the Press and the racegoing public she was always known as the "flying filly". As a 3 year old she maintained her spectacular speed and was unbeatable over 6 furlongs. She formed a great attachment for a gelding, Lakers, and according to her trainer, Dick Dawson, Lakers accompanied the filly to every race meeting she attended.

The Aga Khan owned 17 Classic winners, including five Derby winners; he bred 13 of them between 1929-57, not bettered since the 39–45 war; he was also leading owner 7 times.

Having taken over the Ismaeli Imamate in 1885 at the age of eight, he held the job for 72 years and was wont to say, "It's not all jam being God." However short he may have been of jam, he made up for it in precious stones – which he was weighed against; the source of his immense riches being his then 12 million subjects who contributed up to a tenth of their wealth to the "Living God" – supposedly to be spent on good works. He became such a name in racing that it prompted Bud Flanagan, the comedian, to quip, "I am getting to be so big that they're calling me the Aga Cohen."

A

AGA KHAN – Karim   b.1936

Grandson of the 3rd Aga Khan and inheritor of the title in 1957 at the age of 20, descendant of the prophet Muhammad and spiritual ruler of some 15m Ismaeli moslems around the world. He has also inherited his grandfather's love of racing. He kept most of his horses in France for a period after his 1989 Oaks winner Aliysa was disqualified after a dope test, though he won the Derby three times, firstly with the ill-fated Shergar in 1981, then with Shahrastani in 1986, whom he later syndicated for $16m, and again in 1988 with Kahyasi.

The Shergar story is a sad one. After winning the Derby by an unprecedented 10 lengths (Walter Swinburn up) the Irish Derby, and the King George VI, the Aga retired him to his own Ballmany stud on the Curragh at a syndication value of around $18m. He was kidnapped after only one season, presumably by the IRA, who demanded a £2m ransom, and after it was not paid, he was never seen again.

His racing, tourism and other businesses was not going so well by the mid-nineties. While not critical in the light of his estimated £3 billion fortune, it is not what his contributing Ismaeli subjects want to hear. After all if the "Living God", as they call him, is going to be a businessman, he should be seen to be good at it.

Karim, or "K" as his friends call him, was married in 1969 to Princess Salima, who, as the model Sarah Stuart was rated by Harpers as one of the 12 most beautiful women in the world. However in 1994, after 9 years of separation, Karim started divorce proceedings, but not before his name had been linked with a host of other pretty women on the international scene. In truth the 49th hereditary Imam is no less of a philanderer than his father, Aly Khan, who was considered too irresponsible to take on the religious duties of the Aga Khan.

AILESBURY – 4th Marquis   d.1894

"Ducks", as he was known to his friends, had about exhausted his capital, which at one time provided him with an income of £60,000 pa, when he was hauled up before his trustees to discuss ways of paying off his enormous debts.

"And now, my Lord," said a stiff old solicitor, "you have forced us to cut down oaks in Savernake Forest that have seen eight generations of your Lordship's family; oaks that are part of the history of England and must now be cut down to satisfy your creditors. What have you to say to this?"

"I'd say," replied the Marquis, "that'll make the bloody squirrels jump, won't it now?" His debts were more than £200k (or nearer £15m in today's money).

"Billy Stomache-ache", as he was also known, was very friendly with The Squire – the wealthy George Abington Baird – until Billy's delectable wife, the actress Dolly Tester, tiring of his drunkenness and bad temper, sought solace with The Squire. She soon decided to return to Billy as the lesser of two evils. The Squire was furious and had her kidnapped, but Billy, with unusual competence, succeeded in rescuing her. This little affair caused Billy to sell Baird Gallinule – later Champion Sire – who he knew to be a bleeder (a tendency to break blood vessels). Baird gambled massively on him in the Cambridgeshire; the horse bled and lost and Ducks was warned off!

ALBUQUERQUE – Duke of (Span.)   d.1994

Best known in England for his 7 attempts to win the Grand National between 1952 and 1976. An indomitable, though foolhardy, spirit who in his own words saw the race as "The greatest test of horse and rider in the world. I said then that I would win the race one day." Alas he was condemned to fail in what had become to him an obsession.

The first time, when 32 years old, he ended up with cracked vertebrae. His next attempt some 11 years later was in 1963 when he was brought down at the 20th fence. However in 1973 when he was 54, riding with a broken collarbone on

A

Nereo, he finished the course for the first and only time, coming 8th behind Red Rum. In 1976 he had his worst fall and by 1977 the Jockey Club had introduced a rule calling for amateurs over 50, very much with the Duke in mind, to have a medical, which the Duke would undoubtedly have failed.

ALNER – Robert   b.1943

His wife, Sally, said of Sir Rembrandt, who they trained, and who was twice placed in the Cheltenham Gold Cup, "If he were human he'd be a lager lout."

ALY KHAN - Prince   d.1960

Son of the Aga Khan, he bred in partnership with his father and had his best year in 1959 when he was leading owner and breeder (through horses such as Taboun (2000 gns), Petite Etoile (1000 gns, Oaks and Champion Stakes) and St Crespin III (Eclipse and the Arc).

The combination of Lester Piggott and Petite Etoile (Gns, Oaks, Champion Stakes) was electrifying; she was a grand-daughter of Mumtaz Mahal and as quirky, as Noel Murless found when he had to exercise her with a grey in front and another behind to avoid the sulks. Her volatile temper exploded when Aly Khan's stud manager walked into her box one evening and prodded her, saying "You're getting a bit fat, old girl," whereupon she swung round, sunk her teeth into his lapels and lifted him off the ground. However, she won the Coronation Cup as a 4yr-old the year when her owner also won the French Derby and the Ascot Gold Cup with Charlottesville and Sheshoon – but sadly all three of them posthumously.

Prince Aly had immense charm and impeccable manners and a zest for the good things of life – including pretty women such as Pamela Harriman, later US Ambassador to Paris, or the ex Mrs Randolph Churchill as she was in 1947, followed by his second wife Rita Hayworth, the actress, and the model Nina Dyer;

all of which kept him in the headlines and ultimately out of the line of succession. The racing public adored him and his charm extended to an ability to pacify outraged husbands – even those who had vowed to kill him. On his father's death he bought out the inherited interests of the Begum and his half-brother Sadruddin, and for a short time controlled an empire, which at his untimely death in a car crash near Paris, included 10 studs in Ireland and France and 100 broodmares, excluding his American interests.

QUEEN ANNE 1702-1714

We owe Royal Ascot to Anne who instructed a course to be prepared at Ascot at a cost of £558 and donated a Queen's Plate of 100gns. This was first competed for in 1712, attended by the Royal Family and a following of fashionable society – as it is to this day. The Hardwicke, Coventry, Jersey, Bessborough, Chesham and Cork and Orrery Stakes are all named after former Masters of the Queen's Buckhounds.

Anne was a martyr to gout from an early age, which caused her to be carried in a sedan chair to her Coronation. She had 17 children – none of whom survived her – by the dim Danish Prince Georg, of whom her uncle, King Charles II, said: "I've tried him drunk – I've tried him sober, but there's nothing to him."

Anne won a King's Plate at York, with her horse Star, the Friday preceding her death – the last Queen to do so before King George VI's wife Elizabeth – the late Queen Mother – did so in 1947.

ARCHER – Fred   d.1886.

Died at the age of 29, "The Tinman", so called by the racecrowds because of the huge amount of money they thought he had won in bets, both for himself and others. His retainers and fees alone amounted to over £100,000 and it is said that

A

no jockey lost fewer races he might have won. His courage was best displayed in Bend Or's Derby win of 1880, when not only riding with one hand disabled, after being savaged by Muley Edris in the May, but he was driven into the rails at Tattenham corner and rode for 50yds with his left leg on his horses neck. Sadly the strain of continuous wasting led to his death before he was 30 in 1886. Some say he committed suicide, but it is more likely that he was delirious with typhoid fever when he shot himself with a gun, which he kept in his bedside table. Ironically it was a gun given to him 13 years previously by the trainer of Stirling on whom he had just won the Liverpool Autumn Cup.

Over such a short period he rode the astonishing number of 2447 winners – including 21 English Classics. His record number of wins in a season was 241.

The most famous of all the Victorian Flat jockeys, he headed the list of winning jockeys for his last 13 seasons; quite a feat even without his weight problems. He often had to lose half a stone in 24 hours by the aid of "physic" and Turkish Baths, and from 1878 to the end of his career (1886) he could never ride at less than 8st.7lb.

A clever and close observer of life, Fred, according to his close friend Capt. Machell, once said to him regarding the sporting Duchess of Montrose, who had just proposed marriage, "I don't think I had better do it, do you, Capt.? And anyhow it wouldn't make me a Duke!"

After he was savaged by Muley Edris, Lord Falmouth, the horse's owner, took him to some of the best men in London, but they seemed unable to get his arm right. Eventually he was advised to see Sir James Paget, the surgeon, who bound up the wound. Fred asked him if he would be fit for the Derby. "Yes I think you can go" said Sir James. "Actually, I meant shall I be fit to ride?" replied Fred. "Better drive, better drive," said the surgeon, who was quite unaware of Archer's profession. On being told he was eager to know how much he would lose if he failed to fulfil his engagement, Archer said, "About £2000" (about £160,000 today). "I only wish my profession were half as profitable as yours," said the eminent man.

ARMYTAGE – Marcus   b.1964

Won the 1990 Grand National and Whitbread on Mr Frisk and has written a column in one of the dailies for a number of years. In that role he has come by some wonderful one-liners, mainly in the Owners and Trainers bar, as when he commented on former jockey Clare Bryan's new company Kinky-Monkey, selling fetish clothing. "A friend asked her to make some leather cuffs, and one thing led to another."

He also wrote of Jimmy George, marketing director of Tattersalls, at Santa Anita for the Breeder's Cup in 2009, who at 45 looked 10 years younger. When asked to produce some I.D. by a barmaid before she would serve him a drink, he was like the proverbial dog with two tails.

Q. "Why do you drink so much whiskey?" A. "It's the taste of the water – not the whiskey." On being dressed down by his wife for passing on state secrets, one man replied "Darling, secrets are things you tell to one person at a time."

A friend of his asked a West Country trainer how much he wanted for a certain point to pointer, who replied, "I think I'm going to frighten you by asking £3000." "In that case," said the friend, "I'm going to frighten you even more by offering £300." "Well," said the trainer, "I'm going to terrify you by accepting your offer."

He also wrote of the 2009 Velka Pardubicka – the world's toughest jump race held in the Czech Republic – that it had been won by the world's oldest professional jump jockey, 57yr old Josef Vana on Tiumen; a tactical masterpiece by the 5th time winner as a jockey, 6th as a trainer, riding his 23rd race.

ARMSTRONG – Frederick "Sam"   d.1983

Although he started training at Middleham in Yorkshire, he was keen to move south, which he did in 1946 at the invitation of the Maharajah of Baroda, to Warren Place – now Henry Cecil's yard – in Newmarket. The year before, he had purchased an own brother to Dante for him at a record £28,000gns who, as Sayajirao, won the Irish Derby and the St. Leger with Edgar Britt up. When Baroda died at the age of 48, Armstrong said of him, "Poor chap, they were all after him. He died a victim of wine and women." He also won the 2000gns in 1948 with My Babu ridden by Charlie Smirke for the same owner.

Sam was a great tutor of apprentices, like Willie Snaith, who was top of the 1949 table. Sam said, "I like them to weigh no more than 4st. 7lb. at the age of 14."

ASMUSSEN – Brian "Cash" (US)   b. 1962

Top ranking American jockey based in France since 1982, several times French champion, who has made a habit of coming over here and making off with our top prizes, particularly at Royal Ascot.

Of Lingfield and Epsom he said, "The first time a French horse comes to the top of the hill, he's going to think the earth has dropped from under him. The only time horses here meet anything that steep is when they come down the ramp out of the horsebox". He was the first American to ride a winner for the Queen when partnering Reflection at Chepstow.

In 1977 he changed his name to "Cash" – presumably to reflect his ability to garner the "folding stuff". After all in the five years preceding his move to France to ride Stavros Niarchos' horses he did win $20m on American tracks! However Cash believes the greatest challenge is to form a true partnership with a horse and ride according to their needs. "I don't think you have to blow up a mountain to move the sonofabitch – you might be able to just pick it up and ease it over."

ASMUSSEN – Steve (US)   b.1965

The first U.S. trainer to send out 500 winners, in the 2004 season. He said, "I understand it's a vain act, but one I'll be proud of."

ASTAIRE – Fred   d. 1987

Film star and master of the dance linked anecdotally with another dancer and entertainer, Freddie Starr, through one of photographer Patrick Lichfield's dimmer, but nonetheless glamourous model girlfriends. On hearing at breakfast that Fred Astaire had just died, as reported in the morning papers, she exclaimed, "What a shame, he was so young!" Having never heard of Fred Astaire, she mistakenly thought they were talking about Freddie Starr, of whom she was a fan. Astaire was in his eighties.

Both artists co-incidentally were racehorse owners; Astaire with a few good winners in England before the war and a great punter besides – aided and abetted by his friend the jockey Jack Leach. When Jack rode Adam's Apple to win the 1927 Guineas, beating Call Boy, the future Derby winner, he told Fred, "Don't be a mug all your life – back Call Boy, he's a certainty." However, when he came out of the weighing room afterwards Fred was grinning and jumping about like a wild man and said, "You don't think I'd listen to you do you? I had a tenner on at twenties."

Starr confines his activities to steeplechasing and reached his zenith by winning the 1994 Grand National with Miinnihoma.

ASTLEY – Sir John   d. 1894

An exemplary Victorian turfite and sportsman. In 1879, at 16 st. 6 lb. on the 6 yr. old Drumhead he beat Mr Alexander on Briglia, 16 st., for 500 sovereigns over a mile and a half at Newmarket. In 1881, the year his best horse Peter won both the Hunt Cup, after stopping for a kick at the half-way stage, and the Hardwicke Stakes, as well as running in the Gold Vase, all three engagements over the one Royal Ascot meeting, he appeared in the Royal enclosure wearing a short coat. The Prince (later Edward VII) took exception to this and told him he should wear a tail coat. So the "Mate", as he was always called, appeared the next day with a pair of large buttons sewn on the back of the same coat. He showed himself to the Prince, saying he hoped His Highness would be satisfied; luckily the Prince saw the funny side of it.

B

BAERLEIN – Richard   d. 1995

A great racing journalist and tipster who having urged his readers to back Shergar at 20-1 for the 1981 Derby, duly named his new Sussex house after the horse that paid for it. He also tipped Morston to win the 1973 Derby; he obliged at 25-1. He was a fearless critic of the Jockey Club, once observing, "It took 15 years of pressure to get a photo-finish camera, 20 years for overnight declarations, and 15 years for starting stalls. Workers didn't start the 'go-slow'; the Jockey Club got in first and subsequently patented it."

His father, an amateur racquets champion, once for a bet played and beat a pro, using a policeman's truncheon instead of a racquet. He also retired to his library at the beginning of one weekend, with coffee and sandwiches to decide whether there was an afterlife. He emerged on the Sunday evening, declaring – "No better than 7-4 against." Richard, a great oyster enthusiast, once claimed he'd consumed 12 dozen at a sitting. Richard wrote in *The Observer* in 1978, "Artificial Insemination is a crazy idea, who wants 100 Mill Reefs anyway?"

BAILEY – Sir Abe (S.A.)   d.1940

A South African owner/breeder on a lavish scale over here, who kept a number of trainers on the hop, having made a huge fortune in the SA gold rush alongside the Joels, and gambled equally hugely, losing about £1m on the British Turf. He rarely put less than £5000 on one of his own horses, which he frequently sold *en bloc* if they were not good enough. Son-in-Law is thought to have won him about

£200,000 when he won the 1915 Cesarewitch and went on to sire countless brilliant winners. In all he won 400 races in Britain worth £300k. He was a member of the Jockey Club and the following quote assures him of a place in racing history. "It is said that all those who go racing are rogues and vagabonds. This may not be true – but it is true that all rogues and vagabonds go racing."

BAFFERT – Bob (US)   b. 1953

U.S. trainer said, "That's the beauty about losing. Everybody drops you like a burnt match." "I'm not superstitious, but I have this thing about black cats. When I was walking Point Given from the barn to the track, a black cat bolted in front of us. I froze. We were the favourite and finished fifth." A reported saying from the not at all superstitious trainer about his 2001 Kentucky Derby loser.

BAILEY – Jerry (US)   b. 1957

Jockey who had won 15 consecutive races on Cigar, said of him to *The Independent* in January 2006, "I didn't get into this game because I loved horses. But when I found him I came to love horses. He was so genuine, so charismatic."

When he was 48 and about to go onto TV in January 2006, he said: "Though I miss the thrill of the physical competition which I have been accustomed to for the past 31 years, this new seat will be far less dangerous than the old one. It also includes lunch."

BAILEY – Kim   b. 1953

After winning the 1990 National with Mr Frisk, jump trainer Kim failed to break his Cheltenham Festival duck until 1995 – his 18th season – when he did so in spectacular fashion with a Champion Hurdle (Alderbrook) and a Gold Cup (Master Oats).

By a strange coincidence, both David 'Duke' Nicholson and Josh Gifford both took 18 years to train their first Festival winner. But as Kim said, "I'm not that concerned that I have never trained a Festival winner before. Many of my rivals have never trained a Grand National winner."

Alderbrook, who was a Group class performer on the Flat with Julie Cecil, actually won the Champion after only his third outing over obstacles.

BAIRD – George Alexander   d. 1893

Died at the comparatively young age of 31. A Scots multi-millionaire, who was shunned by late Victorian society, both for his lack of manners and the low-life he cultivated, and who George Lambton described as, "A good judge of horses, but a damn bad judge of men." His income was about £200k pa (£16m. today) and when asked once how many horses he had in training, he replied, "Damned if I know."

His ambition was to become a leading gentleman rider and he rode anywhere he could get a ride as a Mr Abington (to fool his Trustees), but he was known as "The Squire" to his cronies and the racing public. He was both disliked by his peers for his predatory sexual activities, and by his fellow jockeys for his habitual rough riding. In 1882 having threatened to put the Earl of Harrington over the rails in a Hunters Flat race if he didn't give way – he was reported for foul riding by Harrington, who lost his temper when, afterwards in the weighing room, the squire had drawled by way of an apology, "My mistake, my Lord. I took you for a farmer." This led to his being warned off by the Jockey Club.

After his reinstatement two years later, he won both the 1887 Derby (Merry Hampton) and the Gentleman Rider's Championship, in the same year which meant a sight more to him!

Ever keen to seduce a married lady, he openly befriended the actress wife of his erstwhile friend – the Marquis of Ailesbury – another dissolute young man.

However she quickly tired of him and returned to her husband, whereupon the Squire had her kidnapped. The Marquis, with unusual competence, managed to rescue her and got his own back by selling him at auction a wrong 'un (Gallinule), on which Baird lost a fortune in the Lincolnshire of 1889. Having disposed of him for only £900, the horse later became Champion Sire in 1904 and 1905 for his new owner, breeding Triple Crown winner Pretty Polly.

BALDING – Andrew b. 1972

The jockey turned trainer, brother of Clare Balding, the BBC presenter, is quoted as saying, "I had a dream that his bridle broke before the start and I had to borrow one and then the horse won. Quite bizarre – it's what actually happened," trying to convince himself that his horse Phoenix Reach had actually won the Hong Kong Vase.

BALDING – Clare b. 1971

"Premature ejockulation," the BBC commentator's graphic description of an unseated jockey, 2007.

BALL – Alan d. 2007

Ex-Arsenal and 1966 World Cup hero who became an owner while he managed Southampton, had his first horse Daxel with Barry Hills. Piggott rode it into 4th place and Ball asked him afterwards what he thought of his future. Lester looked him straight in the eyes and said, "Glue."

Ball was also in a syndicate with ticket tout Stan Flashman and footballer Peter Marinello, which owned the aptly named Go Go Gunner. The horse was running in a Newmarket maiden, which Piggott said he would win and Ball had £200 on when it romped home. Although he had a broken leg, Alan was determined to lead him in, hobbling all the way to the winner's enclosure. " It was the greatest day of my life," he said, "even better than Wembley."

BARBOUR – Frank

Eccentric Irish trainer and wealthy linen thread manufacturer from Co. Meath where he had replicas of several of our famous fences laid out on his gallops. This enabled him to send out Koko to win the 1926 Gold Cup and produced Easter Hero, whom he sold in 1928 to Capt Lowenstein for £7000 with a £3000 contingency payment if he won the National – about £320,000 today. After three false starts Easter Hero set off in the lead, treating all with disdain until he took off outside the wings of an open ditch and landed plumb on top.

Easter Hero proceeded to win the Gold Cup two years running in 1929-30. Not bad for an extremely inaccurate jumper, albeit with ability, when Barbour bought him from his impoverished owner. However, he only won one race for his new owner, who was lost without trace while flying over the North Sea. He was then sold for the second time in a year to Jock Whitney, the American millionaire.

BARNES – Simon

"Horses will break your bones, your bank and your heart." His quote in *The Times*, November 2005.

BARRY – Ron   b. 1943

Champion jump jockey who rode the Dikler to victory in the 1973 Gold Cup. Now an inspector of courses, he described his reason for retiring after his final winning ride at Ayr in 1984 on the aptly named Final Argument: "I wanted to go out on a winner – not a stretcher."

At the same meeting Ron led a jockey's chorus of, "Show me the way to go home." As he explained afterwards, "A couple of lengths covered the field for the first half mile and I thought the proceedings needed livening up a bit, so I started singing. Somebody else joined in, then another and pretty soon we were all on a top note."

He rode Red Rum at Haydock Park in 1978, the year after his 3rd and last Grand National win, and is quoted as saying, "I know he doesn't like it; he knows he doesn't like it; and he knows I know he doesn't like it."

BASTIMAN – Robin   b. 1950

Trainer, when asked by *The Spectator* in August 2006 what he felt about his sprinter Borderlescott, said "I soon knew he was a good horse because I've got so many bad ones."
"I've got plenty of flat caps but I ain't got a topper," the Weatherby trainer revealed his hope for a first Royal Ascot runner in 2006.
After his biggest success with Borderlescott in the 2006 Stewards Cup, the modest trainer credited his children, Harvey and Rebecca, for his victory and commented, "I am really only the tractor driver these days."

BECHER – Capt. Martin   d.1864

Apart from winning the Vale of Aylesbury (1834) and the Cheltenham (1837) Steeplechases he is chiefly remembered for his fall from Conrad into the first of the two great brooks at Aintree in the first Grand National of 1839, which henceforward bore his name. The second was named after Mr Power's Irish horse Valentine, who also deposited his rider into the water.

Capt. Becher was a very athletic chap whose party trick was to get round a room without touching the floor. Unfortunately, he had to retire in 1847 after a very bad fall – from his horse, that is, not from the furniture.

B

BELL – Michael   b. 1960

The Newmarket trainer, showing a certain amount of false modesty when his horse Motivator won the Derby, is reported to have said according to the *Racing Post* in 2005, "I am so lucky to have had this horse and not ballsed it all up."

BENNET – Capt. "Tuppy"   d. 1924

Top-flight amateur rider who won the 1923 Grand National on Sergeant Murphy. In the same year as leading amateur he was only one winner behind the leading pro. F.B. Rees.

He was chased round the paddock by the redoubtable Mrs Hollins with an umbrella on one occasion, after he had remounted her horse, Turkey Buzzard, no less than four times in the National. Sadly he will also be remembered for posthumously instigating the introduction of compulsory crash helmets, after he was fatally kicked in the head after a fall at Wolverhampton, at the comparatively young age of 29.

BENSON – Charles   d. 2002

Racing correspondent for the *Daily Express* (The Scout) during the seventies when he won the *Sporting Life* naps table – the tipster's championship – in 1977. He was also well known as a seriously good backgammon player and a heavy punter. An Old Etonian and habitue of the Claremont Club, he was also one of the Lucky Lucan set, and presumably to his dying day was one of the guardians of the secret of his whereabouts.

At one time or another he was part of both the Karim ("K") and Sally Aga Khan, and the Robert and Susan Sangster, entourages, and was known for never betraying a confidence. On one occasion to pacify K, who had read a trumped up story involving Sally in the William Hickey gossip column, he signed an affidavit against his own paper, only to be suspended by his editor, before he could turn the tables on "that little toad Dempster" the Hickey reporter, and be reinstated. He was squiring Lady Charlotte Curzon around at the time, but was banned from the house by her father, Lord Howe. Three years later when the old gentleman was soliciting his help when the press were coupling her name with George Wright, a petty criminal found dead in his bed in suspicious circumstances, he gave the rather ludicrous explanation for the ban as, "Nothing personal, I assure you. It was just that we are a totally motor-car family and you are a horse man. No more than that."

Always broke by the standards of the company he kept, some were happy to entertain him for his acerbic wit, others for his services as a social consultant.

BENTINCK – Lord George   d. 1848

Early Victorian owner and gambler and second son of the Duke of Portland. On the eve of the 1843 Derby he backed a horse of his to win £120,000, then on the morning of the race laid off his bet to restrict his outlay to £7000 – just as well as the horse failed to get a place. However he still landed £30,000 on the winner, Cotherstone. In 1845 he was actually £100,000 (£17m) ahead on betting alone. According to his cousin Greville, "Lord George desired to win, not so much for the money as for the trophy of success after a great coup." An unlikely story, as by 1841 he had 60 horses in training, another 100 at stud and 3 large training establishments, and he relied on betting to keep it all going.

He spent the last 24 years of his life promoting and organising racing at Goodwood, which as the Senior Steward of the Jockey Club from 1821, he was well able to do. During this period he revolutionised the Start with his "advance" flag, although there were still 16 false starts in the 1840 Oaks. He also forced trainers and jockeys to come out on time for races, and much more. However, Lord George was not above running up the odds himself, as he did with his horse Elis. Ten days before the 1836 Doncaster St Leger, when the horse was known to be 250 miles away in Sussex, the bookmakers happily laid him 12-1 for the race, knowing the horse couldn't walk the distance in the time. However, Bentinck and his trainer, the notorious John Day, transported Elis in a van pulled by 6 horses at 80 miles a day. The first " Horsebox" arrived in Doncaster 2 days before the race, which Elis won easily.

After selling all his bloodstock to devote himself to Parliament, Surplice, whom he had bred himself, immediately won the 1848 Derby. Afterwards he groaned to Disraeli, "All my life I have been trying for this and for what have I sacrificed it?" He was dead before the year was out.

BETHELL – James   b. 1952

Trainer. Paying tribute to the presenter of Channel 4's Countdown, he said of Richard Whitely, keen racegoer and owner and one time mayor of Wetwang, "He loved his racing and I'm so glad we managed to have a winner for him with Old Mare of Wetwang."

BEAVERBROOK – Lady Marcia   d. 1994

A Greek Cypriot tobacco merchant's daughter, she was widowed by two millionnaires – Sir James Dunn who left her an estimated $33m and in 1964 by the press baron, who left her nothing, stating in his will that she was already adequately provided for. Nothing daunted she spent over £1.5m in the sales ring between 1966 and 1976, often with little to show for it. She spent a then record 81,000gns on Bigivor, who never even raced for her, and a further 202,000gns for a Mill Reef colt, Million, whose winnings amounted to £4,376. Her horse Terimon was second to Nashwan in the 1989 Derby at 500-1; bookmakers learned that day not to offer those kind of odds again.

She loved her horses dearly – "I don't mind about the jockeys," she would say. "They are paid to be there, but nobody asked the horses." After Rampage died in a race at Ascot she walked down the course with her trainer Dick Hern to bid him farewell – in floods of tears. She also loved dogs and once chartered a plane to fly her and her two puppies to Canada to save them travelling freight on a commercial flight. It was her practice to use seven letters in naming her horses and her colours were, not surprisingly, predominantly beaver brown.

BERNARD – Jeffrey   d. 1997

The well-known punter and, for a time until being found paralytic at an official engagement, racing hack for the *Sporting Life*, was also an author who wrote the Low Life column in the *Spectator*. His anecdotes are legion, being a keen observer of mankind – more often than not from a barstool.

While with the *Life* he wrote, commenting on the Cheltenham Festival, "It attracts the best crumpet of any racecourse in England – mind you, you've got to be a millionaire to talk to any of it, but if all the mink at Cheltenham was stitched together, it would cover the course."

He comments that Doug Marks, the Lambourn trainer, was wont to flannel his owners, of which Jeffrey was one with a part-share in a filly called Deciduous, with such encouraging words as "…she galloped so well at work this morning, she's bound to win a race," or "… he's jumping out of his skin," or again, "he can catch pigeons on the gallops." Bernard's favourite bit of exaggeration was the one a lot of trainers use after a win, even if the horse only got up by a neck: "He won doing handsprings." Best of all is the definitive statement he quotes from the hardnosed bookie discussing the many victims claimed by the Turf – "Yes," he said, "this racing game tames bleedin' tigers."

The laureate of Soho, a regular of the Coach and Horses, where he drank Vodka, lime and soda in copious quantities until diabetes forced him to give up the lime, was the

B

eponymous hero of *Jeffrey Bernard is Unwell*, and was further celebrated by the refrain "Jeff bin in?" in Michael Heath's cartoon strip The Regulars in *Private Eye*.

The late racing journalist and author who devoted his life to alcohol, once, when he owed Victor Chandler senior twenty quid in unpaid bets and had been avoiding him for weeks, he saw him come into the Member's bar at Newbury and hid under a table. A few minutes later a hand appeared under the table clutching an enormous whisky. Victor's face followed saying, "Have a drink Jeff, I thought you might be thirsty!"

He tells one against himself when he was with the Irish trainer Mick O'Toole, who when he pulled a filly out of her box in his yard remarked, "There's a nice little filly we've got here." To which JB replied, "She looks as if she'll stay 3 miles in time." "Jasus Jeffrey you're a fool," Mick retorted, "She couldn't stay 2 miles in a f.....g horsebox!"

Of the other sort of filly he says trainers tend to refer to them as if they were one of their horses. Apparently Fred Winter was once heard to refer to another trainer's mistress as "a very moderate sort." One morning in Lambourn, seeing what he took for a truly magnificent carthorse cropping the grass verge, he said to the man holding it " I bet he could plough a field by himself in 10 minutes." " This is the Dikler," said the offended stable lad. It was five years before Fulke Walwyn would speak to him again and the horse went on to win the Gold Cup.

His finances improved when he began the "Low Life" column in the *Spectator* in 1978, but this didn't deter him from cadging off his friends or making an illegal book in the Coach and Horses, which led to a mere 9 policeman and 3 customs officers descending on him in 1986 to make an arrest. As he wrote in his own obituary, "He gradually drifted into writing a series of personal and, at times, embarassing columns about his own wretched life." The late and now permanently unwell journalist wrote, "What a pity people don't take as much trouble with their own breeding as intelligent race horse owners do." "When I die, I'd like to be buried at Chester, if there's room." He wasn't; so perhaps it was full.

In 1987 he said, "I once spent the night with a girl in a ditch at the Pond Fence at Sandown... perhaps I was pointing out to her that obstacles present peculiar hazards."

He said the same year, "The racing world is stuffed with lunatics, criminals, idiots, charmers, bastards and exceptionally nice people."

BERRY – Jack   b.1937

Jump jockey turned trainer in 1969 after, as he says "About 46 wins and a bone broken for every one." His rise to prominence is all the more remarkable since he started with nothing, and his autobiography is aptly titled *Its Tougher at the Bottom*. Since when he has published three more, culminating in *Better Late Than Never* (2009), the proceeds going to the Injured Jockeys' Fund, for whom he has raised a great deal of money over the last 15 years. Training at Moss Side, his first winner on the Flat was a 20-1 outsider, Fiona's Pet – ridden by his wife Jo. On 30 May 1981 the whole family were in action; Jack at Kempton and Jo and the two boys at Ayr.

After winning the Ayr Gold Cup in 1988, he saddled more winners in 1990 than any other trainer – 127 – and in so doing broke a 58 year old record for a Northern trainer. One horse he trained, O.I. Oyston, helped raise money for charity in 1989 when he was let into a field, divided into squares, each one of which had been sold off to raise £1000. The horse's droppings were to designate the winning square and he eventually kept the eager punters waiting 40 minutes before he obliged. In 1991 he beat Henry Cecil's records for both the fastest 50 and the fastest 100 winners. He has a propensity for wearing red shirts ever since he bought one at Ayr races when he was only 24.

BETTS – John

"Straight from the horse's mouth is nothing but hot air," observed the author in 1945. The same is equally true 60 years later.

B

BIDDLECOMBE – Terry   b. 1941

He was Champion jump jockey three times between 1964 and 1969. At Stratford in 1964, after dropping his whip, and failing to get any of his fellow jockeys to lend him theirs, despite his offer of a tenner, he grabbed one out of the hand of the nearest and used it to ride home the winner by a head.

Terry was a very flamboyant character, but his weakness was his weight and his lifestyle. Mercy Rimell reckoned he didn't get much sleep the night before a race, one such race being Gay Trip's second National, which was certainly one of Terry's off days. She also said, "I am sure he won more races for us that he should have done, than races that he lost. I can't say more than that."

Terry was a tremendous opportunist, though he often won carrying 6-8 lb overweight. However in France, if a jockey is more than 2lb overweight, he has to be replaced, and the night before he was due to partner Gay Trip in the French National at Auteuil, Terry announced he would have to spend the night in the Turkish Baths. "I bet he doesn't," said Fred Rimell – so he went with him to make sure he did. The next day Terry weighed in at exactly 2lb overweight. He has ended up with trainer Henrietta Knight, where he has had quite a lot to do with a horse called Best Mate, winning the Gold Cup three years in a row. In March 2006, on admiring Philip Blacker's statue of Best Mate, is reputed to have said, "Look at that power and movement and muscle. It reminds me of me in bed." No comment from trainer Henrietta Knight, Lord Vestey's sister-in-law, at her husband's slightly boastful statement.

He also said on Best Mate's death in November 2005, "I haven't cried because it was a good way for him to go." However, Simon Barnes of *The Times* said, "It was a great life, and in a way, a great death. A life worth celebrating; a death worth grieving for."

Graham Sharpe, however, in his book *1000 Racing Quotations*, said of Jim Lewis, the horse's owner, in reply to J.L's saying, "He'll be up there in the sky now taking on Arkle – and he'll probably beat him" – "He can have 10-1 with me – any day!" In 2005 he was described "As part Just William, part Max Miller with more than a passing resemblance to Charlie Blake."

BIN LADEN – Osama   b. 1957

A business associate of Osama said in December 2004, "Osama liked horseracing. But when they started playing music he would get up and walk out because music was haram" (forbidden by Islam).

BIRD – Alex   d. 1991

Son of a bookmaker and a successful owner, his wagers were well in excess of a million pounds a year after the war. But the weak markets at the smaller meetings later forced him to confine his larger investments to the major meetings.

When photo-finishes were first introduced, Alex placed himself on the winning line and saw an optical illusion prompts the public to think the horse on the far side had won. So when he was convinced that the nearside horse had won, there was no limit to his stake; he once bet £50,000 to win £5000 (£10,000 in today's money). However it was his gamble on the 1954 Grand National that has gone into turf history. Having backed Tudor Line successfully three races in a row, and put all his winnings on at 40-1 down to 100-8, so on the day he stood to win £500,000 in today's money – a record had he won. However Tudor Line had a habit of running wide on the corners, which had been counteracted by a pricker in the three previous races. At Aintree it was left off; he ran very wide and Royal Tan went ahead to win by a neck. The National was always one of Alex's favourites. "The odds are good, the market is strong and the field can be narrowed down to a small number guaranteed to complete the course." This enabled him to win £60,000 in 1950.

BLACKMAN, Mark

The *Racing Post* Weekender columnist commented in March 2005, "If it's female, aged four years or older and is trained by Sir Michael Stoute, back it every time it runs."

BODLE – Tim (Aus)

The owner of 1988 Melbourne Cup winner Empire Rose (a lofty 17.1 hands high) said, "They dig a hole for her to put in her back legs, so Star Way can reach." He was explaining why Windsor stud had to dig a hole 30cm deep in the serving barn floor before Star Way arrived to service her.

BOLGER – Jim (Ire)   b. 1941

The trainer is reported to have said in 2006, "I don't do pressure. Pressure is for tyres and footballs."

BOTTOMLEY – Horatio   d. 1933

Born in the East End of London, the son of a tailor's cutter, the disgraced MP and financier was demanding a betting tax as far back as World War I, when he was Chairman of the Racing Emergency Committee. He himself was a heavy but hopeless gambler and an owner of moderate racehorses on a large scale. Nonetheless he managed to win the Cesarewitch (Wargrave) and the Stewards Cup in 1899 when his 20-1 winner, Northern Farmer, made him £50,000 richer in bets.

One of his ingenious schemes was to buy up all the runners in selling races where there were only 3 to 4 runners entered and then "arrange" the result, having got his bets on before the bookmakers rumbled him. This worked very well until one day the horse he had arranged to win dropped dead on the way to the post; it was time anyway to move on to a new scam as the Stewards were getting suspicious.

He still went to gaol a bankrupt in 1922, when he got seven years for misappropriating trust funds.

During the court case he was asked, "You keep racehorses I believe?" "No," he replied, "They keep me." On his first day in prison he espied a racing crony, a Capt. Peel, sent down for swindling, who was cutting the grass. Bottomley called out to him, "Hullo, still at the Turf, I see?" Later he himself was spotted by a prison visitor in the mail-bag room, who inquired, "Sewing, Bottomley?" "No," he said "reaping." A rogue perhaps, but a humorous one, who died penniless in the public ward of a London hospital, after a lifetime of wine (Pommery was his tipple) and women, most of them drawn from the chorus line and installed in various London flats and hotels.

BOWES – John of Streatlam   d.1885

A son of Lord Strathmore, he would have succeeded to the title, but for a minor matter of his parents omitting to marry until he was nine years old. However as an owner he won four Derbys – the first when he was only 21 with Mundig (1835) followed by Cotherstone, Daniel O'Rourke and West Australian in 1853, when he became the first horse to win the Triple Crown.

Bowes' equally famous ancestor, Sir John Bowes, in 1622 at Richmond in Yorkshire, won a three mile race for a cup worth £12, where the owners of each of the five horses and one mare listed put up £2 each. The winner's tryer (jockey) is also given as a Mr Humphrey Wyvell.

Sir John, it is recorded, was still racing hard at Newcastle in 1633.

BOYD ROCHFORT – Capt. (Later Sir) Cecil   d. 1983

Five times champion trainer, he trained the great Alcide for Sir Humphrey de Trafford. Having won the Lingfield Derby trial by 12 lengths, he was hot favourite for the 1958 Derby when he was injured in his box, and thought to have been "nobbled". However Alcide went on to win the St Leger and the next year's King George VI.

Previously the Capt. had won the Irish Derby with Premonition in 1953 when Vincent O'Brien, trainer of the second horse, lodged an objection which was upheld. B-R was so furious that he got hold of a film of the race and hired a cinema in Newmarket so that he could publicise how hard done by he was! He also refused to run his horses in Ireland for the next 10 years.

B-R liked the public to believe that he didn't back his own horses. However, as he had one in the next race at York one day, a friend nearby said, "How will yours go here Cecil?" To which B-R replied, "Only a lunatic would have a bet in a race of this kind." At this moment his commission agent, Peter (Pierre) Higgins appeared at the foot of the stands and called up, "I've got you 7-2 to the lot, Captain." Much to Boyd-Rochfort's annoyance.

By marrying Henry Cecil's mother he was able to pass on his stables to a worthy successor when he retired in 1968.

BRABAZON – AUBREY "the Brab" (Ire)   d. 1996

Irish jockey whose prodigious feats under both sets of rules gave rise to the lines "Aubrey's up; the money's down; the frightened bookies quake…" Actually the doggerel referred to his partnership with Cottage Rake, whom he rode to win three Gold Cups at the same time as winning two Champion Hurdles on Hatton's Grace – both trained by Vincent O'Brien – between 1948-51. Both were initially unlikely winners as Cottage Rake had only won once over fences and had fallen in his last race, and Hatton's Grace was bought for only 18gns and looked it! In fact both Aubrey and Vincent had to stiffen their resolve before the 1948 Gold Cup by taking a port and brandy after Aubrey had weighed out for the race.

On the Flat Brabazon won both the the Irish 2000gns (1950) and Oaks (1948) when the Aga Khan's Masaka beat Aly Khan's Amina by a length. As his father was not at the Curragh, Prince Aly had to lead in the winner with a smile for the Press as he cursed under his breath at losing the £500 he had on Amina.

BRADLEY – Milton

"He's improved as he's got older. I thought I might do the same, but it was not to be." The veteran trainer of flat racers was referring to his horse, the 8 year old sprinter Corridor Creeper, winning a race at Haydock in 2005.

He was taking over another sprinter called The Tatling for The Prix L'Abbaye in 2004 when he got lost in the red light district of Paris "We were hopelessly lost, we couldn't read the signs, my French was zero and the locals didn't understand a word I said. All we kept getting was hookers offering all sorts of services!"

BRASSIL – John

"Let's be honest, it was a scurrilous race – I just hope we can find another one like it." The trainer on how Glabejet won at Limerick in 2005.

BREASLEY – Arthur "Scobie" (Aus.)   d. 2006

According to Gordon Richards, "One of the all-time greats in the history of the game." Scobie, nicknamed after the Aussie trainer Jim Scobie, came over in 1950 for a season at the invitation of millionaire mill owner Mr J.V. Rank and stayed on as a jockey for 17 years.

He rode Charlottown to win the 1966 "Blacksmith's" Derby, after the Wernhers had sacked Ron Hutchinson at short notice. It was a Derby in a downpour, and

Smythe, fearful of Charlottown's thin-soled feet, took the Lewes farrier to Epsom with him, as he was very difficult to shoe. Needless to say, the horse spread a plate and as one national daily put it, "Derby winner, Charlottown, owned by Lady Zia Wernher, trained by Gordon Smythe, ridden by Scobie Breasley and shod by George Windlass." Scobie's wife May also lost a shoe – in the crush after the race!

One day in 1960 Lester Piggott, who eventually beat Scobie to the championship by 17 wins, came close to putting Scobie over the rails at Wolverhampton when it was obvious he was going to win anyway. Scobie was furious and was determined to hit Lester where it hurt most – in the pocket – and chose the valuable King George VI & QE Stakes to exact his revenge, where Lester was on the wonder filly Petite Etoile. Accordingly he boxed Lester in on the rails so that by the time he had found a way out, Jimmy Lindley had the race won on Aggressor. Lester knew perfectly well what had gone on, but when the press asked him how he'd had failed to win, his priceless remark was, "I think they cut the grass the wrong way."

BRITTAIN – Clive   b. 1934

A Wiltshire sausage-maker's son, he came late to training, having spent 21 years as assistant to Noel Murless, before using his gambling winnings to start training in 1972. He was later backed by Capt. Marcos Lemos who bought Carlburg Stables to set him up in 1974. Clive repaid his good faith by winning the St Leger in 1978 with the Captain's Julio Mariner at 28-1 and again in 1984 when Pebbles won the 1000 gns, the Eclipse, the Champion and the Breeder's Cup Turf.

Brittain is always first trainer out on the Heath, because he believes "Horses tend to work more honestly in the dark." Quirky maybe but his eagerness to have a tilt at aristocratic opposition with apparently modest animals has earned him the title of Don Quixote and once second place in the Derby at 500-1 (Terimon 1989).

By 1991 he had jumped to 4th place in the trainer's table with £1.2m. in prize money including the 2000 gns with Mystiko.

Brittain said " I wouldn't make much as a writer, but I don't do too badly as a trainer."

The irrepressible trainer said to the *Racing Post* in 2006 "I know how to train, I know when I've got a good one and I know what to do with them. I'm not afraid of anything – not even when I'm lying on the ground being kicked"

BROGAN – Barry (Ire) b. 1947

A N.H. jockey of the 60s and 70s, who apparently often used a "cheating" saddle to fool the Clerk of the Scales. The trick was to weigh out with the mini lightweight saddle and then exchange it for the standard saddle held by a waiting accomplice. Once at Newcastle, by using a convenient rear window to pass the "cheater" back to the next jockey, no fewer than five jockeys weighed out with it!

Barry rode many winners for Ken Oliver before coming South to ride for Fulke Walwyn, winning the King George VI on The Dikler (1971) and the Hennessy on Charlie Potheen (1972). Unfortunately his weight problems and highly strung nerves forced him to hand in his licence at the end of the 1974-75 season after only nine years as a professional.

BROOKS – CHARLIE b.1963

Old Etonian jump trainer who, at only 25, took over Fred Winter's yard at Lambourn, where he started off as a stable lad and later commented, "I think all Eton boys should be made to work as stable lads. It would knock all the arrogant crap out of them."

However mounting debts forced him to sell the yard, "I managed to pull off a master stroke by buying the yard at the top of the market and selling at the bottom," he said. This led him in 1995 to try to market his services for his new yard owner, by doing a mail-shot to owners, a normal business practice which was seen as flagrant poaching by other trainers. One journalist commented, "How dare you, Charlie – anyone would think you're trying to run a business!"

"Champagne Charlie's" boyish charm, which also allowed him to poach John Francome's pretty ex-wife and model Miriam, hid enough ambition and professionalism to help him to a Champion Hurdle and a Hennessy Gold Cup.

Having spent £220 in acquiring Norman Williamson's jockey's board at an auction, the ex-trainer said, "Norman is now hanging above my bed for the moment and I'm very pleased with him."

In 2005 he said to one of the dailies, "Don't ask me why but going racing is what low-life bums do in New York." He also said, "Charisma has bypassed the current crop of Flat jockeys."

BROWN – Capt. Keith

The Aintree starter, who made his name a legend in what was meant to be his last race, the 1993 Grand National, the race that never was. With 39 starters, the 65 yards of tape sagged in the middle due to the weight of rain that had fallen since lunchtime, with the result that two horses broke the tape for a false start. A while later, after its repair, he sent them off again, with those on the inside getting a clear start, but on the outside the tape got snagged around jockeys' necks and horses' legs, and despite the cries of the redoubtable Captain, which were lost in the noise of wind and crowd (nor did his flag unfurl), 30 of the horses raced on. The advance flagman, Ken Evans, in front of the first fence, apparently didn't stay to raise his red flag, preferring instead to leg it to safety.

In the end the "race" was ultimately won by John White on Esha Ness – only to be declared void. Whatever blame is laid at the door of an aging army captain and a panicking flagman, the buck must surely stop at the Aintree management. How an international event like the National, with millions worldwide watching the event, could depend on tape and flag, with all the modern-day electronic devices that were available, remains a mystery to most people.

BUCKINGHAM – John   b. 1940

Jump jockey whose big moment came in 1967, when riding 100-1 chance Foinavon, he was able to pick his way through the carnage at the 23rd fence in the National, when the riderless Popham Down brought down most of the field, and keep the old horse going to the line. He later turned valet and his book *Tales from the Weighing Room* has some good stories about other jockeys.

One concerns John Southern, ensconced in a WC at Fontwell, where the doors had no locks. John, having dealt with this problem by propping his foot against the door, was surprised by the next candidate, with his leg stuck out like a false one, reading the *Sporting Life*. He had forgotten the door opened outwards. Neil Curnick, a West Country jockey, as an antidote to a terrible stutter, used to thump his chest and, if necessary, jump up and down as well. One day at Newton Abbott, John saw him disappearing into the loo before his first race and called out "Hey Neil, novice chasing then?" which caused poor Neil to hop into the loo on one leg belabouring himself.

He recounts a typical Francome/Smith Eccles prank played on Andy Turnell, where Franc said, "You must ask Steve about his Mum. She's just won a piano competition." When Steve reappeared Andy said, "Hey! What's all this about your Mum playing the piano?" Steve looked him straight in the eye and said, "Talk sense. My Mum's got no hands." Andy wanted the floor to open up and swallow him until the other two began to guffaw with laughter.

BULL – Phil d. 1989

One of the most influential figures in British racing since the Second World War, he sat on many committees, and commissions as well as the Racehorse Owners' Association. In 1947 he produced the first Timeform (weight for age) ratings for the Flat season and his organisation in Halifax now publishes annually *Racehorses of 1920* with a worldwide reputation. Nowadays a full set of Timeform annuals can fetch thousands!

His father, a Captain in the Salvation Army, was wont to chalk uplifting messages on various walls in Doncaster. On one occasion in 1901 the slogan read, "What shall we do to be saved?" below which a wag had written, "Back Doricles for the St Leger." This he did and landed a 40-1 winner and the Sally Annie had lost Phil's dad for ever. However the Sporting Pink henceforward appeared amongst more serious literature for young Phil's edification and he responded to both.

Phil has never been one to suffer fools gladly, and when Weatherbys refused the name Ho Chi Minh for one of his horses he registered it under the name Ho Mi Chinh. His submission to the Royal Commission on Gambling in 1977 included the words "Racing belongs to the people, not to the owners, not to the Jockey Club, and especially not to the owners and breeders" (63% of the Jockey Club were).

An owner who once said his favourite racing story was about the woman who goes up to the bookmaker to have a double with two horses in the same race. The bookie explains patiently that it can't be done – but she'll have none of it, so in the end he says, "OK, George, book her a double" and the two horses run a dead-heat! Along comes the lady to draw her winnings and as he pays her out he says with a grin, "Lady, you must have known something to make a bet like that." To which she replied, "Yes, and so must you to try and put a lady off a good thing."

Apart from racing his other two loves were chess, where he was unbeaten for 25 years, and once, when blindfolded, he managed two wins and a draw against three opponents he was playing simultaneously, and snooker, where even his chum, the great Joe Davis, found it difficult to beat him.

He owned about 350 horses in his time, and won practically all the major Flat races, except the Classics, putting his betting gains at about £400k. Bull believed that bookies are vital to the public's interest in racing, and has said, "With betting, what you are selling the punter is the prospect of profit, or at least the illusion that he may profit. If you raise the tax to the point where you destroy that illusion, then you will kill his incentive to bet." He also said that after half a century of the Tote, 95% of all bets are at bookmaker's odds – pretty conclusive evidence of where the punter's preference lies.

BUNBURY – Sir Charles   d.1821

The first President of the Jockey Club, and something of a dictator as it was a lifetime appointment; nor was he afraid to tread on Royal toes, as evidenced by his enquiry into the inconsistent running of the Prince's (afterwards George IV) horse Escape.

It is sometimes said that he tossed a coin with the 12th Earl of Derby to decide who should give his name to the inaugural Derby in 1780, a race he won with Diomed for a purse of 1075gns. He also had the winner of two more Derbys – in 1801 (Eleanor) and 1813 (Smolensko). But he is best remembered for giving his name to the Bunbury Mile at Newmarket. Diomed then went to America to found a very successful line, but his best horse was actually the champion 18th Century sire Highflyer whose progeny won 974 races worth £140k (or over £50m today). Although he bred him in 1774, he unfortunately sold him first to Lord Bolinbroke and then in 1779 to Richard Tattersall who founded the eponymous bloodstock auction house and the horse's name lives on with the Newmarket Yearling sales that are named after him.

BURRIDGE – Jimmy   d. 2000

Midge & James. The breeder and part owners (together with his son Richard and Simon Bullimore) of Desert Orchid, winner of the 1989 Gold Cup, and uncrowned king of Kempton by reason of his then record four victories in Boxing Day's King

George VI Chase – winning record prize money of £652,802. Worth considerably more today.

He survived an emergency operation for a twisted gut in 1992 (the horse not his breeder) and was "...a great show off and loves an audience. You can see him light up and rise to the occasion when we take him into the paddock," according to David Elsworth's travelling head lad – Peter Maughan. In fact, if he wasn't the centre of attention he would go into a major sulk, as in 1988 after his stable companion Rhyme 'N Reason had won the National and the many visitors to Elsworth's yard passed by Dessie's box to give homage to his (then) more illustrious neighbour. Once Dessie realised what was going on, he about-faced and presented his rump to the public for the rest of the afternoon.

At the end of 1980 Jimmy asked a local trainer to look at a rather unimpressive grey yearling he couldn't make up his mind about, since on the one hand he had been gelded, and he had a badly swollen hind (due to an embedded thorn). After one look at this plain-looking fellow he said, "get rid of him." However Jimmy couldn't sack a member of the family; just as well, as the horse was destined to become the most popular chaser since Arkle and for nine years the focal point in Jimmy's life. "Worried Burridge" was not the man to meet on the course before Dessie had raced – probably after an agonising 12 minutes wait to see whether his horse would ever get up again after somersaulting over the last hurdle in his first ever race. On this occasion Dessie was merely winded. Monty Court of *The Racing Post*, wrote that he was not so much worried about whether Desert Orchid was going to Cheltenham as he was about Jimmy's chances of getting there – since he was last seen leaving Sandown with all the spring in his step of a man about to go to the gallows! As an example of his popularity, on one of the Open Days at Ab Kettleby Stud, 2000 people came and paid as much as £120 for one of his lead ropes (for charity)

Less popular was Rodney Boult, head lad at Whitsbury. By the time Dessie had finished fourth in the Victor Chandler Chase at Ascot in 1991, Boult had seen him run seven times and it was the seventh time he had seen him beaten – a jinx which dogged him to the end. If Rodney was the kiss of death, Richard Burridge's brown overcoat was their insurance policy – whenever Dessie fell or was pulled up it coincided with Richard not wearing it! He raced in the colours of Jimmy's son Richard, who when Dessie started over fences, so did he, since it became a ritual for him to jump the last fence in the dusk.

Lester Piggott rode his sire Grey Mirage to several victories, and in the 2000gns where Desert Orchid was third favourite, said admiringly, "That Desert Orchid is just like a human being. He knows exactly what he is doing in a race. He is a star."

When Desert Orchid won The Cheltenham Gold Cup in 2005, a course bookie said, "All the punters wanted their money – and I knew what Custer felt like!"

He even has been sent a Christmas card addressed simply 'Desert Orchid, Somewhere in England'. He received it.

BUTLER – Gerard

When contemplating the draw at Chester in 2006 the trainer said to *The Racing Post,* "When they had chariot racing, the gut drawn widest was in the same boat as trainers today. You just have to get on with it."

C

CANNON – Tom   d. 1917

One of the best riders of his day. Apart from winning the Derby on the filly Shotover in 1882, he won 12 other Classics. He only weighed 54lb at the age of 15, when his first mount threw him over the rails and left him unconscious; unruffled he rode his first winner the next day.

As rider, trainer and teacher it is doubtful if any man then alive had more of all three skills. His sons Mornington and Kempton each won the Derby, as did two of his other pupils – Jack Watts – four times, and Sam Loates, twice.

He was also a shrewd businessman. When in 1888, the Scottish millionaire, George Abington Baird, wanted to retain him, Cannon realised he was a hire and fire merchant and demanded a three year contract at £3000 pa – the whole to be paid in advance. As everybody in England wanted him at the time, Baird had to pay up.

CARBERRY – Paul (Ire)   b. 1974

A jump jockey in the Francome mould, who never let his sense of fun get in the way of winning the big races (like the 1999 National on Bobbyjo). He once unloaded a horse from a trailer in a pub car park, went for a spin, and then rode it into the pub. "Amazing," said his owner, "that looks just like my horse. Hang on a minute, it *is* my horse."

Like most jockeys in Ireland he hunts twice a week, so trainer Noel Meade is never certain he'll be fit to ride, but that's part of the package – as when he was an apprentice. He wasn't much good with a broom, but when they discovered he had a knack with 'nagging' young horses, that was the end of his apprenticeship.

Speaking of the difficulties of riding Harchibald (narrowly beaten in the 2005 Champion Hurdle), he said "He's just like an aeroplane. The trouble with this aeroplane is he hijacks himself."

CARNARVON – 6th Earl of   d.1987

In dress something between a bookmaker and a comedian; in character both amusing and mannerless, kind and unscrupulous; in racing a good judge but a poor manager of his own horses – all in all something of a paradox. However, he rode a number of winners on the Flat as an amateur (including seven races on Patmos), where he was known unkindly as "the flying pig". His policy as a breeder at Highclere of "better sell and regret, than keep and regret" resulted in his selling Blenheim as a yearling, prior to winning the Derby of 1930 for the Aga Khan, and King Salmon as a two year old before he ran second in the Derby and won the Eclipse.

'Porchey' would present unsuspecting guests, especially Americans, with a signed photo of their host in full regalia of a Peer of the Realm – together with a bill for £25. He adopted the same ruse as a means of promoting sales of his autobiographies, by sending his victims a signed copy with a bill inside. However if you were a friend in need, he wouldn't let you down.

CARNARVON – 7th Earl of   d.2001

The owner of Highclere Stud and the Queen's erstwhile racing manager, referred to by his friends as "Porchey", as was his father, and described by

C

them as having an unerring eye for a fast horse, a high pheasant and a pretty woman.

He tells a story of when he was a gentleman rider and, as Lord Porchester, due to ride his horse "Lights o' London" at Ayr. He was sufficiently keen on its chances to advise a professional punter with whom he was friendly, to back it. However en route to Euston and the 'sleeper' he thought he had time to drop in on the Embassy Club, where a fanciable young lady agreed to share his berth on the journey north. However, as the lights of London had already dealt his owner-rider a mortal blow, the horse took complete charge, made his effort far too early, and lost by half a length. An expensive evening for Carnarvon, who had backed his own fancy, but much more so for his somewhat irritated friend who had correctly worked out what had happened.

CARSLAKE – Bernard "Brownie" (Aus)   d. 1940

So called because of his sallow complexion, another result of hard wasting, which forced him for years to live on "a cup of tea and hope". Known for his sardonic wit, he used to say "Don't believe anything you hear, and only half of what you see."

A certain amount of rumour surrounded the ante post betting on the 1924 St Leger, which Brownie won for the Aga Khan on Salmon Trout, since the bookies, and in particular, a friend of his, Mo Tarsh, started laying heavily against the horse. Years later Carslake admitted he had thought the horse wouldn't stay the trip, and had instructed Tarsh to lay him to lose, although "He was determined to give him the best ride possible." He must have been fairly 'boracic' to chance his arm in this way, since betting alone would have led to his being warned off if the horse had lost.

It took seven Classic rides without his winning the Derby, and he was another jockey where weight and wasting problems brought about his early death at the age of 54.

CARSON – Willie OBE   b.1942

Probably the strongest of all the post-war lightweight jockeys, his vigorous style has been described as "all kick and push" and, according to Eddie Hide, another jockey, he might not be a tactician, but horses just ran for him. In 1981, on a filly that broke both her forelegs, he had, in Steve Cauthen's words, "The worst fall I have ever seen," and a three month mandatory lay-off – but he still rode 114 winners! However he was kicked in the chest by a horse at Newbury in 1996, which finally forced him into retirement six months later at the age of 54.

The 1994 Derby was perhaps Willie's greatest victory, when he brought Erhaab from way behind with a late charge to overhaul King's Theatre. As he said afterwards, "It was carnage out there with so many horses jostling for position and they were lucky only one horse came down. They just shouldn't allow so many bad horses to run." As Piggott was fifth, he also said, "Us Grandads did all right, didn't we."

Business-Age magazine in May 1994 rated Carson 14th richest sportsman in Britain (behind Piggott and Eddery), with £6.65m. A man of wildly swinging moods, Willie's second wife said, "The secret of being happy with Willie is to accept that racing is his first love, and any woman must come second." Willie's determination and will-to-win on the course, and his wise-cracking cackle off it, helped to earn him the title The People's Jockey.

"It's like attaching a factory chimney to a bungalow," Giles Coren of *The Times* wrote in 2005 of Willy Carson's Royal Ascot top hat.

The same year he said, comparing racing to soccer and the huge amounts players get under contract whether they play or not, "In horse racing if you don't turn up you don't get any money and what you earn depends on the number of wins you have."

C

CHANDLER – Victor   b. 1951

One of the top betting houses in London until he moved his operation to Gibraltar in 1999 to offer punters tax-free betting. V.C. recalled Princess Anne's remark when he was interviewed by *The Racing Post* in 2006 and she had just met him at some charity event: "So you're the man who has lost the Chancellor so much money?"

CONNOLLY – Eric (Aus)   d.1944

Favourite maxim of the Aussie high-roller was, "Money lost, nothing lost; courage lost, everything lost." He was said to have won £200,000 on a winning double in 1930, but still managed to die broke.

CATTERMOLE, Mike   b. 1961

He is reported to have said, "I remember sitting in this office in North London with bullet holes in the window, thinking this isn't my sort of scene," reflecting on his time as an unemployment benefit officer (*Racing Ahead*, 2005).

CAUTHEN – Steve (US)   b.1960

Kentucky born jockey, who by the age of 18 had made the front cover of *Time* magazine as "Athlete of the Year" after setting a new mark for prize money earned in a single season, with $6.2m and 487 wins, and had won the US Triple Crown with Affirmed (1978). However, after 110 consecutive losing rides at the end of the same season, he signed with Robert Sangster to ride in Europe. Sangster had seen the headline in *Time* magazine, "Superbug hits bad patch" (bug in the US means an apprentice). As a result he became the first American jockey since Danny Maher in 1908 to win the British championship, which he did in 1984 and again in 1987.

Cauthen rode so flat against the horse that one Belmont punter opined, "You could serve drinks on The Kid's back at the furlong marker and you wouldn't spill a drop before he hit the wire." He tended over here to win from the front, which was a legacy from riding in America, where the horses go flat out from the start, but he became a superb judge of pace. In both Slip Anchor's Derby (1985) and in Reference Point's (1987) he made every yard – the first time a Derby winner has led from the start since Coronach ran away with Joe Childs in 1926.

Willie Carson once chastised him for doing something stupid: "I called him an idiot, or maybe worse. Steve replied coolly 'Yeah! But a rich one,' which put me in my place – coming from The Kid." He returned to the States in 1993, as his wife said, to play golf.

CECIL – Henry   b.1943

The most successful British trainer of the eighties, whose 180 wins in 1987 smashed John Day Junior's record which had stood for 120 years.

True to his somewhat superstitious profession he confesses to always stopping his car on the way to the races to put in petrol: "If I don't fill it up, I don't win." He also won't wear anything green: "I hate green – most of my family have died wearing it, including one ancestor who fell down the stairs in it." However, he also said, "It used to amuse me to wear outrageous clothes, but I've grown out of that a bit now. But I like to make a joke of myself, then you've got people off guard; they think you're a fool – then you move in." Cecil also collects white shoes and is teetotal. Commenting on that well known sartorial disaster area John McCririck, he said, "One has to admire him for his stamina and enthusiasm – he certainly adds a bit of colour, although his dress sense leaves something to be desired." Still with his mind on wearing apparel, he said: "The only tip I can give on jumpers is where to buy them in London!"

He once said, "Trainers who spend their time prostituting themselves at cocktail parties get the owners they deserve." He went on to describe one such uninformed owner, who, when his trainer said "I'm afraid he's still a bit green," replied, "He was brown the last time I saw him."

His British humour is sometimes lost on American hacks across the Pond, as when he was approached by one at the Santa Anita Breeder's Cup races in 2009. The local man asked the ten time champion trainer what he thought of the place "I'm not sure yet. I've only been here five minutes," replied Henry. On being pressed he went on, "Well, it's better than Wolverhampton." "Oh! I've never been there, so I wouldn't know." "Come to think of it, nor have I!" added our Henry.

Second wife Natalie's bossiness in the yard led to one of the lads suggesting, on being told by Henry that she had suggested the pigeons messing up the yard should be shot and hung up, to discourage the others, that it might be easier to string up Mrs Cecil. His present whereabouts is unknown.

He was quoted in 2007 as saying, when preparing his two Oaks runners, including Light Shift, the eventual winner, "I thought I'd got the job done as long as I didn't put the wrong saddle on, which in the old days I often did when I had a drink."

He said to *The Independent* in May 2005, before his classic winning comeback, "I don't want to give up by being made to give up." In July 2006, having just won "another bit of silver" at Sandown, he said, "I'm rather pleased it's a glass thing. We used to win all those silver trophies but we only had the one daily woman, and you just can't clean them all."

CHANNON – Mick   b.1948

The ex-Southampton footballer (46 England caps) now turned trainer, when asked why he switched to racehorses has a blunt answer, "Why didn't I stay in football? Because I didn't want to kiss anyone's arse. That's why!" In fact after McMenemy, the Southampton Manager, had bawled him out for all of three minutes once, Mick asked him, "Have you quite finished, gaffer? How many more times do I have to tell you that football is only my hobby!" In fact while he was still playing he bought a stud and bred a Hennessy Gold Cup (Ghofar) and a Tote Gold Trophy winner (Jamesmead). In 1994 he dismissed rumours that he might become the Saints Manager by saying, "I prefer racehorses to footballers. They don't talk back." He also said earlier, "I'd like to be remembered as a trainer who trained racehorses, not just as a footballer who won a few races." His motto apparently is "Proper planning prevents piss-pot performance."

In 2006 he said, "It's little things that make English racing special, like the Derby being run on the worst track in the world." He later added, "Racing has shot itself in the foot by moving the race to Saturday. Now it's just like any other Saturday fixture."

His pal Alan Ball, when Southampton Manager, recalled the confidence-boosting instructions Mick gave to a jockey before a hurdle race: "Just keep remounting." Mick's own favourite pre-race briefing was when he told a jockey that he was a cowboy and all the rest were Indians." He asked what that meant. "Ride for your f*****g life," I replied!

Talking to *The Times* in May 2005, "It's not for the faint-hearted this game. Horses are there to be raced. If you don't want to have a go – don't own racehorses – certainly not with me." Talking to the *Mail on Sunday* in August 2005 about Godolphin's penchant for taking back the best two year olds to train as three year olds with they themselves, "My job is to train them, not fall in love with them." In March 2006 he said, "The Guineas are too early – I found two polar bears on our gallops this week, and a penguin nicked my scarf."

CHAPLIN – Henry   d. 1923

Later Squire of Blankney Hall in Lincs. and friend of the Prince of Wales. He owned Hermit, winner of the 1867 Derby of whom it was said, "He destroyed a Marquis, avenged a commoner, and attained Turf immortality." The Marquis was Harry

Hastings, a dissolute young man who made off with Chaplin's fiancée, Lady Florence Paget, the Pocket Venus, a tiny beauty half London was in love with, and married her while preparations for her wedding to Henry Chaplin were still going ahead. Chaplin took himself off to India for a year's big game hunting to try and forget, and on his return, plunged into frenzied activity on the Turf, which included buying Hermit, with Hastings the underbidder. It was said of him at the time that he bought horses as though he were drunk, and backed them as if he were mad. However, Hastings conceived an irrational hatred for both the man he had wronged and the horse, and laid £120,000 against him when he became Derby favourite. Despite breaking a blood vessel on a trial gallop, Hermit won by a neck and broke the Marquis in the process. The magazine *Punch* carried the following post-Derby jibe: "Who will dare say that racing is a sinful amusement? Think of the money carried off from a Rake by a Hermit for the benefit of a Chaplin!"

CHARLES I 1625-1649

The King was interested in bettering the breed as well as racing. When Parliament seized the Royal Stud at Tutbury in 1643 there were 139 horses in all, valued at £1982, including a number of Barbs and Spanish horses and many of Eastern descent.

Mention is made of Charles racing in Hyde Park by John Aubrey, the historian. Apparently Charles "had complaint against Henry Martin (Knight of the Shire of the county of Berkshire, which he later raised against the King) for his wenching." It happened that Henry was in the Park one time when his Majestie was there going to see a race. The King espied him and sayd aloud, 'Let that ugly rascal be gone out of the parke, that whore-master, or else I will not see the sport'."

CHARLES II 1660-1685

The 'Merry Monarch' restored racing as well as the monarchy. He established race meetings at Windsor, but raced mainly at Newmarket, which became headquarters of the Turf during his reign. He later gave his nickname 'Old Rowley' to the mile course. He conducted a good deal of State business from Newmarket, where he was attended by the whole Court, including an assortment of mistresses, notably Nell Gwynne. According to Pepys, who commented agreeably on the purgative action of the spa waters (hence Epsom Salts), he attended Banstead Downs races in 1667 with Nelly.

Chasing about racing certainly gave Charles the time and opportunity to father no fewer than 13 illegitimate children – without of course producing a legitimate heir. Nell, a one-time comedienne at the Theatre Royal, Drury Lane, had learned how to deal with 'The Pit'. On one occasion the mob mistook her for the King's catholic mistress, the French Duchess of Portsmouth; "Be civil, good people," Nell shouted from her coach, "I am the protestant whore!" which delighted and disarmed the ugly crowd. Once, when an astrologer offered his services to the King, he was immediately taken to Newmarket "to foretell winners."

CHARLTON – John   d. 1862

Flat race jockey who died of consumption at the age of 33, but not before he had achieved everlasting notoriety by 'pulling' the Derby and Oaks heroine Blink Bonny, whom he had ridden in both races, in the 1857 St Leger, which went to Nat Flatman on Imperieuse. A riot took place at Doncaster after the race, not so unusual at a time when switching, nobbling, poisoning and pulling of horses often interfered with the chances of a favourite.

CHARNOCK – Lyndsay   b. 1955

A Northern lightweight jockey who would almost certainly have followed his father down the pits if said parent hadn't apprenticed him to Cheshire trainer Ronnie Barnes. In those days that meant working 12 hours a day and being locked up in a dark cupboard for the next 12 hours to prevent you growing! Luckily Barnes released him by "popping his clogs".

C

Once trainer Charlie Booth said to him after riding a badly judged race "If I was 7st-10lb, Charnock, I'd have been champion jockey." "If you were 7-10, Charles, I'd have punched the daylights out of you by now". He went to India where he rode 120 winners and found a wife (her five brothers rode there). Once he had to force a way through rioting punters to get to the start without getting lynched. He turned to the nearest jockey – appropriately it was Kipper Lynch – and said "It took a lot of guts getting to the start. But how the f..k are we going to get back?"

On an another occasion at Newmarket he won a race, despite having had a fall and broken his ankle on the way to the start. When praised for his bravery he said, "I knew the connections had backed it heavily and I can tell you, it would have been a lot braver to get off the horse than to ride it!"

CHETWYND – Sir George   d. 1917

A Warwickshire Baronet, whose considerable income could never hope to pay for his string of horses, and indulgent lifestyle. The gap between income and expenditure possibly led him to an arrangement with Charlie Wood, the wealthy champion jockey, whereby the two of them controlled the policy-making at the heaviest betting stable in the country, Chetwynd House at Newmarket, which was owned by Wood. As the stable's fancied runners usually won, after being backed down to very short odds by the stable, rumours were rife, and these eventually led to an accusation by the Earl of Durham and the most famous court case of the period in 1889.

The basis of the slander was that Wood bet in large sums on horses that he not only rode, but in reality owned, although they ran in Chetwynd's name. It was axiomatic that he also pulled horses on Chetwynd's instructions to make money out of them. In the ensuing libel action Chetwynd claimed damages of £20,000 and on hearing the verdict of "one farthing damages" he apparently made the memorable comment, "Damn short odds !"

CHILDS – Joe   d. 1958

Although never champion jockey, he won 15 Classics between 1912-1933, including three Derbys – and he gave all his riding fees to his regimental funds, those of the 4th Hussars – the last on Coronach in the 1927 Derby. Fred Darling, Coronach's trainer, knew the horse liked to be given his head, and instructed Childs "to make all". Coronach won by five lengths, despite Joe's swearing throughout the race, and he was still fuming as he walked into the weighing room, quite a lot richer, and snorted "What a bloody way to ride a horse." He also muttered the marvelous one-liner, "The bastard ran away with me." Many people believed him. Joe had a hair-trigger temper, which made for some withering ripostes to people in authority such as to his troop NCO: "What I don't know about grooming a horse, you certainly couldn't teach me"; and to a steward, "You were not at the gate, so you couldn't have seen what you say you did."

When he landed the 1000gns for King George V in 1929 on Scuttle, the King presented him with a cane which became his most treasured possession. Every time he won for His Majesty he sent out his valet for champagne, so he could give a toast to "My Governor."

CHURCHILL – Lord Randolph   d. 1895

Like his son, Sir Winston, he took up racing late in life, when he became sick of politics, and began buying yearlings on a large scale in 1887. To his friend Sir Fred Johnstone, who said at that rate he would soon be broke, he replied a trifle arrogantly, "Nearly all you people who go racing are fools and no really clever man has yet taken it up seriously – but now that I have done so I shall succeed." He almost made good his words when L'Abbesse de Jouarre won the 1889 Oaks and the Hunt and Manchester Cups. He really loved his horses and his pockets were always bulging with apples and sugar. After the Abbesse had gone to stud and he visited her after an absence of 12 months, as soon as he entered the yard,

C

she started squeeling and kicking until they opened her box, when she rushed at Randolph trying to put her nose in his pocket like a dog, at which tears came to his eyes.

CHURCHILL – Sir Winston   d.1965

A keen and lucky owner, his first horse Colonist II, which he bought at the age of 75 – won 13 races, including the Jockey Club Cup. But Churchill refused to send him to stud saying, "I don't want to end my days living on the immoral earnings of a horse." He then proceeded to put a tax on betting, although he was strongly against limiting bookmaker's activities to the racecourse since he "didn't want to throw half a million people out of work." Once when Doug Smith, the jockey, wrote apologising for losing a race, the cryptic reply came, "Dear Smith, I am sure you did your best. Yours, Churchill."

However off the racecourse, Churchillian anecdote is legion; many of his best one-liners revolve around alcohol, the services and politics: "Always remember I have taken more out of alcohol than alcohol has taken out of me," and "The traditions of the Navy – Rum, Buggery and the Lash!" A less well known story, told by Sir Hugh Foot (Lord Caradon) when Churchill, visiting him when he was Governor of Jamaica, returned from a triumphant tour of Kingston, and turning to him said, "Haven't seen so many blackamoors since Omdurman."

He was renowned for his repartee, as when Lady Astor said, "If you were my husband, Winston, I should flavour your coffee with poison." "Nancy," he replied "if you were my wife I should drink it!"

His comments on various notables of the day are worth recording: on Field Marshall Montgomery: "In defeat unbeatable; in victory unbearable." On Stanley Baldwin's retirement: "Not dead. But the candle in the great turnip has gone out." On war and politics: "In war you can only be killed once. In politics many times." On Joseph Chamberlain: "Mr Chamberlain loves the working man. He loves to see him work."

In his twilight years, staying at a friend's villa in Monte Carlo, after lunch Winston closed his eyes and seemed to drop off to sleep – whereupon an aging American guest, Daisy Fellowes, turned to her host and said, "What a pity so great a man should end his life in the company of Onassis and Wendy Reves" (another American whose interest in Churchill had occasioned some malicious gossip). To Daisy's dismay, an eye opened and he said, "Daisy, Wendy Reves is something you will never be. She is young, she is beautiful and she is kind." With that his eye closed.

COLLINS, Con (Ire)   d. 2007

An inscription on a gift to Ireland's longest serving trainer read, "I'm not 80, I'm 18 with 62 years of experience." Sadly he died two years later.

COMBS – Brownell (US)

Son of 'Cousin Leslie' from whom he took over the running of Spendthrift, one of the great Kentucky stud farms of the early 1980s. The farm went public in 1983, but Brownell was spending like a lunatic, to the dismay of the shareholders, who tried to oust him in 1984, when they found on the one hand he was giving beneficial contracts to his own companies, and on the other he was selling stallion nominations to girlfriends at prices which enabled them to sell them on at profits in excess of $100,000.

Brownell had also got into debt and by 1985 his interest payments were $6.3m. while his yearlings only fetched $2.5m. at Keeneland.

He was soon defending himself against writs from investors, who maintained the farm was overvalued at the time of the placement. He won but by then the farm was bankrupt and he sold his 4.6m shares to his sister for a nickel each! One 280 acre parcel went to Khalid Abdullah for a mere $3m.

C

Apart from greed and mismanagement on a spectacular scale, father and son had failed to acquire a top Northern Dancer stallion, and thereby missed out on the foreign buyer's mega-dollars in the boom years.

COMBS II – Leslie (US)   d. 1990

Owner of Spendthrift Farm, Kentucky – known as "Cousin Leslie" and a great salesman and promoter of horseflesh. "Have I got a horse for you! This sir is a running horse if ever I saw one, and this little itty-bitty contract I've got for you to sign is something you are never going to regret. Yessir. Hey boy! Bring them mint juleps over here."

The great American sires Nashua (1956) and Raise a Native (1961) stood there and founded a new dynasty while Cousin Leslie perfected the art of stallion syndication. As early as 1970 he was selling yearlings for over half a million dollars, such as the Raise a Native colt who was destined to become the English Champion 2 yr old Crowned Prince.

Covering sessions went on to 10pm at night, and on one occasion one of the men yelled at Seattle Slew (champion sire in 1984) who was a shy breeder and took time to get 'warmed up'. When the V.P., Arnold Kirkpatrick got to hear of it, he paraded the breeding shed staff and told them "You're a bunch of minimum wage-earners. That horse earns about a million dollars a day (actually his nomination fee was $750k) If he wants Mouton Rothschild, candles, and a violin quartet, get it for him. OK?"

COOPER – Robert

Of *The Sportsman,* said in October 2006, "I often think of Leicester as a Longchamp of the Midlands!"

COUSINS – Eric   d.1996

The Cheshire trainer and great handicapper whose shrewdness in laying out horses for the big handicaps matched that of Atty Persse, Boyd-Rochfort, Ryan Price and more recently Reg Akehurst. He also rode 50 winners as an amateur under N.H.Rules, including eight on the popular Creggmore Boy, a lively veteran of 22 when he was retired from racing!

His great feat was to win the Great Jubilee Handicap at Kempton Park four years running, starting with Chalk Stream in 1961 – the race which achieved added significance by starting a remarkable race career for its owner Robert Sangster and the building of his bloodstock empire. In fact the horse often acted up at the start, so Robert arranged with Eric from the stands to signal him on the rails only if the animal got away, so that he could still get a bet on with his friendly bookmaker. He did, and at 8-1 won £800 – the equivalent of £8000 in today's money.

CROCKFORD – William   d. 1844

Victorian proprietor of the gambling hall in St James' St., who was quite capable of handling bets and losses amounting today to millions, as he did in 1842 when the Earl of Eglinton won £30,000 – something approaching £5m in today's money – when his filly Blue Bonnet won the St Leger.

He was part of a betting syndicate which had laid out a huge sum on his filly, Princess, to win the Oaks of 1844. However Crockford, who was ill in bed on the day, rather inconveniently died of apoplexy before the race was run, which automatically cancelled all bets. However, the gang concocted a plan to ensure they could collect their winnings, when the filly won – as she duly did. First one of them took a carrier pigeon to Epsom, saying as Crockford couldn't leave his club, the bird was to be released to bring him the news. Next they dressed the corpse and sat it in the bow window at Crockford's in full view of the many carriages that had to pass by on their way home from Epsom. The bets were collected, but the story got out to provide yet another turf scandal.

C

CRUMP – Neville   d. 1997

The jump trainer who saddled Sheila's Cottage in the 1948 National, turned to John Proctor, her owner, when it looked as if they were going to win, expecting him to be roaring his horse home. Instead he was polishing off the remains of a flask of brandy. "Look here, aren't you interested?" he asked, "we could be winning the bloody National, you know." John looked quite unconcerned and replied, "Neville – you look after the horses and I'll see to the drinks." Either way they won. Two days afterwards at a photo-call the mare proceded to bite off the top of Arthur Thompson's (the winning jockey) finger.

Crump won it again in 1952 and 1960, and the Scottish version five times.

CULLOTY – Jim   b. 1973

Best Mate's jockey said, after the horse won The Cheltenham Gold Cup for the third time in 2004, "It's nice to be important but it's more important to be nice" – slightly twee remark!

"Whenever I've had a fall lately, I've been left feeling dazed, which I didn't in the old days." Having won three Gold Cups he decided to retire in July 2005.

CUMANI – Luca (Ita)   b.1949

Son of a leading Italian trainer, Luca started training in this country on his own account in 1976. His first Classic win – Commanche Run in the 1984 St Leger – was classic Piggott who only got the run by 'jocking off' Darrel McHague, Cumani's American stable jockey; as Ivan Allan, the horse's owner claimed, "There's only one St Leger and only one Lester."

However, it was Pat Eddery who brought him his first major success with Tolomeo in the 1983 Arlington Million, of whom Cumani said "Mine's a hell of a horse. The pot's big enough, so why not have a shot." His second overseas coup was in the 1994 Breeders Cup Mile, when Frankie Dettori, who he had taken on as an apprentice, gained a three length victory on Barathea – only the third British win in the 11 year history of the series.

Cumani quotes include, "I don't believe in luck; just fast horses." And on Sunday racing, "We will need to have a closed day so everybody can have a breather." On bookmakers he said, "They are like leeches." In *The Racing Post* (2006) he said, "The racing culture you have is second to none. It's the only place I know where racing is part of the national fabric and not a niche sport." On why he intends to stay in England rather than return to his native Italy. He said to *Pacemaker* in 2006: "If a horse that I have trained races against one that I have bred then I want the one that I have trained to win. Racing is my profession. Breeding is my passion."

"Cumani knows that keeping the women in his life sweet with a nice horse to ride is much better value than a shopping trip to Gucci and he gets a win percentage for his trouble," his former trainer revealed to *The Sportsman* in 2006. This explains why the Italian handler likes to set his wife Sara or daughter Francesca up with a fancied runner in ladies' races. In 2006 his daughter, Francesca, complained, "If there's ever any mention of me training, there's an immediate reaction from my Dad, which is "Absolutely not".

CUNLIFFE – Percy d.1942

An old Etonian who owned the Druid's Lodge stables on Salisbury Plain, which gave its name to the Confederacy (sometimes called the Netheravon Syndicate) he put together to hit the bookmakers during the early years of this century. There were four other members, whose skill, judgement and resources were necessary to bring off their many coups, which at today's values often brought them millions of pounds – Wilfred Purefoy, Holmer Peard, Captain Frank Forester and Edward Wigan. Cunliffe and Purefoy masterminded the trials and selected the races, while the trainer Jack Fallon only had to get the horses fit. In fact as he didn't know the weights, neither he nor the stable lads could interpret the trials. Nonetheless, they were subjected to a strict curfew – and were even locked in at night.

One of the greatest coups they brought off was with Hackler's Pride in the 1903 Cambridgeshire, before which the mare was run unfit to fool the handicapper. Meanwhile the lightweight Jack Jarvis was booked to ride. In the event, the filly was "wonderfully handicapped with about 20 lb in hand" and bets were placed by a network of agents, who couldn't be traced to Druid's Lodge. A supremely fit Hackler's Pride won by a comfortable three lengths; the coup was reportedly worth £250,000, worth today a staggering £10m. Jack Jarvis received a present of just £125.

CUNNINGHAM – Graham

The journalist commenting on jockeys, said in December 2004: "One of the only trades where an ambulance follows you around at work."

D

DAVIES – Hywel   b. 1956

Jump jockey who partnered Last Suspect to a shock win at 50-1 in the 1985 National and, according to Scudamore, a friend you could do without at a Steward's enquiry for his unintentional talent for dropping one in it. Once when he was supposedly reassuring Scu's wife, Marilyn, about his behaviour on the jockey's tour of Australia, he said, "Oh yes, he was very well behaved; when he was on the dance floor he only had a kiss and a cuddle – nothing more."

When touring in America in June 1985, he had to spend so much time in the sauna to keep his weight down, he took on an extreme pallor. So much so that one of the coloured lads, who was bringing his horse out of the barn said "Man that's the whitest white man I ever did see. Ain't yo got no sun in England?"

John Buckingham tells the story of once when Hywel shared a car to Ludlow with Johnny Francome and a couple of other jockeys. On the way back they stopped for petrol and, with all of them in the kiosk together, Hywel bought a coke. As they drove off he said, "Cheers to whoever bought the coke," but noone owned up so he reckoned he'd won a freebie and didn't think anymore about it. Not so the pranksome Franc, who got one of his friends to ring up that evening purporting to be the Chief Constable of Gloucestershire. After admitting to the heinous crime, he was told that unless he could give an explanation, the C.C. would have to consider taking action. Hywel was beginning to get into quite a sweat over the whole business, until bursts of laughter made him realise that he had been had.

D

He has some claim to immortality by having "died" three times; after falling at the last at Doncaster in 1984 on Solid Rock, he had to be revived three times on the way to hospital. The next time he rode there he fell again! He once listed his favourite recreation as 'sleeping'.

DAWSON – Daniel   d. 1812

A Newmarket tout and horse poisoner, who was eventually hanged before a crowd of 15,000. Not only had he been found guilty of plying his trade in Newmarket, but in 1808 two horses died after drinking from the troughs on Town Moor, Doncaster just before the St Leger, and he later, while under sentence, confessed to being the perpetrator. Apparently he was hired by two bookmakers called Bland, who were never subsequently brought to book. Quiet mannered and a man of some education – he spoke fluent French – Dawson first poisoned the wrong troughs on the Heath (each trainer had his own), and thirteen of J. Stevens horses were taken ill, instead of two of Tom Perren's, in a yard adjacent to Stevens', who were strongly fancied for the 1809 July Stakes. Two years later he did the same to Richard Prince's troughs, introducing the poison under the locked covers by the simple expedient of using a syringe and a tube. Some horses refused to drink, alerted by the strong smell, some recovered, but three died an agonising death. The Jockey Club offered 500gns (about £175k today) for information and the reward achieved its purpose. Dawson was sentenced under an Act which made it a capital offence for "maliciously destroying horses and cattle".

DAWSON – Matt   d. 1898

One of the great Victorian trainers, who enjoyed extraordinary success, particularly with Lord Falmouth's horses, with Fred Archer as his stable jockey. His Classic record was 28 victories, including six Derbys, although the unbeaten St Simon, the greatest sire of the century, did not win a Classic.

He disliked heavy betting and despised those who had an eye to the main chance, like Archer, who he was actually very fond of, calling him "That damned, long-legged, tin (money) scraping young devil". The year Dutch Oven won the St Leger (1882), Archer tried to beg off the ride, thinking Geheimness had a better chance; Matt wouldn't hear of it and when the filly won in a canter, the punters were certain Fred had pulled her in her two previous races. Amazingly fillies took the first three places.

Even at exercise Matt would wear a tall hat, varnished boots, and a flower in his buttonhole. He had no time for bad horses, and on one occasion advised the Duke of Portland to put a very highly bred filly in a selling race. The Duke remonstrated, "Surely its a pity to sell one bred like this?" To which Dawson replied, "Well she's a damned bad specimen of a damned good breed; get him out of here, Your Grace."

Although he led a simple life, he was generous to a fault, particularly where his horses were concerned, and died leaving only £20,000. His motto was "Damn the blunt (money)."

DAWSON – Richard (Ire)   d. 1955

Until 1931, when he had a disagreement with the Aga Khan, Dick Dawson was one of the most successful trainers of the period, starting with Drogheda in the 1898 National and ending with Blenheim's Derby in 1930.

He also trained the phenomenal sprinter Mumtaz Mahal for the Aga Khan. When Dawson tested her against a good filly to whom she was giving 28lb, her dazzling speed caused him to say, "I was so astounded I nearly fell off my hack." Her brilliant two year old career led to her being unbeaten over six furlongs as a three yr old.

Although an Irishman, Dawson looked neither Irish nor a trainer, but resembled an old-fashioned schoolmaster, with a drooping moustache, pince-nez and dress more suited to the classroom than the stable yard.

D

DAWSON – Tom   d. 1880

Took over from his father George to train at Middleham and was known to his fellow Yorkshireman as "King o't'Moor." He won the Derby with Ellington in 1856, and again in 1869 with Pretender, the last Northern trained horse to be successful in the race at Epsom.

On Ellington, he won the huge amount of £25,000 (say £4.25m), but left it on the luggage rack in an old hat-box at Northallerton station on his way home. Calmly advertising for it to be returned as an item of no particular interest to anyone save its owner, he received it back intact. When convalescing at the age of 70, he left his bed to see a trial on The High Moor, caught a chill and never recovered.

DEMPSEY – Eddie   d. 1989

Irish rider of the 100-1 winner of the 1947 Grand National, Caughoo, he was widely rumoured not to have completed the course in the fog, taking a short cut from the fence before Bechers and joining in again after Valentines. Dempsey said, "It wasn't a great day for seeing…" but Ginger McCain (Red Rum's trainer) always maintained he hid under the Canal Turn and only went round once. The whole affair involved Eddie first in a punch-up and later in a law-suit in which he was completely vindicated.

During the war he had previously won three races on the great Prince Regent in Ireland, before wartime restrictions were lifted and the horse could race in England where he won the Gold Cup in 1946.

DENNIS – Barry   b. 1942

Bookie who is best known for his weekly Bismarck on Channel 4's Morning Line said, "This buffoon has cost the industry £7m. The real winner was virtually un-backed but the horse we have to pay out on was a heavily backed favourite. Her eyesight can't be trusted," talking about serial offender Jane Stickels. She reoffended the following Monday by calling 9-4 favourite Welsh Dragon the winner, but later corrected herself in favour of 14-1 shot Miss Dagger.

He said of Belgian superstar jockey Christophe Soumillon in 2006, when interviewed by *The Sun*, "He's so cocky that if he was a sweet he'd eat himself." He also said of Andre Fabre, "The French don't win our greatest race – simple as that and we should take great delight when Visindar is stuffed. His trainer thinks he's Napoleon and in fact is the most sullen man on the planet."

Apparently, in trying to get back the £50 he just lost to trainer Mickey 'Sumo' Quinn, he lost the double or quits he offered him for a foot race over half a furlong saying, "Blow me, he went so far clear and ran backwards, laughing at me."

"Knowing the old Essex foghorn, who started betting at Romford dogs in 1968, it would not surprise me if topless girls were hired as his settlers," *The Sun*'s Claude Duvall on the opening of the high profile bookie's first betting shop in Romford in August 2005.

DERBY – Isobel Countess of   d.1990

Wife of the 18th Earl, whose forbear, the 12th Earl, instituted the Derby in 1780, was passionately interested in racing, breeding the filly Tahilla, who won seven races, including the Sceptre Stakes at Doncaster.

In 1952 at the Stanley (Derby) seat at Knowsley, near Liverpool, a footman went berserk with a machine gun (apparently acquired for £3 and a pair of trousers) and after firing 37 shots he entered the smoking room where Lady Derby was dining alone and shot her in the neck, leaving her for dead, before shooting the butler and the under-butler. One aspect of the case which caused a great deal of comment in post-war Britain was the number of servants in the Derby's employ. Prime Minister Churchill is said to have remarked, "It's nice to hear of a house where you can still get a left and a right at a butler."

Actually they were fairly grand; the Earl's father, the celebrated statesman, was known as the King of Lancashire and the loyal Lancastrian toast at the time was "God save the Earl of Derby and the King."

DERBY – 12th Earl of   d. 1834

Having in 1773 leased a house at Epsom called The Oaks from his uncle, General Burgoyne, Lord Derby and his friends founded a race for three year old fillies over a mile and a half in 1779, which he won with Bridget. As this was rated a success, a second race for colts and fillies was proposed for the next year, this time over a mile. Lord Rosebery said a century later, "A roystering party at a country house founded two races, and named them gratefully after their host and his house, the Derby and the Oaks. Seldom has a carouse had a more permanent effect." In 1784 the Derby distance was increased to its present 1.5 miles. He won the race himself in 1787 with Sir Peter Teazle.

By the mid 1860s the Derby had established itself as the most important event of the racing year, in fact it had become "the Blue Riband of the Turf" according to Disraeli. Derby Day was essentially a great public holiday, when Parliament did not sit, and people went in their thousands to Epsom, not so much to see the race, but to enjoy all the fun of the Fair on the Downs. For years Barnum's Show occupied a site on the rails between Tattenham Corner and the winning post.

DERBY – 17th Earl of   d. 1945

Famous as an owner/breeder he bred 19 Classic winners between 1916 and 1945, and owned another, both records which have not been beaten last century. This included three Derby winners, one of which was Hyperion (1933) – later to become the most prepotent sire between the thirties and forties while still under his ownership.

Towards the end of the last war *Horse and Hound* mistakenly referred to "Lord Derby's stallion" as "Lord Derby – the stallion." When the Editor phoned to apologise it is said His Lordship merely expressed his pleasure at being so flattered.

As an owner he made famous the familiar black jacket and white cap of his colours and as a breeder his stock still influences thoroughbred lines worldwide. Unfortunately his son died before him and his grandson sold the great Stanley House stables in 1976.

DE TRAFFORD – Sir Humphrey   d. 1971

The tall and immaculately dressed Sir Humphrey was a member of the Jockey Club in its more autocratic days. He also owned Alcide, who when hot favourite for the 1958 Derby was found to have damaged himself in the Boyd Rochfort stables, or more probably he was "got at". As he went on to win the St Leger and the King George VI as a 4 yr old it was thought he would have won the Derby. However Sir Humphrey won it the next year with Parthia, and decided to celebrate by retiring to bed at 7 pm with two boiled eggs. He told the actor and owner Robert Morley, "I would have liked to have celebrated, only as I had a horse running the next day, I had to get to bed early." Oh well! what can one say?

DETTORI – Frankie (Ita)   b. 1970

Son of the 10 times champion jockey of Italy, Frankie took the British championship for the first time in 1994 with over 200 winners, including his first Classic victory on Balanchine in the Oaks. When he started the season with a 35-1 double at Southwell, trainer David Chapman said, "I used to think jockeys were only as good as the horses they rode, but Frankie is something special." One of his more colourful nicknames is The St. Mark's Square (Venice) Bum Pincher!

D

He came to England in 1989 to work for Luca Cumani, and by the time he was 19 he had topped 100 winners in a season to beat Piggott's 35 year record. As Brough Scott said, "He has something else, something you don't learn, something that you can recognise in any sport, something that sets him apart. It's the gift." Put another way, " Just occasionally a jockey comes along with a bit extra – takes the right decision without seeming to think about it, and that's what makes him so exciting."

Frankie has an incurable sense of fun and delighted in taking the mickey out of Lester Piggott, whom he much admired, with such encouraging remarks as, "Hey Larry (his pet name for Lester) – they gonna stuff you full of paper – and put you in a museum." Or, "Hey, old man, they should have retired you years ago." Lester would mumble, "What's he on about?"

He rode the temperamental filly and sprinter Lochsong for Ian Balding of whom he said, "She's like Linford Christie – without the lunch-box."

Champion jockey in 1994 and 1995 when he had 216 winners. In September 1996, at the Ascot Festival, Frankie won all seven races on the card, much against the odds, particularly since his last mount, Fujiyama Crest, was no more than a 10-1 shot forced down to 2-1 by the weight of doubles and trebles on its rider. Punters cried all the way to the bank; one couple, Mr and Mrs Bolton, won £900,000 (their cheque was limited to 500k) for an outlay of £216, but the betting industry paid out over £30m. As one spokesman said, "The fifth was expensive, the sixth was disastrous, and after the seventh it was time to put the lights out."

His trademark flying dismount, usually reserved for Group I wins, was in evidence twice that day, the first time after winning the QE II Stakes on Mark of Esteem, who was not expected to beat the favourite, Bosra Sham, and then again to celebrate his 'Seven Up'. He said afterwards after being interviewed by the BBC's Julian Wilson, "I warned Julian not to touch me because I was red hot."

Ten weeks earlier he had won six races in a day for the first time, split between Yarmouth and Kempton, only to have a horrific fall at Newbury the very next day, which put him on the sidelines for two months – such are the highs and lows of racing.

He was very complimentary to 24 year old Canadian riding sensation Jayne Wilson when he said, "I have ridden against her and there is no way to tell whether she was a boy or a girl. She's different to any woman I've seen in the past," quoted in *The Times* 2006.

He also won the Derby in 2007 with Authorized and said "Get the f**ckin' bubbly open!" He was equally emotional when the plane he was sharing with Ray Cochran crashed in 2001, when he said "We're dead mate, this is it, we're gone."

Luca Cumani said of Frankie shortly after winning The Japan Cup with Alkaased in 2005, "When he came to England he was basically a pest and he is still a pest. But he is probably the best rider we've seen in the world for a very long time."

"It is up against a different kettle of 'orse." His language is instantly understandable as he explains why St Leger winner Sixties Icon was up against it in the 2006 Arc. "The sun always seems to be shining at the racetrack when Dettori is around," quotes Hugh McIlvanney in the *Sunday Times,* 10 September 2006.

DEVONSHIRE – 11th Duke of   d. 2008

Andrew Devonshire was a member of the Jockey Club since 1956 and was the lucky owner of Park Top. She was originally bought for Bernard van Cutsem, to pass on to a new American owner, but when he heard she only cost 500gns he decided to offer her to his old friend, Andrew Devonshire, who commented, somewhat icily, "But I used to own her dam. She was useless." Nevertheless, he took the filly who went on to win on 13 occasions, including the Coronation Cup and the King George VI Stakes. He likes to say of racing, "On the turf, and under it, all men are equal."

The Duke tells the story when, as a young man, he sat between the Duke of Norfolk and the Archbishop of Canterbury at a banquet, "Ignoring my presence, they talked across me throughout the meal, calling each other 'Your Grace' the whole time. Then and there I vowed I would not be addressed thus, and ever since have insisted, whenever possible, on the use of my Christian name, Andrew."

His ancestor, the 8th Duke, who held Cabinet office, was said to be "A decent gentleman who yawns during his own speeches and prizes the triumphs of the turf and the boudoir above those of the forum."

He believes Gold Cup Day to be racing's day of the year, since steeplechasing is still a sport, whereas flat racing is now a business. "Compared to Cheltenham, Epsom, alas, is very déclassé." His early recollections are amusing "I wasted my education at Eton, where I was a horrible boy – dirty, lazy and useless – Cambridge was a washout. Too near Newmarket. But the Army turned me from a filthy useless boy into something approaching a man." However he goes on to say, "When you consider my advantages, I've achieved absolutely nothing. It's quite shaming."

Andrew's method of naming horses has embraced houses, streets, towns and countries – as with Chatsworth, Watling St., Tenby and Uganda; sometimes even grouse moors, like Park Top. One of his weaknesses is yellow socks – another is snoozing after lunch.

DEWAR – John. A   d. 1954

He inherited his first Classics winner – Cameronian (1931 2000gns and Derby) from his uncle, Lord Dewar, who in 1928, when he bred him, uttered the prophetic words, "He will win the Derby, but I may not live to see it." Tom Webster recalls a Hoover salesman called to demonstrate his latest model just before the race. His wife told him, "If Cameronian wins, I'll have it." The chap wasn't a racing man, but he shouted as loud as anybody while he listened to the race with the rest of the family.

Later he won the 2000gns again with his best horse, Tudor Minstrel, in 1947, who couldn't act left-handed and only came fourth in the Derby, which caused his jockey, Gordon Richards, a good deal of public disapprobation, since they were convinced he had pulled the animal.

DICK – Dave   b. 1924

A swashbuckling jump jockey from Liverpool, whose timing, fearlessness and powerful finishes won him the Gold Cup on Mont Tremblant in 1952, and allowed him to profit from the unfortunate Devon Loch's collapse in 1956 to win the National on ESB.

Dave usually spoke his mind, and according to Josh Gifford, one day at Leicester when the fences were particularly badly built, and D.V. Dick had fallen no less than three times in the same race, the Clerk of the Scales asked, "Have you seen the doctor?" "It's not me that wants the bloody doctor " Dave snapped "It's the stupid bastards that built those concrete shit-houses out there."

Six foot tall and built like a middleweight boxer, he could have been mistaken for one, when one day, after being beaten in a tough gruelling race on a hot favourite, as he was riding back, he was bad-mouthed by a raucous punter, who accused him of pulling the horse's head off. "Say that again," said Dave, and after the foolhardy man obliged, Dave dismounted, gave the reins to a willing bystander and proceeded to deal with the fellow in a sufficiently uncompromising fashion as to require him to be carried to the ambulance room.

With the Maktoum family in mind, he once summed up the Arab's unique empathy with horses in his inimitable way by saying, "The Arabs were racing horses when the average Briton was still covering himself in woad, wearing a bearskin and chasing their women into caves with a club."

D

DILL – Victor Lt-Col MC   d. 1986

An Old Etonian best known for his part in the Francasal betting coup affair, for which he was jailed in 1954 for 18 months. Santa Amaro was secretly switched with an inferior animal called Francasal in a Bath Selling Plate. Just before the "off" the gang, of which poor Dill was a member, as the judge said, "Purely to lend respectability to the affair", placed £6000 around the country in the knowledge that the bookmaker's blower phone line had been cut so they couldn't shorten the odds. He duly romped home at 10-1. However as suspicions were aroused, payment of off course bets was withheld on the advice of the National Sporting League, the bookmakers association.

At the time Dill was working in a bookmakers office for £5 a week. In 1949 he had previously set up as a bloodstock agent in Maisons Lafitte, near Paris, where he was often seen in his monocle and corduroy cap, riding an old-fashioned English bicycle.

DILLON – Mike

Ladbrokes marketing supremo said in 2006, "It's the craziest betting race I've ever seen in my life." He was referring to the amount of money put on Deep Impact from mainly Japanese punters to win The Arc, which forced the odds down to 1/10 on the Pari Mutual, so that the eventual winner Rail Link went off at 24/1 instead of a predicted 8/1.

DOBBIN – Tony   b. 1972

In 1994 the jump jockey showed extreme excitement on winning at The Cheltenham festival when he said to his valet, "Did you see me on the radio?"

In discussing the festival with *The Racing Post* in March 2005 he said, "The best Cheltenham I ever had was when it was off for foot and mouth; it's not been a lucky meeting for me."

DONOGHUE – Steve   d. 1945

One of England's favourite jockeys between the wars – he was quite a character with not a lot of responsibility combined with prodigious talent and a lot of Irish charm. His early successes with Atty Persse's stable led to the cry, "Come on Steve!" becoming part of the English language.

He first won the Derby with Pommern in 1915 and another five times over the next 10 years, and a total of 14 Classics by 1937. However he had an eye for the main chance, as when he persuaded Lord Derby to release him to ride Jack Joel's Humorist in the 1921 Derby, which he won, and again in 1923 when he talked Lord Woolavington out of his retainer so he could ride the eventual winner, Papyrus.

In 1913 he partnered the wonder grey "rocking horse" – The Tetrarch, so called because his powerful quarters made it look as if he always won at a canter. He was never beaten, even in one race when he was left at the start, and Donoghue rode him in all his six starts as a two year old. The following spring he rapped a fetlock joint and had to be pin-fired and on damaging the same joint early the next year The Spotted Wonder was retired to stud to become champion sire on his first crop,, and later to pass on his genes to Mumtaz Mahal – the Flying Filly. She was probably the fastest horse in the history of the Turf.

However Steve was probably best known for his Royal Ascot partnership with Brown Jack, since between 1928 and 1934 they won 14 times, including the Ascot Stakes once and the Queen Alexandra Stakes six times! "I loved the old fellow like a brother," Steve said, and at his retirement dinner in 1937. Brown Jack's owner, Sir Harold Wernher, arranged for a radio receiver to be placed in his box, so Donoghue could send his old pal a message. The groom swore he recognised the voice.

The six times Derby winner (between 1915 and 1925) reckoned Gay Crusader, the 1917 Triple Crown winner, was the best horse he ever rode, but his empathy with a horse could be uncanny at times, and with George Lambton's Diadem, with whom he shared 13 wins out of 22 races, he one day in 1919 rode her with a broken wrist – "She seemed to know I was injured for she helped me in every way, and we won by a short head. She wanted nothing more than a kind word whispered in her ear and she would strain every nerve in her body." For Donoghue Humorist hung on to win the 1921 Derby by a neck, despite only having one lung, as was made evident less than a month later, when he was found dead in his box with a lung haemorrhage.

In 1937 he went out in a blaze of glory, with two Irish Classics on Phideas. and the 1000gns and Oaks on Exhibitionist and wrote, "I love horses with all that is in me Some people think of them as animals. I think of them as friends – my greatest friends."

DOUGLAS-HOME – William   d. 1992

Son of the 13th Earl of Home and brother of Sir Alec Douglas-Home, the Prime Minister, William was a brilliantly witty writer of light comedies, including in 1970 "The Jockey Club Stakes".

His best horse was Goblin, which at his death still held the seven furlong record at Newmarket. He was then entered in the Derby when he appeared to have his tail caught in the starting stall, before getting off to a poor start. In fact he had fallen asleep, but still managed to come tenth out of 25.

His next coup was at Wincanton, when with Lord Oaksey in the saddle, he asked afterwards, "How did you find him John?" "He should think about some other sport," Oaksey replied, "like golf."

His many practical jokes include one where he smuggled a stuffed crocodile out of the family seat in the Borders, before escorting his mother and some other ladies for a walk in the gardens. As they approached a bridge, his accomplice launched it into the stream. "Did you see that, Mother?" said William excitedly. "How interesting," replied Lady Home quite unperturbed, "I hadn't realised they came so far North."

D

DOUMEN – Francois (Fra)   b.1940

Jump trainer of King George VI and Gold Cup 1994 winner The Fellow on being asked about what he thought of the Cheltenham roar said, "It's something you don't find anywhere else in the world. Maybe the Romans were doing this in the arena, but only here do we get it now."

He also said in 2004, as Baracouda won the Long Walk Hurdle for the fourth time, "I can't be humble when I talk about Baracouda. The bottom line is, we love you." "He kept all his rivals out of the handicap, and I did enjoy it, seeing all those other jockeys starving to do the weight," said the trainer in 2005, looking back at the golden days of his great staying hurdler Baracouda.

DOWDESWELL – Jack   b. 1918

The former champion jump jockey (1946-7) was drinking a gin and tonic in his local after being discharged from hospital, after yet another accident, when fellow jockey Dave Dick swaggered in and asked, "How did you get on, Jack?" Jack blushed a deep red and stammered, "I had to have fifteen stitches in my old man." "Fifteen stitches, you're boasting," boomed Dave to a hushed bar.

He also broke his collar bones so often that in the end he had them removed and wore a kind of cricket pad over his shoulders instead. His injuries finally forced him to retire and take up training in 1960. Few braver men have ridden under NH Rules.

He said of Lambourn trainer Ted Gwilt who was celebrating his 90th birthday in May 2007: "I was treated like slave labour. Gwilt was a right bastard, a miserable old sod, and he never gave rides to apprentices."

D

DOWN – Alastair

The TV presenter said in 1994 of Willie Carson winning the Derby, "I seriously doubt if many other jockeys in living memory would have won on Erhab." The same year he recalled the halcyon days of stewarding when he said, "Eventually the pool from which they were selected was extended beyond the registered blind, the chronically inbred and those whose ear trumpets or searing gout problems render them half sharp or pathologically vicious." Just before the 1994 Grand National he said to *The Sporting Life*, "Any fatalities will immediately be laid at our door in triumph by those who profess to love animals, yet still relish the odd corpse to add grist to their mill."

He also said in January 2002, "I can never understand why people get so excited when J.P. McManus has £100,000 or whatever on something, it's all just small change to him."

DUFFIELD – George   b. 1946

After his first winner, Syllable at Yarmouth in 1967, trainer Jack Waugh gave him the following assessment: "You were bloody hopeless." Despite this, Duffield dedicated his autobiography to him.

DUNLOP – Ed   b. 1968

The trainer did not believe in the excuse offered for Ouija Board's poor running in The Dubai Sheema Classic in March 2006: "I know it was suggested that she was unsettled by the noise of the fireworks, but that theory is totally invalid in my opinion."

"I was never going to be a jockey and I am far too stupid to do anything else. But I am not daft enough to think I got the job for any other reason than my name." A quote from John Dunlop's son, Ed, trainer of Ouija Board, in the *Daily Mail*, 13 June 2005.

DUNWOODY – Richard MBE   b. 1964

Top jump jockey, who took over the crown from Scudamore in 1992/93. In March 1993 he was up in London to collect the Jump Jockey of the Year Award for the second time, when after dinner at the Hilton Hotel, the jockeys repaired to the Plaza at about 1am to continue the revelry. After a couple of false fire alarm calls, the police finally arrived at about 4.30am and told everybody to go to bed. One of them, Roger Marley, remonstrated with them, pointing out that he was a resident, whereupon the police bundled him into a van; Richard stood up for him and was immediately invited to join him – in handcuffs! The police at Paddington Green let them off with a caution after four hours in the cells. Unfortunately, the *Mirror* had a tip-off, which provided a good start to Grand National week; the starter of course ensured a sensational ending (the National was declared void).

He was the fourth jockey ever to score 1000 wins and by 1999 he had broken Peter Scudamore's record of 1699 winners. However, his almost obsessive race for the 1993/4 title with Adrian Maguire, who was all of 43 wins ahead in the January, led him to give his rival a double bump at an unimportant race at Nottingham in March 1994 after Adrian had delivered the ultimate insult of getting up on his inside, earning himself a 14-day suspension for intentional interference. He eventually won by five wins, After it was all over he said, "I don't know if I can go through all this again – I want to enjoy the last five or six years of my career."

DURACK – Seamus   b. 1951

Irish jump jockey nicknamed Baboon because, according to Carl Llewellyn, "Believe it or not he's proud to be the hairiest jockey on the circuit and rejoices in that nickname."

D

DURHAM – 3rd Earl of   d. 1928

Elder brother of the well-known trainer George Lambton. Although he won the Oaks in 1927 with Beam, it was the slander case brought against him by Sir George Chetwynd, following a speech he made at the Gimcrack Dinner of 1887, for which he is chiefly remembered.

Lord Durham wasted no time in castigating jockeys who "Bet in large sums and are the virtual owners of horses which run in other people's names." He went on to say that one well known jockey not only did this, but pulled horses to make money out of them. Warming to his theme he referred to an aristocratic racing stable that had been conspicuous for the in-and-out running of its horses. He subsequently confirmed that he was referring to the champion jockey, Charles Wood, the Newmarket trainer Richard "Buck" Sherrard, and that the offending owner was the former senior steward, Sir George Chetwynd. Wood certainly owned the Chetwynd House Stables, and had been accused of pulling horses during the season, and Chetwynd, a compulsive gambler, certainly controlled the stables and needed money to support his lifestyle. Chetwynd demanded an apology or satisfaction – a duel; neither were forthcoming, and in 1888 the stewards refused to renew Wood's licence. In June 1889 the case came to court, where Chetwynd claimed £20,000 damages (about £1.6m); he won a Phyrric victory, since damages were assessed at a farthing. Chetwynd resigned from the Jockey Club and retired from the turf, but Wood's licence was restored in 1897.

DUVAL – Claude

The racing journalist said in *The Sun* in 2006, "Never get involved in incest, Morris dancing or betting odds-on." Apparently this was advice from his Dad.

DWYER – Martin   b. 1975

The flat jockey said, "Doctor Who and all The Daleks wouldn't keep me away," referring to his ride on Sir Percy, having had a tumble at Bath the night before.

E

EASTERBY – Mick   b. 1931

Trained for the Flat at Sheriff Hutton in Yorkshire. Mick had a name for successful bargain hunting; Lochnager cost 600gns as a yearling and was syndicated for £260,000, and Mrs McArdy, a £1000 filly, was sold to stud for £134,000. Workboy was another cheap buy at £600, which he sold for his owners for £50,000. As he said, "Everything's for sale around here, including me."

His main jockey, out of the 80 or so who rode for him, was Eddie Hide, of whom he once said, "It's brains that win races; I don't give a bugger about style." He also regarded his elder brother, Peter, as the brainy one in the family: "That's why I like to mix with him."

He is also known for making one or two injudicious comments, such as in an interview with Alistair Down on Channel 4 in 2006 when he said, "You made me look a c**t once, I'm not a c**t twice."

EASTERBY – Peter   b. 1929

Christened Miles Henry, Peter ran a very successful mixed stable at Malton. He is remembered for the dual purpose gelding Sea Pigeon, a son of Sea Bird II, who after winning two Chester Cups (1977 and 1978) and an Ebor, had a brilliant hurdling career including two Champion Hurdles (1980 and 81). Peter had another dual Champion Hurdle winner in Night Nurse (1976 and 1977).

E

He also trained the aptly named Saucy Kit (by Hard Sauce – Reckitts), the 1967 Champion Hurdle winner, who being an entire, went to a stud managed by his former jockey, Roy Edwards. When the horse passed away in 1980 Edwards said, "He loved grey mares – he was covering one before he rolled off dead. But he still got her in foal!" What a way to go and what an epitaph!

EDWARD VII – King 1901–1910

As Prince of Wales, he bred Persimmon to become in 1896 the first Royal Derby winner for 108 years, and he won the race twice more with Triple Crown winner Diamond Jubilee in 1900 and with Minoru in 1910 after becoming king. Minoru was later exported to Russia where, it was alleged, he was seized by the Bolsheviks and executed for being an aristocrat. After Persimmon's Derby the crowd broke through the police cordon, patting the Prince on the back and shaking his hand with cries of, "Good old Teddie," which prompted Bismark to remark to Disraeli, "You will never have a revolution in England as long as you keep up your racing." When he went on to win the St Leger the North Country crowd went equally wild, and the police had to escort the Prince back to the stands, whereupon some wag shouted out, "Never mind, Teddie – we'll come and bail you out." He was ridden both times by the lugubrious Jack Watts, whose expression prompted Richard Marsh, his trainer, to slap him on the thigh and shout, "Don't you know you've just won the Derby for the Prince of Wales?" Jubilee year saw the Prince also win the National with Ambush II.

Although a keen racing man, racing was not his first love as his nickname, "Roger I", would seem to indicate. In fact at his Coronation his ladies' stall was referred to as "The Loose Box". Princess Alexandra appears to have been fairly tolerant of her husband's mistresses – actresses like Lily Langtry and La Goulue, the Moulin Rouge dancer. She even turned a blind eye to the society women to whose bedrooms he padded at country house weekends, but she wasn't too happy about "My Darling Daisy" – Lady Warwick – though it amused her that Mrs Keppel, although 20 years her junior, was a good deal stouter.

However, he was a stickler for form as when he saw Lord Harris at Ascot in a brown bowler and enquired "Goin' rattin' 'Arris?" When the Russian Ambassador asked him if it was correct to go to race meetings while still in mourning (for Queen Victoria), he replied, "To Newmarket, yes, because it means a bowler hat, but not to the Derby because of the top hat."

Queen Victoria was distinctly unamused by her son's love of racing, and before Royal Ascot in 1867, when he was 28, she requested him to limit his visits to two days as "...your example can do much for good and a great deal for evil." Needless to say, the Prince ignored her. However by 1870 the Marlborough House Set, which the Prince gathered about him, had involved him in various scandals, starting with a subpoena in Sir Charles Mordaunt's divorce suit. In 1891 he was subpoenaed again in the Baccarat Scandal, when Sir William Gordon Cumming tried to defend himself against an accusation that he had been cheating. Towards the end of his mother's reign he said, "I don't mind praying to the eternal Father, but I must be the only man in the country afflicted with an eternal Mother." When referring to Goodwood in the early 20th century he described it as a garden party with racing tacked on.

EGREMONT – 3rd Earl of   d.1837

A big owner of the pre-Victorian era, he won the Derby five times by 1826, which is still a record, although it has been equalled by the old Aga Khan. However some of them were almost certainly four year olds! His trainer, Bird, on his deathbed, admitted winning the Derby twice with four year olds by the simple expedient of slipping two year olds into the yearling paddock. As there were some 300 horses at Petworth, where the management was fairly lax, bordering on the non-existent, this ruse was unlikely to be discovered. Certainly Lord Egremont knew nothing of the deception; he was far too wealthy to be motivated by greed – giving away £20,000 (about £7m today) to charity every year.

The discontinuance of his great annual race meeting at Petworth Park in 1801 led to the Duke of Richmond establishing the Goodwood meeting the same year.

E

ELIZABETH – The Queen Mother d. 2007

The Qiueen Mother has long been associated with racing as an owner, particularly under NH Rules, and in May 1994 she had her 400th winner, the majority trained by Fulke Walwyn at Lambourn, who took over from Peter Cazalet. After her 200th winner in 1969 she said, "It's one of the real sports that's left to us; a bit of danger and a bit of excitement and the horses, which are the best thing in the world." Her first, and at that time only, horse Monaveen, who she shared with her daughter Elizabeth, broke a leg at Hurst Park and had to be destroyed. He was the first horse to run for a Queen of England for 235 years, when Queen Anne's Star won a race at Ascot in 1714. Her most disastrous time on the course must have been when Devon Loch collapsed inexplicably on the run-in to winning the 1956 Grand National. But her ability to "treat those two imposters Triumph and Disaster just the same" was never more apparent as when she was commiserating with Dick Francis, her disappointed jockey, the tearful stable lad and her trainer – Peter Cazalet – saying as she patted Francis on the shoulder, "Well, that's racing I suppose."

With her graceful and understanding ways she was also politely dismissive. To a Boer from Johannesburg, who said he could never quite forgive the British for conquering his country, she replied, "I understand perfectly. We feel very much the same in Scotland." As Morgan-Owen, the portrait painter, said, "She is the perfect grandmother. She drinks gin, goes racing and is accessible to everyone."

ELIZABETH I 1558–1603

A year into her reign one of racing's oldest surviving trophies, the Gold Bell, was donated by the wife of the Governor of Carlisle to initiate racing on 'Kynges Moor'. Previously in 1511, Chester Corporation had gifted a silver bell of an annual value of 3 shillings and 4 pence to be competed for on the Rood Eye and another was awarded for the first recorded race at York in 1530.

The Queen maintained a racing stud, and she attended the races at Croydon in

1585, where 34 shillings were expended on a stand for her use. There was also racing – probably a match between two horses – at Ayr in 1576 when a quarrel over the fairness of the start led to both the starter and his assistant being shot in the leg.

Deeds bearing the date 1600 refer to racing on Wheatley (Town) Moor, Doncaster, and a Yorkshire historian relates that gambling was already "Injuring the fortunes of many individuals, private matches being arranged between two gentlemen who were generally their own tryers (jockeys)."

Good Queen Bess provided us with a classic anecdote at the expense of Edward de Vere, the Earl of Oxford, who some would have us believe wrote Shakespeare's plays. "The Earl, making a low obeisance to the Queen, happened to let a fart, at which he was so abashed he went to travel for seven years. At his return the Queen welcomed him home and sayd 'My Lord, I had quite forgotten the fart'!"

ELIZABETH II – Queen since 1952

Her Majesty is quoted as saying, "If it were not for my Archbishop of Canterbury I should be off to Longchamp every Sunday," which probably says it all! However even if the Queen's love of racing is not shared by her consort or her heir, no doubt her mother, sister and race-riding daughter, who at Redcar in 1986 became the first Royal winner since Charles II in 1685, used to share in her success and profit from her undoubted knowledge. In fact it is a widely held belief that the first newspaper the Queen used to pick up in the morning was *The Sporting Life*.

Early success as an owner and breeder followed her accession with both Guineas, two Oaks and a St Leger – the last two with Dunfermline in 1977.

The night before the Coronation in June 1953, with the Derby the following Saturday, one of her ladies in waiting vouchsafed, "Ma'am you must be feeling apprehensive?" The Queen absent-mindedly replied, "Yes, yes I am, but I still think

E

my horse will win." The horse was Aureole and it came second. The fact that the Queen definitely finds racing exciting is amply demonstrated to anyone watching her in the Royal Box when one of her horses is first past the post.

ELLIOTT – Charlie   d. 1979

Rider of 14 Classic winners as well as the first King George VI & Queen Elizabeth Stakes in 1951 on Supreme Court, Charlie has the following recollection of Nimbus' Guineas and Derby wins in 1949: "The ordeal of two photo finishes put one hell of a strain on his owners – Mr and Mrs Glenister. One of them fainted on Guineas Day and the other on Derby Day. I can't be sure now (1976) which one flaked out on which day, but I know they did the double!"

ENGELHARD – Charles (US)   d. 1971

A platinum billionnaire and insomniac who liked to talk all night drinking Coke, he was owner of Northern Dancer's greatest son, Nijinsky, winner of the Triple Crown and Irish Derby in 1970. He also won the Irish 2000gns on a disqualification (Kings Lake), but lost it again on appeal.

The great Russian ballet dancer, Vaslaw Nijinsky, said on his deathbed he would come back as a stallion; if Nijinsky was the result, he obviously passed on his temperament, for without O'Brien's magic touch Nijinsky would have been impossible to train.

Trainer Fulke Johnson Houghton remembers Piggott riding Engelhard's Ribero in the 1968 St Leger after an abscess in the horse's mouth had burst the night before. Lester never once touched him with the whip and literally lifted him over the line. Engelhard would pay anything for Ribot's offspring and, apart from owning the Irish Derby winners Ribocco, and Ribero, he also owned Ribofilio who was second in both the Irish Derby and St Leger.

FABRE – Andre   b. 1945

He once said, "I hate mediocre people. I just don't take the time to talk to them." He also said, in 1993, "When I go racing it is to work. I don't have the time to say hello." Just before he had a shock winner at 133-1 in the 1993 Breeder's Cup Classic he is quoted as saying, "I get fed up with hearing complaints about the tracks out here. It is silly They are fair with wonderfully designed bends." On The Derby, the French trainer said to *The Sportsman* in 2005, "It's too hard a race for three year olds. It has not produced a decent stallion in years and lives on its reputation."

FAIRFAX-BLAKEBOROUGH – Jack OBE MC   d.1976

Died aged 93 after a lifetime in racing as amateur rider, judge at Northern meetings, owner/trainer as well as racing journalist and writer of 112 books on the subject.

In JFB's first race as a judge in 1919, when he had to sort out a close finish between eight Hurdlers, one punter shouted, "He isn't fit to judge a donkey race on Redcar sands." In his memoirs JFB recounted several stories about jockeys. John Osborne once received so many instructions from an owner before a race, that he said after failing to get in the frame: "There isn't a course long enough to carry out all the orders you gave me." And to another owner who blamed him for not "coming on" according to instructions, "I couldn't come on without the horse."

At Haydock "Speedy" Payne was hauled up before rather a grand lot of stewards to explain his riding and addressed them as "My Lords, Dukes, Admirals, Colonels and gentlemen: when I rides and wins they say I ride foul; when I rides and loses they says I pulls. I have a wife at home, some money in the bank and I doesn't care a damn what you does with me!" The stewards were so amused that they let Speedy off without even a caution.

Conversely, Bob Harper, who rode around the turn of the century, told JFB that he had slipped out of the saddle so often at country meetings, when he found he was going to win on unbacked horses, that he had become quite a circus performer! Obviously you can't compare falling off to order with a genuine accident.

Jim Snowden, who rode more often drunk than sober, was, according to William I'Anson the Northern trainer, the best jockey he ever saw in either condition. Once, after a drinking bout, Snowden arrived at Chester to ride and remarked to his landlord that the town was very quiet for a race-day. "Race-day," came the reply. "Why Jim, the races were last week." When a judge, one of the most glaring errors he ever saw was at Thirsk in 1911, when Ask Papa was judged winner by half a length from Formamint, when it was obvious to all that the latter had won by at least two lengths. All the more remarkable as there were only two at the finish and their colours were quite dissimilar, although mistakes were not uncommon before the photo-finish.

He also wrote of the gangsters who operated, mainly on the race-trains, in the 1890s up to the First World War. Hopeful punters (pigeons) and successful ones (sitting ducks) all had pockets full of cash and were prey to either the Birmingham or the Glasgow Boys – the two main gangs. Their methods varied from card-sharping and pick-pocketing to blackmail; bookmakers were forced to donate to bogus charities – with threats often backed up by ex-pugilists. However they met their match at Shrewsbury in 1878 when Lord Marcus Beresford and some of his pals (who were exponents of the Noble Art) gave them a good thrashing.

F

FALLON – Kieron   b. 1965

Irish jockey of explosive temperament whose talents on the track – three times champion and winner of three of the first four classics in 1999 – have been more than matched by his antics off course. Firstly his manhandling of fellow jockey, Stuart Webster at Beverley in 1994 earned him a six month suspension. Then in his first season with Henry Cecil, his riding of Bosra Sham in the Eclipse, brought public criticism from the trainer, lost him the ride in the Champion, which in turn spurred him to over 200 winners and the title by the end of 1997. Then by Goodwood in 1999, with 116 winners under his belt, he had been sacked as first jockey to Warren Place by Cecil after his second wife and erstwhile stable-hand, Natalie, had bragged to a "friend" that she had had sex in a shower with an unnamed jockey. Cecil immediately assumed it was Fallon, but some say it was a deliberate bit of misinformation by Natalie to get her own back for another bit of stable yard frolicing on the part of Henry. Thus 32 year-old Natalie added the champion jockey to the champion owner and 40 of his horses (Sheikh Mohammed's reaction to her criticising his removal of one of his horses to Godolphin in 1995) as Warren Place losses. Henry was even more displeased when Kieron took him to Court; Mrs Fallon wasn't too pleased either, but Kieron went on to win his third championship riding for Sir Michael Stoute.

He was quoted as saying, "Racing should do away with the totting up system – where your riding offences are kept on file until you hit a certain level – who was the clown who invented this one? You do your suspension, and then if you get another some time later, you get another ban, just for good measure." Jamie Spencer (top jockey married to TV presenter Emma) would agree with him. He will go abroad and do winter racing just to avoid totting up points for the flat season.

F

Fallon returned from an 18 month drug ban for failing a second drugs test in France in September 2009 after winning the champion jockey race six times. The drug affair caused a breakup with the Ballydoyle operation and Aidan O'Brien, but he said at the time, "I love racing, I know nothing else. Outside riding, I find life a little more difficult. When I'm on a horse, it's completely different. Nothing bothers me; whereas I feel uncomfortable around different people. Maybe I think they're better than me" – an inferiority complex perhaps?

After winning the Irish derby on Hurricane Run, he said, "For years I've dreamed about winning this race ever since I was an apprentice with Kevin Prendergast – it means everything."

He said to *The Times* in September 2005, "When I went to America they asked me question about why I had been arrested. When I said it was about race-fixing the guy just looked at me and said, 'Isn't that your job?'"

His trainer Aidan O'Brien said of him, "Nobody wants to win as badly as he does. He's an absolute master of his craft – like none before." "The Morning Line when John McCririck is not on it," was his response on being asked what his favourite TV show was. (From *The Sportsman*, June 2006.)

FALMOUTH – 6th Viscount   d. 1889

Victorian turfite, and son of a parson, who loved racing for its own sake, and could afford to do so without betting; his only recorded bet being 6d on his own Queen Bertha before she went out to win the 1863 Oaks. However, his tally as a stakes winner was extraordinary for those days, creating a record in 1878 with £38,000 prize money. To give some idea of what this meant at the time, 50 years later when Lord Derby was winning owner in 1927, the value of his races won was only £40.355.

In 1883, Mathew Dawson, his trainer and Fred Archer, the champion jockey, presented him with a silver shield, on which were inscribed the winners of his two Derbys – Kingcraft (1870) and Silvio (1877) – three Oaks, St Legers, 1000 & 2000gns (his 16 Classics included two trained by John Scott) the Champion and the Great Challenge Stakes – all trained and/or ridden by the doners.

FARELL – Sid (possibly apocryphal)

An Edwardian trainer who has gone down in racing lore for a certain telegram he is purported to have sent to one of his noble patrons, who being 'something in the city' seldom got to the midweek races and therefore required a cabled report from his trainer, that evening of, his horse's performance. However, the noble Lord was somewhat taken aback when he received his first bill, and saw the cost of this method of reporting, which led him to remonstrate with Sid on his lack of conciseness.

The next week his cable was considerably shorter and read – "SF, SF, SF, SF." He immediately contacted his trainer and complained, "Brevity is one thing, but this is ridiculous." "Oh! I thought you'd understand," said an unrepentent Sid. "It's quite simple really – Started Farted Slipped and Fell See you Friday Sid Farell."

Sid was also known for never letting the truth get in the way of a good story!

FINNEY – Albert   b. 1936

Son of a bookmaker, the actor and owner of a horse called Synastry bought up all the tickets for one performance of a show he was in so he could take the day off to see his horse run. That, and reimbursing the bar for loss of profits and buying six tickets on Concorde so that he and his friends could see the race, cost him £25,000. It was the Kentucky Derby and the horse was a non-runner!

F

FITZGERALD – Mick   b. 1970

The Irish jockey in 2006 recalls his reaction to a fall: "I think I've broken my left collarbone. It couldn't be the other one as I've already had it removed."

Johnny Murtagh said to him at the beginning of his career: "Mick, if you want to do this job you've got to realise you're not a normal person." He also said, "Relationships come a very distant second to racing." He said just before he retired in December 2005, "I am an optimist, but I'm also a realist. You tend to be once you've broken your neck."

FLATMAN – Nat   d. 1860

The first officially recognised champion Flat jockey in 1846, a position he held for a further six seasons. A natural lightweight, he only won one Derby, on Orlando in 1844, and this on the disqualification of Running Rein, who was later found to be a four year old.

However, he is best known for riding Voltigeur in his two matches against The Flying Dutchman and his jockey Charles Marlow. The first one – the 1850 Doncaster Cup – he won, but Marlow was tight as a tick and conceding 19 lb. The second one in May 1851, over two miles of the Knavesmire for £1000 a side, he lost.

He never recovered from a kick he received in September 1859 and died about a year later aged 50, with 10 Classics to his credit. Always in great demand for his skill, he was also honest and could keep his mouth shut about stable form.

FORDHAM – George   d. 1887

Champion jockey from 1855–1869, excluding only 1864 and 1866, and towards the end of his career the great adversary of Fred Archer. According to John Osborne, one of his contemporaries, "Fordham rode short, after the new American style, and Archer long. Fordham rode more with his hands than Archer and didn't punish his horse as much as poor Fred. I should think he was a better jockey than Archer all round."

He was nicknamed "the Kid" for the way he kidded the other jockeys, and also "The Demon". Archer confessed after losing one race to him that, "He never could make out what old George was up to." He would often feign distress to encourage his opponents to make their effort too early and then pounce.

He was so good with fillies, being very sparing with whip and spur, that they provided him with 13 out of his 16 Classic wins, including the 1000gns seven times. He managed to win the Derby once on Sir Bevys in 1879, but his biggest disappointment was on Lord Clifden in the 1863 Derby, where after 34 false starts he looked round, only to let Tom Chaloner on Macaroni pip him at the post. Apparently he wouldn't go in to dine that evening, but sat on the stairs, sobbing his heart out.

George was only an astonishing 3st 12lb when he won his first race in 1851 at the age of 14. Once before the Royal Hunt Cup, Archer started to curse his senior, and George told him he would teach him a lesson. Sure enough he soon found a race where he could hold him up and stop him winning – "I do not think Archer will ever take a liberty with old George again," he said. George spoke as he found and when the Duchess of Montrose dismissed him, as she was in the habit of doing with her jockeys, he informed the Pink 'Un (*The Financial Times*), which reported: " The Duchess of Montrose has requested Fordham to send in his cap and jacket. He did so instantly, for fear the Duchess might change her mind."

Once, after being tipped only £5 after winning a valuable race, he decided to even the score. After beating another horse owned by the miserly owner, he said in the unsaddling enclosure, "Look sharp I'm a bit short on weight," knowing the man had overheard. Sure enough the fellow soon appeared in the weighing room, ready to lodge an objection, only to see a gleeful George weigh in at the correct weight.

F

Actually he was not that motivated by money, and refused a retainer for £1500, when Mr Stirling Crawfurd was only retaining him for £1000 pa. His main failing was, like a number of Victorian jockeys, drink; before the 1872 City and Suburban he and his trainer, Henry Woolcott, knocked off a whole bottle of port, which the latter brought to stimulate the horse. He then went out on the more sober animal and won the race.

FORSTER OBE – Capt. Tim   d. 1999

Best remembered for saddling three National winners, the first of which, Well To Do, was willed to him by his owner who had paid only £750 for him as a three year old. Tim only made up his mind to run him half an hour before the 1972 race declarations closed. The second time in 1980 with Ben Nevis, he instucted the jockey to "just keep on re-mounting", while the last time in 1985 he sent off Hywel Davies on Last Suspect with the encouraging words, "I'll see you when they've caught the horse." An immensely affable man, he was rarely able to look on the bright side, and was known for his pessimistic humour.

More recently he trained both Paddy Hartigan's Martha's Son to win the Queen Mother Champion Chase after only jumping one fence in public during the preceding 16 months and Hugh Sumner's Dublin Flyer (£201,000 prize money). A steeplechasing man to the end, he said, "One day I'm going to stand for Parliament, and if I get in my first Bill will be to abolish Flat racing and my second will be to do away with hurdlers."

FRANCIS – Dick   d. 2010

Jump jockey who will always be remembered for the 1956 Grand National, when riding the Queen Mother's Devon Loch to within 50 yards of victory, the horse suddenly collapsed under him to give ESB the race. Although never explained, it was thought at the time he may have tried to leap a shadow, or was upset by the roar of the crowd.

Apparently he still had to tie his arm to his side before he went to bed, because if he got his elbow above his head while he was asleep, he dislocated his shoulder. He turned professional in 1948, became champion jockey in 1953/4 and retired in 1957.

Starting as a contributor to the *Sunday Express*, he published his first thriller with a racing background in 1962 – *Dead Cert* – and over 40 novels later divided his time between Berkshire and Florida. For his first three years, he co-wrote with Tony Lakin, a Sussex breeder, then with his wife of 53 years until she died in 2000, and since 2004 with one of his sons, Felix. His other son Merrick said in September 2005, "Racing thrives on an element of skulduggery."

FRANCOME – John   b. 1952

Seven times champion jump jockey, whose antics have taken up almost as much print as his wins! He actually rode a record 1138 winners between 1970 and 1985, thus breaking Stan Mellor's record of 1035.

A renowned practical joker, he was also a shrewd entrepreneur and describes himself as having been "not so much a jockey as a businessman who rode horses." He rode the unfortunately named Stopped in the 1978 Imperial Cup and came in third, to find himself the subject of a Stewards' enquiry and later a hearing at the Jockey Club's Portman Sq. H.Q. After the hearing he told Fred Winter that he had never stopped a horse in his life, to which the Guv'nor replied, "Son, if I thought you had you wouldn't be standing there, you'd be lying down." His answer was to go out and win the Gold Cup for Fred 13 days later. He eventually was cleared of the charge.

His first day at Uplands started well when he went into the stable to muck out his horse after first switching on his transistor radio. The horse broke its head collar then started haring round the stable before "Franc" managed to cut in and turn it off. Apparently 26 other horses within earshot were putting up a similar performance

F

and four other head collars were broken and one horse got out onto the Guv'nor's lawn.

He recounts a number of occasions when he was the subject of the Guv'nor's sarcasm – after one misunderstanding Winter said, "That's all right, son, it's not your fault," and JF breathed a sigh of relief before he continued, "It's my fault. You're so f——g stupid I should have written your instructions down on a blackboard."

He wrote in 1985: "I think the main reason I spent so much time in the Steward's Room was that they quite rightly detected, and resented the fact, that I rarely took them seriously."

When riding with Steve Smith Eccles, one of his pranks was to pin a pair of tights to a steward's collar while the other one distracted him. "Franc" was always having brushes with the stewards, often for failing to ride out horses for the minor placings; his last such appearance at Portman Square was when he was fined a swingeing £2500, which coincidentally came only two weeks after he had referred to them as "cabbage patch dolls" at the Race Writers' luncheon. On another occasion, a permit holder from Wales, called Bryn Thomas, was hauled up at Hereford with JF to explain why his horse had run so badly. He stormed in, slapped his cap on the table, and demanded to know why they were wasting his time. The stewards explained that even the Queen's horses were subject to enquiry. "Aye I know," said Bryn, "but when she gets home she hasn't got 70 f——g cows to milk."

Unfortunately, Franc's misplaced humour at enquiries often led to him getting a stiffer penalty than he might have done; however, his humour wasn't only reserved for stewards. Jockeys are often in a hurry to get to meetings, and once on the way to Leicester he went through a red light at 70mph. A policeman saw him and stopped him two miles out of town and asked him if he realised, etc. "Yes, officer, you don't want to hang about when you go through them on red," said Franc. Everyone laughed at the subsequent court hearing (except PC Plod), but he still got banned for three months.

F

His generous spirit got him into trouble sometimes, as when on the morning of the 1982 Schweppes Handicap Hurdle he offered Scudamore and Smith Eccles the chance to share the £600 prize, whichever of them won, which he duly did on Donegal Prince. Being a man of his word he gave the other two a cheque each for £200 before he left the course. The following Monday he recounted the story in *The Sun*; three months later the Jockey Club started an investigation which ended in all three getting a week's suspension "for receiving presents from persons other than the owner of the horse he rides in that race." A ludicrous affair, considering the amount of money involved and that the spirit of the law was not impugned.

His sportsmanship was again evident when "Scu" had broken his arm near the end of the 1981/2 season with a lead of 20. John rang him and said if he could catch him up he would hang up his boots for the season and share the championship – which he did on 120 wins. By June 1984 he had beaten Mellor's record and by the November had lowered Josh Gifford's record for the fastest 50 which had stood for 18 years. He hung up his boots at the end of the season. When he retired he shared championship honours with Fred Winter, who was then leading trainer, and for whom he had ridden 575 winners in his career.

He was wont to flirt with the pretty wife of a friend of his, who decided to pull both their legs by teaching the parrot to say "Knickers off – Johnny Francome's coming." This joke worked like a treat until the local constabulary called in to investigate a robbery, and on hearing the "tip-off" decided to question Francome.

According to *The Sun* he had these plans for his 52nd Birthday celebrations in December 2004: "I planned a day of group sex for myself and 20 of my closest friends – all of whom are women." When he was asked the question by *The Sportsman* in 2006, "Who is your favourite actress?" he replied "Jenny Pitman". He also in the same interview said "Gynaecologist" when he was asked to give an alternative career. He has also been described as the Hugh Grant of televised racing by the *Daily Mail* in February 2005.

"Always more Jilly Cooper than Norman Mailer," critic Jackie Dineen said of Francome's novels in 2004.

F

FREUD – Sir Clement "Clay"   d.2009

The Liberal MP and sometime owner in the late 60s of a yearling called Overseas Buyer, so named in order to claim all his running costs against tax, since Harold Wilson's last budget had disallowed all entertainment unless for an overseas buyer. His attitude to expenses showed a similar creative talent when working on those dog-food commercials for Quaker in the 70s (Minced Morsels – the ones with the bloodhound called Henry in them. Ed.) He put the horse with Toby Balding who said, "Come and see him work; we'll put you up." Clay brought his pyjamas; he was meant to ride out!

He recounts the time when a woman standing beside him as the runners for a novice hurdle were led around the ring, said Country Pride would win. He pointed out that all 10 runners had Country Pride on their saddlecloth to acknowledge the race's sponsor. As Clay says, "She opined I was a smart-ass."

Working for the *Sun* at the time as a Sports writer, his editor persuaded him to have a go at race-riding, even though it meant losing two stone. Helped by Balding he took out an amateur's licence – in Ireland – and, starting at Naas for one of Toby's braver owners, rode what he could get for 18 months, including a challenge match for £1000 against his friend Sir Hugh Fraser at Haydock, which he won riding Winter Fare, collecting some bruises and broken ribs on the way. The bookies were offering 5-1 on either rider finishing alone. Freud put up 22 lbs overweight, or 22 tins of dogfood!

He is quoted as saying about Newmarket, "Throughout the land the British class system has gone to pot... at Cheltenham the Queen Mother shook hands with a bookmaker's clerk who had a cigarette in his mouth.... but at racing's HQ (The Jockey Club) the feudal system is still going strong."

He started gambling at the age of eight when at a Devon boarding school. Mr Rogers ran the local garage, took bets illegally, and was a miserable old sod. Once when a 2d each way bet had come up at 13-2 Clay raced to the door to collect.

Rogers looked at him over his glasses and said, "How old are you, boy?" To which Clay replied, "About a day older than when you took my money."

He recalls in his book *Freud on Course* once at Folkestone in 1964, he was watching a pin-fired, wall-eyed gelding called Bullfrog limp around the ring after winning a selling race. The auctioneer started the bidding at £100 and Clay raised his racecard. "Do I hear guineas?" the auctioneer asked. He didn't. And Clay was an owner. It lasted precisely two months. The horse went lame and he sold him for only a slight loss. Lucky owner. Uri Geller became his racing partner when he opened a fete in Freud's constituency. He won at 2500-1; He always won he said – how embarrassing! Anyway, they bought a young filly together, which they called Spoonbender. Uri came up with some quite impressive reasons why she always ran so badly.

Clay as a punter visited every racecourse in England, and a good few in Ireland. Once when he was invited to Killarney he was asked whether he'd prefer to fly from Stansted or Luton, which is a bit like saying, "Would you rather have leprosy or syphilis?"

Freud said, when he wrote about his trainers in 1998, that as far as cooking was concerned, Venetia Williams depends heavily on her deepfreeze and M&S. "St Michael and I do have a very close relationship," she replied. (This from a woman who only takes one National newspaper – the *Telegraph*: "Good paper for bedding down horses".)

His one-liners were many and varied, but all of them good value, as when W.C. Fields (the American comic) was given a glass of water and asked what he thought of it. He replied, "I don't know what it is – but it won't sell."

Another was while sitting next to a brace of ex-warriors (Chelsea Pensioners) on a park bench, shortly before he died, he heard one say "You know those pills they gave us in the war (1939-45) to take our minds off women? – Well! I think mine's just beginning to work." And again the old pre-war *Punch* cartoon featuring public

F

school man and office girl at Victoria station on a Monday morning. She: "If I'm pregnant, I don't know what I shall do – I think I shall kill myself." He: "Oh! I say that's frightfully decent of you."

His rarified brand of humour even extended to the Royal Ascot Racing Club of which he was a member (and part owner of Motivator – 2005 Derby winner), when he observed that the RARC had done for racing syndicates what the Boston strangler did for door to door salesmen. He apparently didn't particularly rate journalists either when he said in 2005, "Hacks do not reveal their sources – unless of course the money's right."

In 1990 he wrote a series called "Behind Enemy Lines" which examined the life of bookmakers and was prefaced by his own view: "The human race, to which so many of my readers belong, tend to rank bookies as socially unacceptable – 'gents' rather than gentlemen. Many of them are aware of this and call themselves turf accountants." Maybe the heading for Freud's last column should have read "Oh God ! Our help in wagers past."

In September 2005 he said, "Until an authority offers prize money to whoever wears the most comfortable boiler suit and finds ticket sales decreasing as a result, I shall continue to resent dressing just to watch it." He said in the *Racing Post* in 2006: "If you mind losing more than you enjoy winning – don't bet."

He said in 2006, "The average racegoer's modest ambition is to find a place from which the opportunities to eat, drink, watch the race and urinate are no more than a minute away."

FURLONG – Noel (Ire)   b. 1937

Furlong was associated with the biggest 'crack' ever at the Cheltenham Festival when his horse Destriero won the Supreme Novice's Hurdle in 1991. His winnings were estimated at anything from £1m (by himself) to £3m (by everyone else), and the horse on only his second outing was backable at 6-1. However, the real story lies in what led up to it. Furlong was a wholesale carpet magnate, who in 1985, after experiencing a little difficulty with unpaid VAT on imported shag-pile, decided that the rigours of life in Dublin were preferable to facing charges and a likely sentence in Kingston Crown Court, and jumped bail for £500,000 – a record at the time. However by March 1991 he had found a way to settle with Customs & Excise in order to pave the way for his triumphant return to Cheltenham. The previous December Destriero had romped home at Leopardstown to net his connections between £100k and £150k, which was followed three weeks later by his nine year old The Iliad coming in at 33-1 in a handicap hurdle – where he was laid £10k each way. With these winnings Noel was easily able to settle with the vatman and prepare for Cheltenham!

G

GAINES – John (US)   b. 1928

Owner of Gainesway Stud in Kentucky. By the early 1980s he had 45 stallions standing, including Blushing Groom, third to The Minstrel in the 1977 Derby, but who, after siring Nashwan, the 1989 Derby winner, in 1991 lived up to his name and failed to get any of the 23 mares he covered in foal – and was retired and has since died – presumably of boredom. A breeding farm with that number of stallions would be covering over 2000 mares a year.

In 1984 he masterminded the Breeders Cup to give $10m of prize-money in an afternoon's racing. Each stud farm had to contribute one nomination to each sire; by letting the stallion cover an extra mare it didn't cost them a cent! This was a big incentive for home buyers to continue to pay huge yearling prices, but it didn't stop the crash of 1986 when Gainesway was a hostage to falling bloodstock prices like the rest.

One memorable, if ill-informed, comment when the Lexington racing community tried to shrug off the portents of the impending sale of his pictures was, "I heard one of them's a Claude Monet – that 12 furlong horse sired by Affirmed over in England. Can't understand why Mr Gaines wanted a picture of him in the first place." The sale actually fetched $21m, which prompted another breeder to quip, "Pity Sheikh Mohammed wasn't there, they'd a fetched $41m."

GALBREATH – John K. (US)   d. 1997

Owner/Breeder of Darby Dan Farm, Lexington, Kentucky, apart from breeding 13 American Classic winners, JK himself won two Kentucky Derbys. However it was as owner of the controversial 1972 Derby winner Roberto (named after Roberto Clemente, the Pittsburgh Pirates star on Galbreaths' World Series winning baseball team) that Galbreath first made his name in England. J.K. flew in just before the race to find that Bill Williamson, the veteran Australian jockey booked for the ride, had damaged a shoulder. Despite his protestations that he was able to ride, the 74yr old Galbreath was not risking the Derby on anything less than 100% fitness and told Williamson that Piggott would be aboard. However, to sweeten the pill he promised him the 10% jockey's bonus if Piggott won. The public assumed that Piggott as usual was the villain of the piece and greeted his victory in virtual silence, even though he beat Ernie Johnson on Rheingold by an almost superhuman effort with only inches to spare. He actually gave Roberto a whack on the nose in the final couple of strides, which made him put his head down and so win the race. JK thus became the first man to breed and own the winners of the Kentucky and Epsom Derbys. Later that year Roberto handed Brigadier Gerard his only career defeat, winning in record time at York, and thus denying the Brigadier the chance of matching Ribot's record of 16 wins straight off the reel.

GALEA – Perce (Aus)   d. 1977

A high rolling Aussie punter and who regularly staked six figure sums on a horse said, "I couldn't go to the races and not have a bet. That would be the same as going to church and not praying."

GARRETT – Jonathan

Commercial manager of Scottish Racing in September 2005 opined, "There's been no history of investment in training facilities in Scotland. We have no Malton or Lambourn up here and we need to identify such a place and then develop it."

G

GENTRY – Tom (US)

The son of Olin Gentry, who ran Darby Dan Stud Farm in Kentucky, Tom was a great spotter and promoter of commercial yearlings. He sold Alleged (by Hoist the Flag) to the Sangster Syndicate in 1976 as a two years old – later to be sold back to Kentucky for $16m after winning the Arc in 1977 and 1978. By the early eighties the cabarets at his buyer's parties led the pre-Keeneland Sales entertainment; all of this prompted one Kentucky hardboot to say, "There's more whores in the Hyatt than I've got yearlings on my farm."

In 1984 he picked up $7.9m for 13 yearlings from his Lexington farm; the next year he received $7m for one Nijinsky colt bought by Sheikh Mohammed (Laa Etaab – it couldn't run a yard). But in 1986 the market crashed and by 1987 Tommy had gone spectacularly bust for $14.4m, and this after taking $35m out of the salesrooms in the preceding five years.

GEORGE IV – King 1820-1830

Only four years after he had started racing at the age of 21, 'Prinny' won the 1788 Derby with Sir Thomas, but by 1790 he was running no fewer than 39 horses and was also running into debt. And although the next year he won the Oatland Stakes with a purse of 2950gns, it was just as well a scandal involving his jockey. Sam Chifney (although he was not implicated personally) led him to withdraw from racing. It concerned the running of his horse Escape, where Chifney was thought to have stopped the horse, when favourite, to lengthen the odds for the next day when he had 20gns on him; the horse duly obliged. Sir Charles Bunbury, as Senior Steward of the Jockey Club, told the Prince that no gentleman would run his horse against him if he continued to employ Chifney.

In 1795, to settle his debts, he married Caroline of Brunswick, who was unimpressed both by his looks and the fact that he collapsed in a drunken stupour into her bedroom grate, where he spent the rest of their wedding night. His figure was the cause of Beau Brummel losing his position as favourite, when Prinny overheard him remark to Lady Worcester, "Who is your fat friend?"

His Queen eventually died at the same time as Napoleon, when he was in Ireland, and when a courtier announced his death with the words, "Sire, I congratulate you, your greatest enemy is dead." The King replied, "Is she, by God!"

GEORGE V – King 1910-1936

Known more as a matchless shot, he was keener on racing than was generally supposed and possessed a fair knowledge of the Stud Book. On his coronation the lads at Newmarket subscribed 6d each and gave him a pair of raceglasses. Greatly touched, he insisted on thanking them in person. As an owner he was unlucky, but even so ran the unbeaten two year old Friar Marcus, and Scuttle (1928 1000gns). Once at Royal Ascot, Queen Mary ordered a sporty peeress to be removed from the Royal Enclosure, where she was seen wearing a sailor hat with "HMS Good Ship Venus" emblazoned on the rim.

As an ex-sailor he didn't intend to travel to foreign parts – "Abroad is awful. I know because I've been there" – but he liked risque stories, as when Lord Mountbatten's sister visited Uppsala Cathedral, while Crown Princess Louise of Sweden. The Archbishop, keen to show his command of English as he approached a chest of drawers in the sacristy, made the mind-boggling declaration, "I will now open these trousers and reveal some even more precious treasures to your Royal Highness." He was particularly indulgent to The Duchess of York (the Queen Mother), as on the occasion when she was late for dinner, saying, "You are not late, my dear, I think we must have sat down two minutes early." His attitude to The Prince of Wales (Edward VIII) was made apparent when he shouted, "You dress like a cad. You act like a cad. You are a cad. Get out!" However, the King's much quoted 'last words' – "Bugger Bogner" – were in fact delivered when Bogner Regis was suggested as a suitable place to recuperate from an earlier illness, and not on his death-bed.

G

GEORGE VI – King   1936-52

In 1942 with the nation at war, His Majesty, who, with his Queen, stayed at Buckingham Palace throughout, was a very popular winner of four classics in 1942 with Big Game (2000 gns) and Sun Chariot, who won the Fillies' Triple Crown and in winning the St Leger actually beat the Derby winner Watling St by three lengths. A daughter of Hyperion, she was highly temperamental and neither her trainer, Fred Darling nor Gordon Richards could get her to do what they wanted if she was not in the mood – this led to her only defeat when she refused to take hold of her bit. Afterwards, The King presented Richards with a Munnings portrait of the two of them, which he treasured to his death. The King also won the 1000gns in 1946 with Hypericum, trained by Capt. Boyd Rochfort.

His alarm on hearing of his brother's abdication, due in part to his stammer, prompted him to say to his cousin Lord Louis Mountbatten, "I never wanted this to happen. I'm quite unprepared for it – I'm only a naval officer." His cousin reminded him what his own father had said to the future King George V: "There is no more fitting preparation for a king than to be trained in the Royal Navy." His stammer occasionally lent point to his remarks, as when on a troop inspection he said to Brig. Hinde routinely: "Have we met before?" "I don't think so, Sir," said Hinde, "You should bl-bloody well know," said the King tartly.

GERAGHTY – Barry   b. 1978

He said to *The Racing Post* in 2005, "Noel Mead once said I was a cocky little bastard. I'd say it was probably true – I was always pretty sure of myself. If you don't believe in your own ability then who will?"

The same year he was accused by a racegoer at Listowell that he'd be "Nothing without Moscow Flyer," to which he commented, "As I turned away I thought there might be something in that."

GLANELY – 1st Viscount   d. 1942

Formerly James Tatem, a shipping clerk made good, he was known to the racing public between the wars as "Old Guts and Gaiters" – epitomised by his walrus moustache, loud mouth and florid complexion. However he spent an immense amount on bloodstock and once when he took his seat at Tattersalls for the July sales in a suit of white duck and panama hat, the auctioneer greeted him with "And from which end will you open the bowling, My Lord?" – his other great love being cricket.

Among his many unwise investments he did purchase Grand Parade to win the 1919 Derby, and again in 1934 his 2000gns winner Colombo was favourite to win the Derby. However, Rae Johnstone was boxed in and could only manage third place. His laconic reply to the enraged punters, who thought he had pulled the horse, was "At least no lives were lost." What passed between jockey and owner is not on record, but old G & G immediately cancelled his retainer and fired him as first jockey.

GLASGOW – 5th Duke of   d. 1869

An owner whose madness led him to having his horses shot if they failed to shine in their trial gallops. He also so hated naming horses that they ended up with names like "Give him a Name" or "He is not Worth a Name." He often changed trainers, usually in a moment's irritation.

His strong will was matched by a reckless spirit and, luckily, a practically limitless fortune, so that he could indulge his love of wagering, as when he accepted a £500 bet that he would drive a team from Hawkhead to Ardrossan to beat Lord Kennedy after dinner in the dark. Glasgow, or Kelburne as he was then, lost through taking a wrong turning, and in so doing nearly drove his horses over a cliff into the sea. His face never betrayed the winning or losing of the £50,000 he often wagered. He also scorned the wearing of an overcoat, then a new-fangled luxury, to the end.

G

GLENDENNING – Raymond   d. 1974

The well known BBC radio commentator once said, "He's drawing ahead – it is sure to be Lex – no, it's Harpagon." It wasn't, it was Coronach (the 1927 Derby winner).

GINISTRELLI – Cavaliere Odoardo (Ita)   d. 1920

The breeder, owner and trainer of Signorinetta, who won the Oaks and Derby in 1908, deserves a mention because he, like so many Italians, brought romance to the Turf. He had bred the unbeaten Signorina from St Simon, but she herself proved an extremely shy breeder – in fact she was barren 10 years in succession! However in the next door paddock was a nine guinea stallion called Chaleureux, who Signorina would gallop to greet every morning. The Cavaliere decided to try once again "... on the boundless laws of sympathy and love." The resultant foal from the 18yr old Signorina was Signorinetta.

However, his attitude to his jockeys fell somewhat short of romantic, as William Bullock found after his 1908 triumphs; the Cavaliere did not believe in presents.

GOODWILL – Arthur   d. 1996

Better known as "Fiddler" Goodwill ever since he arrived as an apprentice at Harvey Leader's stable with a violin under his arm. He rode mainly under NH Rules before the war and then took out a trainer's licence in 1945; he soon earned a reputation at Newmarket for his skilful placing of moderate horses to win races. In August 1966 he saddled four winners out of four at Wolverhampton and retired in 1981.

He was also quite good at naming horses, as when in the fifties he had a racemare called Raggotty Anne, named after his wartime Newmarket landlady, Anne Long, whose general disregard of cobwebs and dust was very much in the tradition of Lady Haversham in *Great Expectations*.

GREAVES – Alex   b. 1968

Leading woman rider, whose success on the all-weather surface at Southwell earned her the nickname of "Queen of the Sands". However after winning the Lincoln in 1991, a year later she said, "The chances of me or any other successful lady jockey getting into the big league is nil." A sentiment echoed by Gee Armitage, the jump jockey in her autobiography. It seems to be generally accepted that most women would be exhausted after a three mile Chase and would be beaten by men on the run-in; even Mercy Rimell said she didn't approve of women riders – something about their being the wrong shape! However this cannot hold true on the Flat – witness Emma O'Gorman made the top 50 in 1993 and Joanna Morgan rode in the Irish Derby and the Arc, once beating Lester Piggott in a photo finish. In North America Kathy Kusner, former film star Robyn Smith, and Canadian Joan Phipps, have all proved they can beat men in top-class races. She later married Northern Sprint trainer Dandy Nicholls.

In 1995, Alex, after riding 400 winners on the Flat, orchestrated a gamble on Samah in the H&K Commissions Handicap which reputedly earned connections £1m.

In 2005 she said, "I've always struggled with my weight. I rode nine lots of work the other day in a sweat suit, then got on the treadmill, had a swim – and lost half a pound." She also said, "Being a girl in this game – you have to work twice as hard to prove yourself."

GREEN – Tom

Popular Northern trainer and King of the Platers of the late 19th century, who would have been a great one but for his liking for the drink, moreover he was not always able to restrain his jockeys from indulging themselves. Once, at Catterick Bridge, Jim Snowden, who was about to ride in a Plate told the lad leading the horse round to take off his blinkers. The boy said the horse always ran in them "Take them off" said Jim "its bad enough having a jockey who can't see straight, without having a blind horse as well." Despite his condition he won the race.

G

On one occasion Tom was addressing an after-dinner gathering of Northern trainers after Stockton races and said, "Gentlemen, there is one man here who is a damn thief (usually a term reserved for someone who pulled his horses), and I refuse to sit at the same table as him." Eventually it was decided that they should fight it out; both were big men, but Tom had a fist that could fell an ox and soon knocked out his opponent. That done everyone sat down to a hearty dinner.

GRIFFIN – J.H

A Dublin-born businessman whose fortune made in canned meat earned him the name of "Mincemeat Joe". In 1952 he made a brief but dramatic entry into the Owner's List, which he headed in 1953 with Early Mist winning the National to bring his winnings to £10,015. He then proceeded to buy, on Vincent O'Brien's advice, the chaser Royal Tan and the hurdler Galatian. However on the eve of the National, Bryan Marshall, who was owed £500 from the previous year's race, refused to ride Royal Tan. The row was eventually smoothed over and Marshall duly gained him his second victory – but Griffin hadn't a penny on as he couldn't get any credit on the rails. Galatian then won the Liverpool Hurdle so that their joint prize money again made him winning owner – but the £10,707 was not enough to save him being bankrupted for £80,000 later that year. The luckless Bryan Marshall was a creditor for £2781.

GULLY – John   d. 1863

The celebrated prize-fighter, who later became M.P. for Pontefract, was a keen punter and, as an owner, and won all the Classics once. However he could easily have been put off at the start of his racing career, when, after buying the 1827 Derby winner Mameluke from Lord Jersey, and backing it to win £40,000 in the St Leger, the horse was narrowly beaten after the starter, who was bribed to ensure the horse was left at the start, engineered several false starts until he was! After settling his enormous debts he merely remarked, "It is always convenient, but it is not always pleasant."

Five years later he did win the race with Margrave and in 1846 added the 1000 gns, Oaks and Derby with The Mendicant. In 1854 he completed the set with The Hermit taking the 2000gns and chalked up a second Derby with Andover.

Gully was the first respectable bookmaker, and was considered sufficiently 'gentrified' for Squire Osbaldeston to call him out for a duel – with pistols not fisticuffs. Luckily the Squire's aim was slightly off, which led Gully to make another of his droll remarks: "Better my hat than my head."

H

HAIGH – Paul

Journalist for *The Racing Post*, commented at Japan's Kasamatsu racetrack in July 2005, "The victor, a six year old called Winning Pose, who had managed to run up a total of 106 races without troubling the judge, tells us all we need to know about the tremendous lack of talent that the sponsors managed to attract."

HALL – Sam   d. 1977

One of the great Yorkshire trainers who specialised in big handicaps and one-liners. "Keep yourself in the best company and your horse in the worst," was one of his favourites.

As he trained nine horses for the Racegoers Club in the 70s, everyone a winner and not one costing over £2000, he obviously followed his own maxim. His most successful buy was a little filly called Voucher Book, who won eight times and cost 350gns.

He was also quick to dispose of an animal that wasn't paying its way: "Better an empty house," he would say, "than a bad tenant." He died suddenly at 61, but not before he had sent out his 1000th winner in July 1974.

HANCOCK – Arthur "Bull" (US)

Arthur and his sons Seth and Arthur III – owners of Claiborne, America's greatest stud farm, breeders of two Kentucky Derby winners and owners of a third (Sunday Silence). Apart from the ill-tempered Nasrullah, who Bull had brought from

Ireland, the stallion roster included the English Derby winners Sir Ivor and Nijinsky, together with Bold Ruler and Secretariat among its 27 stallions. Seth syndicated Conquistador Cielo for a record-breaking $36m.

Arthur III left Claiborne in 1972 to found his own stud at Stone Farm, backed by Nelson Bunker Hunt. Unlike his younger brother he was big and athletic, and loved fast cars, women and carousing in general. But, like his father before him, he knew a racehorse and a potential stallion, and bred Hawaian Sound, only narrowly beaten in the 1978 Derby by Shirley Heights. He was apprehensive about some of the things administered to horses, and said to the associated press in 2006, "We're breeding a chemical horse. Nobody really knows the long-term effect of what these drugs will do. It's weakening the breed and it's dangerous."

On one occasion he was courting a lady who continually refused to accede to his persistent demands, preferring her little dog as a bedfellow. Whereupon Arthur grabbed the dog and holding it out the window of her hotel bedroom, which was on the 26th floor, uttered the immortal words, "OK Lady! Take your pick – dog or dick."

HANNAM – Charlie   d. 1947

A Yorkshire gambler who rocked the ring enough times to be called the most successful gambler of all time. Known as Old England, he still failed to settle his losses in the end after losing £36,000 over Domaha's defeat in the 1936 Cambridgeshire, and was never seen on a racecourse again. He started making a small book as a junior clerk in a railway office, then quit as a teenager in the 1880s to take a pitch in Tattersalls, but soon turned from being a layer to a career as a punter. Up at dawn for a drink of milk and soda he did his Form research in time to arrive at the course by midday to glean more information from his contacts. His amazing aptitude for figures allowed him to tell at a glance whether he could back several horses in a race and still make a profit if one came in. He amassed a large fortune in the 1930s and owned a dozen horses as well as buying shares in racecourses and other companies.

His long run of some 40 years as a professional punter was largely due to his refusal to let his judgement be influenced by trainers and jockeys, who have taken many a plunge into the abyss. His nerves of steel allowed him once at Monte Carlo to play billiards for £3000 and then offer double or quits when the odds were 100-1 against him winning. He won.

HANNON – Richard   b. 1945

Has trained near Marlborough since 1970, winning the 2000gns in 1973 with Mon Fils. When Mon Fils won at 50-1, he told the press, "F—k you all, I'll never have to work again. Not until Monday anyway."

He devised a novel version of the three card trick some years ago when his wife had triplets – two boys and a girl. When he had a room full of his Irish drinking chums he would nip upstairs, collect the trio, place them side by side on the sofa and announce they were going to play Find the Lady. Once the bets had piled up he would remove the nappies with a flourish and pay the punters who had found the little girl. Then he'd bellow, "All out of the room while I shuffle the pack," and the game would start all over again. A marvellous source of income until their sex became too obvious.

In 1993 when he had weekend runners in Italy and Germany he was asked where he would go, to which he replied, "I'll tell the owners of the Italian job that I will be in Germany and to the others I'll be in Italy. Meanwhile I will be sitting at home having a bit of roast beef."

When interviewed by *Pacemaker* in June 2005 said about exchanges, "I'm totally against them, I don't agree with them. It bangs racing out to people who like skulduggery and it's just not the way forward to me." His son, Richard Junior, trainer of The Queen's Marching Song, which had just been beaten by Michael Jarvis' Gimasha, apparently said in the August of the same year, "You won't be getting a knighthood Mr Jarvis."

HARLEY – Steve   b. 1951

Also known as The Cockney Rebel (winner of the 2000gns in 2007), which occasioned him to say, "I've lived a life and I've just lived it all over again in the last two minutes. This was as exciting as anything for me – and I've done a lot."

HARTSTON – William

This writer, commenting on Royal Ascot, said: "Nowhere on Earth outside a nudist club is a dress code liable to be quite as fierce."

HARRINGTON – Jessica   b. 1947

The trainer of Moscow Flyer when asked about future plans for the horse in 2004, said "The plan now is to have lots to drink." The owner of Moscow Flyer, Brian Kearney, said the following of her in March 2005. "I'll be guided by my trainer – she will ask my advice and then tell me what to do."

HARTY – Eddie (Ire)   b. 1937

Jump jockey turned trainer who won the Grand National on Highland Wedding in 1969, but said that when he first walked round the course the only thing that kept him there was the thought that other human beings had jumped it. And they had been doing it for quite a while.

On another occasion at Ayr he thought he had won the Scottish National and stood up in his stirrups and waved to the crowd – until the whole field galloped past him – on the last circuit! Afterwards in the Steward's room he gave such a lengthy account of himself that they were too keen to see him go to think about punishing him.

H

HASLAM, Patrick

"One of the advantages of being a trainer past your sell-by date is that what you gained as experience and unless you're a complete pratt, you are then able to recognize and identify the sort of horses you've got," said the trainer, who is certainly qualified to make that remark considering he's had at least one winner at each of our 59 race courses.

HASTINGS – Harry 4th Marquis   d. 1868

Died aged 26. Orphaned at two, he came into his brother's titles and lands in 1851 at the age of 9, played the fool at Eton and by the time he left Oxford he had fallen into the hands of the moneylender Henry Padwick who ruined him by the time he was 26; even though he won more than he lost by betting vast fortunes on the Turf. At 21 he had 50 horses in training with Honest John Day at Danebury and a year later ran off with and married the bride-to-be of one of his closest friends, but soon to be the object of an obsessive enmity, Henry Chaplin, in what became known as the Lady Florence Paget affair (see Chaplin – Henry).

His 25th year was the year of Henry Chaplin's Derby with Hermit, against whom Hastings had laid £120k – out of spite! The same year, 1867, he had a brilliant two yearold filly, Lady Elizabeth, who was undefeated until the Middle Park Plate in the autumn. However this time Fordham rode a badly judged race and she was beaten, costing her owner £50,000. To prove she should have won Harry and John Day, only two days later, forced her into a race for 1000 sovereigns against a three year old, which she won. However, although the winter favourite for the Derby, the effort had ruined her, as her Spring trials evidenced. Strangely, even though they hadn't dare give her a race before the Derby, Harry, after being closeted with " The Spider" – Padwick, withdrew his second string, The Earl, a real contender, and let her run. The public, seeing this, started her favourite at 7-4, but she was never in the race which was won by Sir Joseph Hawley's Blue Gown. Harry had even stood to win £35k on the Earl, who proceded to prove his class by winning the Grand Prix, the Ascot Derby and the St James Palace Stakes, all within a month of being scratched from the Derby.

Hastings had now lost his money and estate, his name, and his health – and in November 1868 he died of TB.

HAWLEY – Sir Joseph 1814–1875

Another eminent Victorian turfist and reforming member of the Jockey Club, who won eight Classics, including four Derbys between 1851 and 1868.

He is best remembered for two scratchings and an objection, none of which enhanced his popularity with the betting public. In 1869 he and his trainer, John Porter, tried out his colt, Vagabond and decided he was a pretty good bet for The City & Suburban. However the news of the trial got out and when he sent his agent to put his money on, he found Vagabond was already favourite. He immediately instructed Porter to withdraw him and enter him for the Grand Met., which as the race was too short he proceded to lose. Next, his horse Pedro Gomez, which was well fancied, was beaten by a short head in the Derby by Pretender, after being almost brought down at Tattenham Corner. However there was a rumour that the winner's owner, a Mr Sadler, had died that morning, which would have made his nomination void. Hawley, without checking, wrote to Weatherbys, the stakeholders and advised them to withhold payment, only to find that Sadler was not only alive, but had been at Epsom watching the race. His second scratching was in the Liverpool Autumn Cup, when he withdrew the favourite, Blue Gown shortly before the race, which was won by the least fancied of his original three entries, coming in at long odds with £500 of Sir Joseph's money on it. By this time The Pink 'Un (*The Sporting Times*) came out with a vitriolic article on Sir Joseph which led to a libel case and Dr Shorthouse, the paper's unfortunate owner, who was sick when the article was written, doing three months in prison.

HAYNES – Peter

The ex-jockey who became starter at The Cheltenham Festival 2005 was quoted as saying in *The Racing Post*, "When I started out in this job I was told that every time you climb onto the rostrum you are only two seconds away from a complete balls-up!"

HEAD – Mme "Criquette"   b. 1948

French trainer and daughter of breeder Alec Head, who also trained winners of both Guineas and the Derby as well as all five French Classics before he retired in 1984. Criquette has also carried off the French Classics, where she is particularly proud of Three Troikas in the Arc and Bering's Derby.

She is best known here for her three 1000gns wins and Anabaa's July Cup win in 1996. "I love Newmarket," she said. "My grandmother, Netty Jennings, was born just down the road at Six Mile Bottom, and her brother Jack, was one of the best jockeys in France." Anabaa was out of racing with a pinched nerve in the back, when Sheikh Maktoum gifted him to Alec Head, who thought he might use him at stud, if he couldn't get him back into racing. When his recovery became apparent Alec tried to return him, but the Sheikh refused saying that presents should always be kept.

"He rode a stinker and I'm fed up… the problem is a clash of personalities between Peslier and myself," was how the trainer lashed out at the jockey who failed to ride her Quiet Royal to victory in the 2006 Prix Maurice de Gheest at Deauville.

HENDERSON – Nicky   b. 1950

N.H. trainer of triple Champion Hurdle winner See You Then, of whom he said in 1987 " He's taken loads of chunks out of me over the years. I give him a carrot every night – and he still hates me." Perhaps he was only trying to tell him that he was sick of bloody carrots!

HERBERT – Ivor   b. 1925

When racing correspondent for *The People*, he wrote, "The number of debs. who lose their maiden allowance by Goodwood (the end of July) is enough to make the owners of most fillies green with envy." He also wrote the story of Arkle, and commenting on the last of his three Gold Cup wins in 1966, when he was distracted by spectators at the 11th fence, and struck the fence with his chest and still managed to get through it, he quoted an Irish supporter as saying, "Sure, hadn't St. Patrick had him well-backed." It was of course St Patrick's Day. Talking of buying stock in Ireland, he said, "A good gas and a drink are three parts of an Irish horse deal."

Ivor was an owner, trainer and rider as well as a journalist and author. In 1957 he saddled Linwell to win the Gold Cup, although it was credited to his head lad, Charlie Mallon, as his activities as a journalist precluded him from being a public trainer.

HILL – Mrs Charmian (Ire)   b. 1917

Owner of the brilliant mare Dawn Run, who carried off the Champion Hurdle in 1984 (easily beating the second favourite, a certain Desert Orchid) and then, after a year off with leg trouble, coming back to make racing history by taking the Gold Cup to become the first horse to complete the double with Jonjo O'Neill in the saddle. She was also the first mare to win the Champion since African Sister in 1939 – ridden by Lester's father, Keith Piggott. Afterwards, Mrs Hill's enthusiastic Irish supporters tossed her in the air in a celebratory "bumps."

Known as "The Galloping Granny", this diminutive lady was the first woman to ride against men under Irish NH Rules at the age of 56, until her Jockey's licence was withdrawn when she was 63. Paddy Mullins, who became her trainer in 1974, bought Dawn Run (by Deep Run) for 5800gns in 1981, and she rode her herself in a bumper the next year only days before the stewards refused to renew her licence.

In her first big race, the Sun Alliance Novices Hurdle at Cheltenham, she was beaten a head by Sabin de Loir, with Ron Barry riding, but afterwards Mrs Hill was offered £50,000 for the mare. Just as well she refused, in view of her eventual winnings. Dawn Run soon established herself as a front runner, and didn't like to be passed as Gaye Brief, the reigning champion, found out in the Ladbroke Xmas Hurdle. Only three months after the Gold Cup, when she was still only an eight year old, she was tragically killed in the Grande Course de Haies at Auteil, which she had won in 1984. She was exercised by her aged owner to the last.

HILL – William   d. 1971

Not only the leading UK bookmaker from 1945 until he died, but an owner and breeder of among others, Nimbus (2000 gns and Derby 1949), Cantelo (St Leger 1959) and Grey Sovereign, a prolific sire of sprinters.

He never bet on a racecourse before 1940, but he did bet on pony races at Northolt before the war, where he was able to amass enough capital to stage his first coup in 1942. This was the year that the King's Big Game had won the 2000gns and was a short priced favourite for the Derby; but Hill was convinced on his breeding that he wouldn't stay and laid against him to the tune of £20,000. His defeat was the foundation of Hill's fortunes, but he was particularly reticent about whether he could have settled up had Big Game won!

He did much the same on Tudor Minstrel five years later, when he discovered that Blue Train, not the Guineas winner, Tudor Minstrel, was the stable's first choice for the Derby. Hill's total liabilities were £175,000 and his accountant admitted he would have needed time to pay if the horse had won. Hill once said, "I don't approve of gambling. I call a gambler a person who bets what he can't afford, or throws money on a roulette wheel. Getting out of your depth – that's gambling!"

He had an acerbic wit, as evidenced by his reaction to some advertising ideas which were presented to him in 2006 – "Call that an advert? I could do better with my knob and a pot of paint!" One of his on-course reps said in 2005 to *The Racing Post,* "One day at Thirsk Terry Ramsden had £100,000 on his horse Chapel Cottage at 9/2 and still went home a loser. I will not see another punter like that in my lifetime." As he was recalling Terry's betting exploits in the 1980s, he was probably right.

HILLS – Barry   b. 1937

The trainer told *The Racing Post* that the clashing of the third placed Alhajjes and the winner Gallient at Newmarket in April 2006 was the result of his own horse running green and the winner being startled by a pair of ambulance drivers.

HILLS – Patrick

Young jockey on advice from his father Richard in 2006 said, "He's always telling me not to drop my hands, possibly because he has done that a few times and knows the embarrassment."

HINDLEY – Jeremy   b. 1943

Newmarket trainer with a good pedigree since his father captained the British Eventing team in the 1952 Olympics. The family also owned the Ribblesdale Stud in Yorkshire. As a race rider his last public appearance was at Haydock on Robert Sangster's Innovator, who carried him round safely, no mean feat on the part of the horse, since Hindley had anticipated his retirement the night before rather overenthusiastically and had to be taken to hospital after the race suffering from what was officially called dehydration.

He bought Kremlin House in 1970 and his first winner was ridden by TV commentator Brough Scott in a Novice Hurdle. He was more successful at Pattern races than the Classics, and in 1977 he won the Cambridgeshire with a horse called Sin Timon, which is Spanish for "without a rudder", since his tail fell out as a yearling, the result of an overtight tail bandage! The next year he bought Clarehaven to which he moved his 70 horses, but his only Classic success before he gave up his licence in the late 80s was the Irish St Leger with Protection Racket.

HISLOP – John M.C. d.1994

Breeder and owner of the great Brigadier Gerard, after the war he rode as an amateur, mostly on the Flat, where he was champion jockey for 13 consecutive seasons. Outstanding over hurdles, his most memorable ride was when he finished 3rd in Caughoo's National in 1947 on Kami. Dan Moore, who was riding the second favourite, looked down on the tiny Kami and said, "I wouldn't ride that pony round here for all the tea in China." His own horse, Revelry, fell at the first fence!

Many of his endless fund of racing anecdote are recorded in his three volumes of memoirs from which the following have been selected:

Capt. Percy Whitaker, the Royston trainer, was liable to be a touch choleric in the early morning, "Where the hell's Rory O'Moore, he's not in the string," he bellowed on first lot one day. "You're on him, Sir," said his head lad as soon as he was able to get a word in. He wrote of Tom Coulthwaite, who sent out the Grand National winners Eremon, Jenkinstown and Grakle, that he boasted when dope-testing was almost non-existant, that he never had to tell a jockey to stop a horse; he stopped them in the stable by fixing their feed. Apparently, he used this technique on occasions to get a horse to run badly in his trials, thus stopping his stable from ruining the market, by backing him themselves.

A good tale about George Todd, the Manton trainer, who gave J.H. a lot of winning rides, was when he discovered a hurdling mare, Miss Blighty, had just come into season when he came to saddle her. As her owner, the elderly and almost deaf Sir

William Cooke, had instructed him to back her for him, he sought him out in the paddock to tell him, that he had halved the stable's commission from £200 to £100. The old man kept nodding his head, saying "That's right – £200." Eventually Lady Cooke came to George's rescue and shouted, "That's right, you stick the lot on, it doesn't make any difference the first half hour." She was right – Miss B. won comfortably by two lengths. One of his own observations was "Jumping at Ascot is like Blackpool with the tide out."

When Brigadier Gerard, after winning his first 16 races, suffered his only defeat at the hands (or heels) of Roberto in the 1972 Benson & Hedges Gold Cup at York, Jean Hislop joked, "He (Roberto) must have been stung by a bee." But he beat the great Mill Reef in the 2000gns. Of breeding, John said, "As I learnt in the hard school of experience, breeding middle distance horses below the top class, for sale as yearlings, is the path to penury." He was asked by Peter O'Sullevan whether the comparative affluence The Brigadier had brought him had made any difference to his lifestyle. "Only that I can now afford to live as I've been doing for the last 20 years," he replied. His friend Robert Morley, the actor, said "I'm furious with John Hislop. He came to my dressing room and told me he'd got a yearling that would win the 2000gns, and I thought he was off his head and took no notice."

One of their friends, when the Hislops bought East Woodhay Stud, near Newbury, was Geoff Harbord and his wife Daultie, the daughter of Lord Vestey. The latter was once running down racing whereupon his son-in-law said, "You're a butcher and you know about butchering, so you've made a go of it. If I tried butchering, I'd probably go broke, but I do know something about racing and its done me pretty well over the years." Their house was run smoothly by the butler, Cotten, who was once seen wading into the stream where his master and mistress were fishing, bearing a silver salver with two dry martinis on it. One of John's favourite precepts was, "Never lay the odds, never travel entirely sober, and never hunt south of the Thames," and his oft heard toast was, "Here's to our softening cocks and hardening arteries." Alas it was the arteries that did for him, as he died after a heart attack out shooting while still in middle age.

H

John was also friendly with another amateur rider called Derek Jackson, who was known for his total disregard for authority. On one occasion at Wye (now defunct), he complained to the stewards about the state of the jockey's lavatories. The stewards said that they had inspected them and considered them perfectly satisfactory. Derek's rejoinder was, "It's all very well inspecting them; you try shitting in them."

J.H. was a journalist after the war, the first 16 years with *The Observer*, which gave him plenty of time for race-riding as well as some good stories about his peers. One of these, who gave his racing selections under the name of Capt. Heath, at the time of a particularly vicious murder by a man called Neville Heath, received a letter expressing considerable dissatisfaction with his efforts, ending with the opinion, "So far as I am concerned, they hanged the wrong Heath." Kenneth Bryceson, one of many formidable drinkers among the racing press, as *News of the World* racing correspondent, had a pretty relaxed ride under its tolerant owner Sir William Carr, until it was discovered that his "Twelve to Follow" contained several horses that were either dead or abroad – exit Kenneth. His Sports Editor, Frank Butler, was once summoned to St Andrews by Sir William who greeted him with, "Hello Frank, what'll you have to drink?" Frank replied, "It's a bit early, Sir William," to which his boss replied, "Damn it man! I didn't ask you the time, I asked you what you wanted to drink."

HOBBS – Bruce   b.1921

Trainer most remembered for winning the 1938 Grand National as the youngest jockey at 17 years old on the smallest horse, Battleship, at 5.2 hands, and on the last entire (Stallion) to have done so. Battleship was bought at two years by Mrs Marion du Pont Scott, millionairess wife of US actor Randolph Scott, and had already won the US Grand National before being sent to England. Trainer Reg Hobbs reluctantly put on £1 at 40-1, "Just in case he had to buy the champagne," declaring he would not be able to see over The Chair. He is the only horse to have won the American and English Grand Nationals and went back to the US to become the leading chasing sire on five occasions.

HOGAN – Patrick (Ire)   b. 1939

Also known as P.P., which many say stands for Punchestown Pat, going back to when he was a brilliant amateur rider, before becoming a bloodstock agent. Apart from advising on the purchase of Rhinegold at Newmarket for 3000gns – the winner of £360k in prize money – it was calculated in 1974 that he had been responsible for the purchase of 200 winners.

As personal consultant to Robert Sangster he selected the Arc winner Detroit for him when she was still a foal. The day after his Arc win, Sangster organised a celebration lunch at the George V Hotel in Paris and Hogan, who, according to Sangster, used to write "George Sank" on his luggage labels, told him he wanted to bid for a yearling he had seen coming up in the afternoon list. Sangster gave him a £50,000 limit, and he bought for 160,000 FF (£16,000) the colt which later became known as Assert and was syndicated at stud for $25m, after winning the French and Irish Derbys.

HOLLIDAY – Major Lionel   d. 1965

England's most substantial owner-breeder in the 20 years following the war will be remembered for his horse Hethersett being brought down when favourite for the 1962 Derby and for Vaguely Noble, who ironically was foaled in the year of his death. Loved by the racing public, he was a difficult man to work for, and was always changing his trainers and jockeys; in fact his dictatorial manner held up his election to the Jockey Club for many years. Nonetheless, as he said, "My trainers say I'm impossible, but they come on bicycles and leave in Bentleys." Despite only winning three Classics between 1951 and 1965, he was leading owner three times. He also topped the breeders list in 1954, 1956 and 1962.

On the Major's death, Vaguely Noble was sold for a spectacular 136,000gns to be trained in France. He proceded to win the 1968 Arc, beating the English and Irish Derby winners Sir Ivor and Ribero, and his progeny includes Dahlia (twice winner of the King George VI & Queen Elizabeth Stakes), as well as Empery (1976 Derby). It was the Major's habit to use the sire's initials to name his horses as with Hethersett by Hugh Lupus.

HOURIGAN – Michael   b.1947

Irish jump trainer said in 2005 when his horse Hi Cloy won at Leopardstown, "The man who never makes a mistake is not a man." The actual winner was Central House, whose jockey stood up to celebrate and consequently mistook the whereabouts of the winning post.

HOWARD DE WALDEN – Johnnie (Scott-Ellis) 9th Baron   d. 1999

One of Britain's richest landlords, owning more than 100 acres of Marylebone in central London, a past Senior Steward of the Jockey Club and owner of two studs in Newmarket and Yorkshire, he bred and ran the 1985 Derby winner Slip Anchor, which didn't stop him a couple of years later confiding in Woodrow Wyatt, the Tote supremo at the time, that he would like to shoot the lot of them. Such are the vicissitudes of racing! However among many other good horses he owned, were Kris the 1979 champion miler (his sire Sharpen Up "Was cheap and fast... standing at £200 down the road") and Lanzarote, who won the Champion Hurdle in 1974. Johnnie claimed to have been quite ignorant about N.H.Racing.

Not a poor man – according to Peter O'Sullevan, "Lord Howard de Walden takes the view that one million is pretty much like another." He has also made one or two interesting asides about the Jockey Club: "If you start working out the average age of the Jockey Club, its absolutely horrifying." "Apart from two others in a smallish way, I'm the only Steward who owns a Flat racehorse. Quite a thought isn't it?" "It has got so ingrained in people's minds that the Jockey Club is an aristocratic, elite, privileged load of nonsense, that we have trouble living this image down."

Between school and Cambridge he was despatched to Kenya to learn something of his father's extensive farming interests. There he found himself among the Happy Valley set. Arriving to stay with some newfound friends, he was greeted by the butler, who said, "Good evening Sir. And who will you be sleeping with, tonight?" A good reply might have been, "I don't know without seeing the menu."

In 1992 he published *Earls have Peacocks*, an anecdotal memoir in which he revealed his only regrets were not learning to dance, to speak Spanish or to fly and that he had never done a course in accounting! Perhaps he will be best remembered for knocking down a pedestrian in 1931 in Munich where he was a student. His German companion said, "I don't suppose you know who that was? He is a politician with a party and he talks a lot. His name is Adolf Hitler." In his memoirs, Johnnie recalls several years later when in the next door box at Munich Opera he lent across and asked The Fuhrer if he remembered the incident. "To my surprise he did and was quite charming about it."

HUE-WILLIAMS – Vera   d. 1992

Vera Skinnorekayou (as she was known in Ruissia) was born in Kiev, and fled the Bolsheviks in 1917, ending up, like so many White Russians, in Paris with her sister Olga and her mother, Baroness Kostovesky, and, hidden in her clothes – her jewels.

The strikingly beautiful Vera married a Major serving with the British Military Mission, of whom little is known, when she was 17. After they split, when she was still only 25, she quickly became an asset-gatherer. She next married Walter Sherwin Cottingham of the Lewis Berger Paint Company, and on his death in 1936, inherited a vast fortune. Her third husband, who she married during the war, was Thomas Lilley, Chairman of the family shoe business, Lilley and Skinner. Thomas died in 1959, leaving her free to marry her last husband, Colonel Roger Hue-Williams, in 1963. With Thomas Lilley, she established herself as a leader of racing's social scene, buying a house within easy reach of Goodwood. Vera entertained lavishly each year, and her parties often included her neighbour 'Porchy' Carnarvon, father of the Queen's Racing Manager. Such a glamorous social life demanded equally glamorous clothes and jewels, collected over five decades, designed mainly in the 30s and 40s, and which amply demonstrated Vera's liking for large stones, one of which – a sapphire – weighed 42.61 carats.

For fifty years Vera was a noted figure in the horse-racing world, founding the Woolton House Stud, near Newbury in the 1940s with Thomas, where they bought, bred and trained many big winners such as Supreme Court (inaugural King George VI and QE stakes in 1951), and Aurelius (St Leger in 1961). They even had 'his and hers' colours – her scarlet with a white V, and his white with a scarlet V. With the colonel, she won the 1000gns, and the English and Irish Oaks in 1971, with Altesse Royale, carrying his colours. Then in 1974 they won the Irish Derby with English Prince.

HUGGINS – John (US)

Walrus moustached American trainer of Volodyovski, winner of the Epsom Derby in 1901. He was once asked if there were many crooks on the American Turf: "None," he replied, "They're all over here in England." His jockey Lester Reiff was generally regarded as one of them!

I

I'ANSON – William

A very heavy gambler himself, he trained at Malton (now Bill Elsey's yard) for the Northern Confederacy, a group who bet on a lavish scale, before he retired in 1912. His father (also William) trained Blair Athol to win the 1864 Derby on his first appearance in public, and won £15,000 (worth about £1.8m today) from his wager. His tip to William Junior was, "Take my tip and don't bet... but if you must bet, then BET." William certainly did and would regularly put £1000 on one of his own horses – more like £40,000 today.

His brother, Robert, considered one of the best riders over sticks of his day, also trained a National winner, Austerlitz in 1877.

J

JARVIS – Sir "Jack"   d. 1968

Son of a trainer and brother to two trainers, he rode the winners of the Cambridgeshire and the Ayr Gold Cup before taking up training in 1914. His nine Classic wins included two Derbys for Lord Rosebery.

In 1951 Lord Rosebery initiated a private test on his filly Snap, who he felt had run far below her usual form, which showed she had been doped. At that time a trainer lost his licence if it was found his horse had been doped to win or lose, although as Harry Rosebery pointed out it made no sense for him to risk using dope to nobble a horse when plenty of equally effective methods were available. However the public were disturbed to think that, had the test been official, the impeccably honest Jarvis would have lost his licence; in consequence a Jockey Club committee was set up to enquire into the whole problem of doping.

Sir Jack had a very short fuse, but never harboured a grudge, and was one of the most generous characters around Newmarket. Also a coursing enthusiast, he won the Waterloo Cup – in fact he was a supporter in one way or another of almost every sport. He died suddenly the year after he was knighted.

JARVIS – Michael

When asked by *The Racing Post* what it was like when he first trained in Newmarket said in May 2005, "There used to be a lot of old trainers, all in their 70s, and the local townspeople thought they were Gods. They didn't pay their bills because they were too good to pay bills."

He also said in 2005, "Either you're womanising or drinking too much or gambling – someone's always got a reason why you're on the slide."

JERSEY – George Child-Villiers, 5th Earl of

A famous Midlands huntsman, whose name in local hunting circles is doubtless still associated with the famous Billesdon Coplow run of 1800. Later he took up racing with a stud at Middleton Stoney, winning the 2000gns, five times between 1831 and 1837 and the Derby three times. However in spite of this splendid achievement, his stud eventually cost him nearly half a million – and this 150 years ago – but since he wasn't a betting man, unlike most of his contemporaries, he had no way of defraying the cost.

He was a tall handsome man who was Lord Chamberlain to William IV and Master of the Horse to Queen Victoria. In 1914 his grandson, who was then Senior Steward of the Jockey Club, was largely responsible for racing continuing, although on a greatly reduced scale, during the hostilities. He also helped to lower the rigid social barriers existing in the Club up to this time.

JOCKEY CLUB – The

Founded in 1750 at the Star and Garter in London, which was the favourite rendez-vous of the jockies (or jockeys) – then anyone who had anything to do with horseracing, but not of course their grooms (or tryers), who later became known as jockeys! Since the Club's intention was to protect itself from undesirables, this certainly included their servants, which is why there are no jockeys in the Jockey Club – much to the mystification of outsiders.

Although to this day they rule English racing with an autocratic air, they have of late had to amend their clubbish ways and broaden their membership to help modernize the sport and indeed to provide the ever-increasing subsidies needed for its survival. Their undoubted knowledge of racing is not always matched by a similar insight into the lives of ordinary racegoers. One very senior older member, a peer of the realm, when discussing the effect televised racing might have on racecourse attendances, said: "I watched TV last Saturday. Frightfully good y'know. But it seemed to me," he went on, "that I couldn't be the only one – and around the country there must have been thousands and thousands of people sitting in their council houses, drinking their port and watching the racing."

In 1986 Brough Scott complain that the powerful Stewards, when interviewed, had little idea what they were talking about; he then went on to criticise their self-election process. Sir John "Jakie" Astor replied: "Oh no! The JC has to be self-electing or you would get delegates; then the media would have to have someone – someone like you – and who would want that?" A wealthy industrialist who had tried for many years to get himself elected, eventually gave up, saying "To become a member of the JC you've got to be a relation of God – and a damn close one at that," showing he finally understood the rules.

Racing as we know it today owes much to the early JC reformers, but it is equally true that it hasn't moved with the times, as is shown by the following comment: Sir Randle Fielden (ex-Senior Steward) gives the feel of the Club with "Do you seriously imagine I'm going to tell Jeremy (Hindley – then one of our wealthier trainers) what he ought to charge? It would be damned impertinence, just as if he were to tell me what I ought to pay my butler."

Lord Cadogan said in 1971, "Our enquiries are not like courts of law. They are more like courts martial."

John Oaksey, who rode as the amateur John Laerence, is quoted in the *Sunday Telegraph* (1974) as saying, "The JC is simply not representative of the thousands of men and women whose livelihood depends on racing. Nor frankly is there much evidence to show that they have tried very hard to alter that state of affairs." The same year Christopher Poole in *The Evening Standard* said, "Eton and the Lancers and no first-hand experience of raceriding is no qualification for stewardship." JC officials are often no better equipped to do their job, which is perhaps not surprising after an advertisement for stipendiary stewards in the *Sporting Life* (1980) ended with the amazing words, "Experience of racing, although desirable, is not essential." However the best story of all concerns a course vet, called up when a chaser fell heavily at a meeting at Hurst Park between the wars, and was unable to rise. The vet decided to deliver the *coup de grace*, missed the horse and instead shot a groundsman in the foot. The horse, no doubt disturbed by the shot, and certainly by the poor man's curses, struggled to its feet and trotted off towards the stables. He won 11 more races during the course of the next two seasons.

The disciplinary committee in 2005 warned off jockey Gary Carter for five years and fined him £2000, saying "He was cheating the connections of the horse he rode and the punters who bet on him."

JOEL – Jack, Jim, Solly and Stanhope

The family has bred and owned Classic horses since 1900 when J.B. (Jack) Joel (1862-1940) a nephew of South African diamond millionaire Barney Barnato, who in turn was a partner of Cecil Rhodes, came back from South Africa, where he too made a fortune as a young man, and won 11 Classics over the ensuing 20 years, including two Derbys with Sunstar in 1911 and Humorist in 1921.

His younger brother S.B. (Solly) (1865-1931) also made a fortune in diamonds, raced on a large scale and never achieved his brother's success. However his sole Classic winner, Pommern, won the Triple Crown in 1915. But he made a betting coup when his horse Polymelus won the Cambridgeshire and he scooped £100,000 – say a million at today's money. The horse then went on to become champion sire five times, producing between 1914 and 1921 no fewer than eight Classic winners.

JOHNSON – Don & Linda (US)

Led the Keeneland sales Breeders List in 1983 with the sale of one yearling to Sheikh Mohammed for $10.2m by Northern Dancer out of My Bupers. It was later named Snaafi Dancer – and couldn't run a step! However this travesty was instrumental in getting the Arabs and the Sangster syndicate to stop competing with each other in the sales ring, which in turn led to the bloodstock crash of 1986. In 1991 their stud, Crescent Farm, filed for bankruptcy, thus confirming that "the curse of Snaafi Dancer lived on..."

JOHNSON – Howard

Has most of his horses with Martin Pipe and is in no doubt why A.P. McCoy left there to join Jonjo O' Neil: "There was all this crap in the papers about furthering his career. That's bollocks. He went to further his bank balance." *Pacemaker* 2005.

JOHNSTON – Deidre

The trainer revealed how she knew the ground was right for her filly Attraction: "My high heels are my penetrometers."

JOHNSTONE – Rae (Aus)   d.1964

Le Crocodile, as he was known to French turfistes, because of his habit of playing a waiting game, before gobbling up the opposition. After being Australian champion jockey in 1931 he emigrated to France the next year. He rode more than 2000 winners in nine countries, including 30 Classics and 12 of these were in this country between 1934 and 1956, including three Derbys; but the Derby he didn't win – on Colombo in 1934 – caused more of a furore, as he was accused of pulling the horse, and as a result parted company with Lord Glanely who retained him. According to Peter O'Sullevan, he was a totally honest fellow; he may have pulled horses – but only for his connections and never against those he rode for.

Rae used to be a compulsive gambler and once in the 1930s, when he was very hard up, he went to Pierre Wertheimer, the owner of one of his Derby winners, Lavandin (1956), and asked for his years retainer in advance. When he got back, his wife Mary, seeing him looking rather downcast, asked him, "What's wrong? Didn't you get it?" "Yes," he said, "But I've lost it." He had called in on the casino on the way home and lost the lot.

Wertheimer gave a farewell dinner for Rae, when he announced his retirement in July 1957. In his speech he showed how acutely conscious he was of how easily a jockey in a matter of minutes, can destroy an owner's hopes and weeks of hard work by trainer and staff. He said, "He needs all the confidence he can be given to ride to the best of his ability." When it was suggested that Frank Vogel, a 65 year old American who was very much a part of the French racing scene, acted as ghost writer for a book on the jockey, Rae, knowing how keen he was on young female company, said, "Frank can't keep his hands off a girl long enough to write a cheque, let alone a book." The job eventually fell to Peter O'Sullevan, the race commentator.

JONES – Warner (US)

Colourful owner of Lanes End Farm – one of the top six Kentucky breeders in the 1980s. He led the Keeneland sales table in 1985 with $20m for eight yearlings and one of these – a Nijinsky colt, later to be known as Seattle Dancer – was sold to Robert Sangster *et al.* for $13.1m – a record which stands to this day.

However the animal, although it won races, was far from top class and never graduated to the Classics – small wonder that the Brethren (Sangster, O'Brien and Magnier) were more than willing to meet the Maktoums at the Summit in the Desert, which put an end to their confrontation in the Ring, and signalled the end for those of the the Kentucky Stud Farms who had borrowed heavily against future profits.

K

KAY – Joyce

She pointed out in her 2005 *Encyclopaedia of British Horse Racing* the undeniable truth that a few high profile trainers and even fewer jockeys at the top level cannot conceal the fact that there are probably no women at the sharp end of the sport.

KELLEWAY – Gay

Royal Ascot winning jockey turned trainer said in April 2005 about Carrie Ford's winning a race at Ascot, "If it was me and I won the race, I'd go up to him (Ginger McCain) and say, 'Kiss my arse'." She also said, "I bought a horse called Old Bailey yesterday and today I flogged him to five barristers I brought racing with me." How convenient!

KELLEWAY – Paul   d.1999

As a jump jockey Kelleway's style belied his particular ability to switch horses off until the run-in, as he did with Bula in the Champion Hurdle in both 1971 and 1972. His frank appraisals of a horse's chances often cost him a ride. "I'm not a fanny merchant," he said, "I don't give owners or trainers the tale. If a horse is a bastard, I say so."

Later as a trainer on the Flat, with a yard of low-budget horses, he still contrived to win seven Group 1 races, which earned him the nick-name of "Pattern Race Paul". His ability to buy class yearlings at low prices produced the champion three year old filly of 1978, Swiss Maid. She was one of a parcel of 12 yearlings purchased for 34,000gns and sold for 325,000gns. She was also so difficult to get into the starting stalls that Harry Wragg, his former boss, offered him 33-1 against ever getting her onto a racecourse. Madam Gay (French Oaks) a £9000 investment, went for £1.4m and Paul also turned a £20,000 colt (Risk Me) into a £1.2m profit.

He was quoted as saying three years before he died, "Ability doesn't get you a glass of water in racing. It's not what you know but who you know."

KERTON – Charlotte

The first female jockey to win in Bahrain, after she rode a double there, reported that, "This guy, a local jockey, actually punched me as I was weighing in and no one did anything about it." *Racing Post* April 2006.

She also said in the preceding March, "The jockeys have said I'm more than welcome to shower in their changing rooms, but I turned the offer down."

KHALID bin ABDULLAH - Prince (Saudi Arabia)

Brother-in-law to the later King Fahad, he is also a nephew of King Abdul Aziz, the founder of Saudi Arabia. As a businessman with extensive US interests, he first attended the Keeneland Sales in 1978, where with his English trainer Jeremy Tree he bought one colt for $225,000 – by In Reality, he named it Known Fact. The horse repaid the investment by wining the 2000 gns (after Nuryev was disqualified), the Waterford Crystal Mile and the QE II Stakes.

Using Humphrey Cottrill and then James Delahooke to buy for him, by 1982 he was spending £3.3m at the Kentucky sales. When Rainbow Quest won the 1985 Arc, he lifted the Prince to No. 2 in the Owners' List, but it wasn't until the next year, when Dancing Brave won the 2000 gns that he had a second Classic win.

He only paid $200,000 for the Lyphard colt, probably because he had a 'parrot mouth'; he lost the Derby by half a length, most people say due to Greville Starkey's poor tactics, and then went on to win the Eclipse, the King George VI – beating Derby winner Shahrastrani in the process – and the Arc ridden by Pat Eddery, who was appointed his first jockey in 1987. The Brave was syndicated for £14m to stand at Newmarket, after being rated the best horse of the decade, but was exported to Japan in 1991. Prince Khalid won two Derbys in 1990, Quest for Fame the English and Sanglamore the French, to which he added the St Leger in 1991 with Toulon.

His horses are with a number of trainers, chiefly Henry Cecil, John Gosden, Guy Harwood, Roger Charlton and Barry Hills. "It is only logical to spread his horses among several stables, as it ensures the limitation of risk," said a spokesman for his organisation.

KA shows little emotion in triumph or disaster, wears nice suits and smokes Marloro Lights. As with the Maktoums, it is difficult to come by much of an anecdotal nature as he rarely talks to the press.

KINDERSLEY – Gay   b. 1930

The former amateur rider, owner and trainer said in February 2007, "I was born at a time when gay meant happy, clap meant applause and only generals had aides."

KINANE – Chris

The former jockey recalled a memorable day's racing when he was assistant to Guy Harwood to *The Racing Post* in July 2006: "I was so desperately disappointed when Dancing Brave lost The Derby I took my frustration out in the garden mowing the lawn and in fact my neighbour's lawn and in fact the whole estate."

K

KINANE – Michael (Ire)   b.1959

Irish Flat racing jockey sees the positive side to an injury sustained in 2005: "I fractured my right wrist – so I won't be able to sign any cheques for a while."

He became the rider with the most wins at Royal Ascot when he turned 46 and greeted his triumph by commenting in June 2005, "The older you get – the more you have to prove yourself."

KING – Jeffrey   b. 1941

One of the best jump jockeys never to have become champion, he rode 66 winners in 1971-2 coming sixth in the table, and won the Hennessy, the Schweppes and the Whitbread before turning to training.

However his bluntness always equalled his ability, as when Inchcailloch finished an unlucky fourth in the 1995 Cesarewitch. When asked if he thought he should have won, King replied, "I don't think. I f.....g well know he should have." Just as well the horse did win the race the next year, although only after an inquiry.

KING – The Rev. J.W.

A sporting parson who raced as "Mr Launde", he won his first Classic in 1856 when John Osborne brought in Manganese to take the 1000gns.

He inherited his family estates at the age of 48, when the last of his three older brothers died without issue, becoming both Squire and Parson, or Squarson as he was jokingly known. His racing exploits were well known to his parishioners, who often benefited from a tip from on high – the pulpit anyway – although his Nom de Course, which he used to protect the Church's good name, may well have escaped his Bishop's notice. However 18 years later he won the race again with

Apology, together with the Oaks and the St Leger, and three Classics in one season was too much for his Bishop, who wrote a letter reproving him. King replied that his family had been involved with bloodstock for generations and he couldn't see how racing them constituted a scandal to the Church, particularly as he never placed a bet or attended a race meeting. He concluded, "I desire to live the remainder of my days in peace and I resign my living, not from any consciousness of wrong, or fear of futile proceedings taken against me in the ecclesiastical courts, but simply to avoid the scandal of such proceedings."

At 73 he married a 21 year old maid at the Hall, and despite the gossip, appears to have had a happy marriage.

KINSKY – Count Charles (Aus)

Won the 1883 Grand National as an amateur on Zoedone, trained by that fine old gentleman W.H.P. Jenkins. As he was inexperienced at raceriding he resolved he would be fit as a prize-fighter; he was, and made nearly all the running and won by 10 lengths. He rode many winners and had a lot of good horses, including Kilmore, who should have won the Paris Steeplchase in 1885, if his jockey, Sly, hadn't taken the wrong course two fences from home. A great Anglophile, he was with the Austrian Embassy when the Great War broke out, and he volunteered for the Russian front to avoid having to fight his friends in the English and French forces. He was 58 at the time.

Charles Kinsky loved hunting better than anything and was a hard rider. Once when out with the Quorn, the Whip came up to the Master – General Sir Reginald Pole Carew – and said, "The Count's had an awful fall. I think he's been killed." Soon after a battered Charles appeared and Polly Carew went up to the Whip and said, "What the devil do you mean telling us the Count was killed?" "Well if he ain't dead now, by God he soon will be," was the answer.

L

LAMBTON – Hon. George   d. 1945

Younger brother of the Earl of Durham he became an outstanding amateur rider, winning the Grand Steeple-chase de Paris in 1888 on Parasang and on another occasion being desperately unlucky not to win the National.

However after a particularly bad fall he decided to take up training at a time when gentlemen trainers were a rare breed, and was appointed private trainer to Lord Derby – the 16th Earl – in 1893 – and afterwards to the 17th Earl, arguably the greatest owner breeder this century, for whom he achieved his greatest Classic successes. His second Derby, with Hyperion in 1933, was the year Lord Derby "retired" him "to spare him the burden and anxiety of running a large stable". At 73 George had no intention of retiring and trained on till his death in 1945.

George's wife Cicely, was considerably younger than her husband and a beauty in her youth. Not without admirers, she had firm ideas on social mores, announcing at dinner once, "Adultery is no reason for divorce." On another occasion, pre-war, George had set off to go racing but, having found he had forgotten his field glasses, returned to fetch them. Meanwhile Cicely was dallying on the sofa with one of the aforementioned admirers, but on hearing George in the hall, called out with great presence of mind, "Don't come in George, the canary's out of its cage."

LEACH – Jack

Apart from being associated with some notable sprinters in the 20s, such as Nothing Ventured and Diomedes for Harvey Leader, and winning the 2000gns on Adam's Apple in 1927, he rode with a number of great personalities; the Australians Frank Bullock and Brownie Carslake; Steve Donoghue, Michael Beary and Charlie Smirke among a dozen others. Their stories are to be found in his marvelous memoirs *Sods I Have Cut on the Turf* and *A Rider on the Stand* – one of them of the time when he was riding in Ireland and had received a cable asking him to recommend a good Irish jockey (English jockeys were banned at the time) for one of the big German stables at a £2000 retainer. He cabled back, "Deposit £2000 in Bank of England and take your pick of O' Donoghue, O'Bullock, O'Archibald and O'Leach." No reply was received.

Another concerned the unpredictable Steve Donoghue, who, having invited him to dine at the Savoy, left the table to answer the telephone, and was next seen 10 days later in Manchester. Rae Johnstone, when he got fed up with being questioned about his losing ride on Colombo in the 1934 Derby, apparently said, "A jockey would have won by 10 minutes."

Of the time when starters were able to fine jockeys for making false starts, he recalled one occasion when it had occured three times and the fines had gone from £2 to £4 and then £8, at which the jockey, who happened to play poker, shouted out, "I'll see you." When weight troubles curtailed his riding, he turned to training, and sent out some good winners from Newmarket between 1931 and 1950, without ever having a Classic winner.

LEADER – "Jack"   d. 1972

Although a fine rider with a few races on the Flat to his credit before he got too heavy, he became known as a mixed yard trainer after the 1914-18 war. He saddled Jack Horner in 1926 to win the National for his owner, the American Charlie

Schwartz, but was unable to see him pass the post as Charlie, in his excitement, thumped him so hard on the shoulders that he fell off the stand.

LEMAIRE, Christopher

"She had a monstrous amount of gas this afternoon." The jockey quipped about his mount Divine Proportion's victory in the Prix De La Grotte in April 2005.

LEPAROUX – Julien   b. 1983

The French jockey who burst on the US scene with a phenomenal run of over 250 winners from 1000 mounts. Trainer Patrick Biancone said, "Every 30 years a new one comes along and I have no doubt that Leparoux is far better than all of the other jockeys I have produced. People come up to me every day to thank me for bringing Juilien to the US. Now that's something that's never happened to me before."

LEVEIN – Craig   b. 1964

Scottish football player who, after purchasing Flash of Realm for his breeding potential, on discovering that he had been gelded four years previously, remarked, "I suppose you could say it was a bit of a cock-up."

LEWIS – Geoff   b. 1935

Rode five Classic winners, including the great Mill Reef, winner of the 1971 Derby. A former Waldorf pageboy, Geoff was appointed Noel Murless' stable jockey in 1970, which enabled him to say he had ridden winners for both Sovereign and Prime Minister – several for the Queen and Tudor Monarch in the 1959 Steward's Cup for Sir Winston Churchill.

He had the reputation for being an expert at one-liners: "It was difficult to get out more than one line because of my stutter," he said by way of an explanation.

LEWIS – Sam

The great money-lender to George Lambton and his peers was Mr Lewis of Cork St and the majority of his clients were also his friends! A driver of hard bargains, he was straight as a die and often showed remarkable kindness to men who were really down on their luck. He had a handsome wife, who always had a pair of the best carriage horses in London, so much so that one great lady, renowned for both her extravagance and her carriage turn-out, asked Lambton if he thought Lewis would give her £600 for her pair of horses – a great deal of money in those days. Lewis immediately agreed, but next morning said, "I can't buy those horses for I've found out she's head over heels in debt and if Mrs Lewis is seen driving them, every tradesman in London will know she's in my hands, and there will be a crash. But you can tell her that I will lend her £600 on her note of hand."

LINDLEY – Jimmy   b. 1954

Although he is now known to the present generation as a race-reader and journalist, he achieved considerable success riding on the Flat, latterly in France, before retiring in 1974. His three Classic successes were in the 2000gns (twice) and the 1964 St Leger on Indiana for Charles Engelhard.

Jeffrey Bernard tells the story of when Jimmy was a regular dinner party guest at the house of Jim Joel, one of his owners. The first time he made his name as something of a *bon viveur* when, noticing that Mr Joel habitually produced a vintage port after dinner, he had the presence of mind to bung the butler a tenner beforehand in exchange for some inside information, so that when the port came round he was able to state with some authority, "Ah! a Croft '37 I think?" Joel was suitably impressed and said, "I didn't know you knew about port, Jimmy," and immediately summoned the butler, saying, "Put the port down to Mr Lindley," (meaning in his will). Encouraged by his success, Jimmy was quick to evince an interest in shooting when on another occasion Joel was showing his guns to his guests: "By God, Mr Joel, those two Purdeys are beautiful things, the best I've ever seen." "Do you really like them?" Joel replied, summoning the butler once again. "Put the Purdeys down to Lindley," he said. Sadly, Jimmy overdid it the next time. At the bottom of Joel's staircase was an enormous statue which probably came from Tutankhamun's tomb, and Jimmy went into his by now familiar routine with, "Goodness, Mr Joel I've never seen anything as wonderful as that." Joel replied, "Don't tell me Jimmy you're interested in archeology too.? Your interests are getting too widespread for me." But it was a nice try.

LINES – Andy

"Men walked around offering the girls beads to take their clothes off – many were only too happy to oblige." (*The Sportsman* 2006). One of the many Kentucky Derby traditions they don't tell you about in the brochures.

LOATES – Sam   d. 1932

A late Victorian jockey, who was never entirely happy with the "monkey on a stick" seat introduced by Tod Sloan, the American jockey. Once riding Nouveau Riche for George Lambton at Liverpool and setting off in true Sloan style, he was soon 10 lengths clear, but then the horse, a difficult brute, began to slow up. After two or three horses had passed him, Sam reverted to his old-style seat, gave the horse a couple on the ribs with the whip and shouted, "That's two for Old England! Now get on with it you bastard." He did too and went on to win by 10 lengths.

L

LODER – Major Eustace   d.1914

He is remembered mainly as the owner/breeder of Pretty Polly, who won 22 out of her 24 races between 1903 and 1906, including the 1904 fillies Triple Crown. Pretty Polly was one of the outstanding racemares of all time, winning the Coronation Cup in a time yet to be beaten, the Jockey Club Cup and the Champion Stakes as a four year old. In 1906 she won the Coronation Cup for the 2nd time, again beating Derby winner St Amant. But in her last race, the 2.5 mile Gold Cup, she was beaten a length, which prompted the crowd and her trainer, Gilpin, to blame her jockey, Bernard Dillon. The truth was she probably didn't get the distance, but the nation mourned and the next day the headline in the *Sporting Life* was "Alas and again alas! Pretty Polly beaten!"

The Major was not known as Lucky Loder for nothing, as he bought Spearmint for a mere 300gns before winning both the 1906 Derby and the Grand Prix de Paris. He himself said, "You may put everything you have into racing – but you will be nowhere unless you have luck."

LODER – Lt. Col. Giles   d.1966

Trainer Derby winner Spion Kop (1920) said, "The only certainty in thoroughbred breeding is the uncertainty." Having inherited Kildare Stud in 1914 from his uncle Eustace, he proceeded to win the 1920 Derby with Spion Kop, the 1000gns with Cresta Run in 1927 and the Eclipse. A shy kindly bachelor, he had been a member of the Jockey Club for 42 years when he died.

M

MACHELL – Capt. James d. 1896

His fame was in no small part due to his association with Isinglass, the Triple Crown winner of 1893, despite the ground being rock hard at both Newmarket and Epsom. It was due to Machell's insistence as Racing Manager to the owner, Col. McCalmont, that he was trained for the 2000gns, since James Jewitt, his trainer, was against it. The dry weather persisted until July the next year when better conditions allowed him to run in the Eclipse, which he won in a canter from the Derby winner, Ladas. The Eclipse in those days was worth twice as much as the Derby, and his 11 wins earned him £57,455, a sum not surpassed until 1952, the record standing, despite inflation, for almost 60 years. On the morning of the race, Jewitt said, "You will see what Isinglass can do today – its the first time I've been able to gallop him properly" (due to the hard ground). He was right, since the horse proved he was a stone better than any other horse in England. In fact he was only ever beaten once when giving 10 lb to Raeburn.

The year Mr Chaplin's Hermit won the Derby, despite breaking a blood vessel before the race, the Capt. had backed him to win £60k, but on hearing the news, got his commission agent to get him out of the bet. Nevertheless, the gallant Captain, smilingly accepted the congratulations of his friends, who thought he had won a fortune ..... and no one needed the money more.

An eccentric in the style of Admiral Rous himself, Jem Machell had physical as well as morals strengths. He could do a standing jump from floor to mantelpiece – and stay up! He also showed a certain fleetness of foot when he beat a Capt.

Chadwick over 100 yards over the Severals at Newmarket. His love of horses led him to retire from his regiment in 1863 when it was ordered to India, because he thought "he could do better at home." He presumably did, as between 1864 and his death, he won 540 races in his own name, worth £110,000 – or about £11m at today's money.

MAGEE – Sean

He started writing for *Time Out* (after his incomprehension at Crisp losing the 1973 Grand national to Red Rum). He wrote his first book when a part time author in 1989 (*The Channel 4 Book of Racing*) and his last on the 2009 Derby winner *See The Stars* which he edited with the help of Racing Post Publications. "The trophy presentation is the post-coital cigarette of a horse race – not the main business, but an essential part of the winding down." (*Racing Post*, March 2005.)

MAKTOUMS – The (UAE)

The racing part of the family are the four sons of the late Ruler of Dubai – Sheikh Rashid. The eldest is Maktoum al Maktoum, the present ruler and something of a figurehead, followed by Sheikhs Hamdan, whose real passion is his horses, Mohammed, who runs the show, and Ahmed, who looks good in a uniform. They're all descended from Sheikh Maktoum bin Butti, who settled the area in the 1830s with a few hundred tribesmen. They now host the world's richest race meeting – the Dubai World Cup with a pot of $5m.

In 1979 the brothers entered the major league by paying a record 625,000gns at Newmarket for a Lyphard colt, which escalated to $20m at Keeneland in 1982, until in 1983 Mohammed paid a record $10.2m for Snaafi Dancer, who unfortunately proved a total failure, both on the course and at stud. After the Snaafi Dancer affair, it occured to the Maktoums that this madness had to stop, and an invitation was sent to the rival Sangster syndicate to attend a secret summit in the desert. This resulted in the "Brethren" and the Bedouin agreeing that they would no longer bid against each other and the big bloodstock crash of 1985/6 was on the way.

We are lucky that the Maktoums have been Anglophiles since their father instilled into them that without the British their lands would long ago have been annexed by Saudi Arabia. The one thing Sheikh Mohammed never does is to get involved in large-scale gambling, since a certain weekend at Kier, the shooting estate in Scotland of the late Col. Bill Stirling. Bill, an inveterate gambler himself, was regaling his guests with stories of his great sprinter Sing Sing – unbeaten in his six two year old races in 1959, only to lose by a neck in the King's Stand Stakes at Ascot, carrying many thousands of the Colonel's cash with him – a lesson the Sheikh never forgot.

The Crown Prince – owner and breeder Sheikh Mohammed has a dry sense of humour, as when trainer Henry Cecil turned to him after a Northern Dancer colt went for $4m after it had been pointed out that the animal was a crib biter, and said, "The man who bought that must be mad." "I know, it was me," the Sheikh replied. However his sense of humour did not extend to accepting criticism from Cecil's new wife, Natalie, of his policy of taking his best two year olds to Dubai to winter and returning them to race under the Godolphin banner with a Dubai ex-policeman Saeed bin Suroor, fronting the operation as trainer, although it was widely thought that it was the Sheikh's strategy that guided his hand. The end result was that the Sheikh's 40 horses were removed from Cecil's Warren Place stables in October 1995.

On another occasion he was asked who was his favourite jockey, which provoked the answer, "The one who wins most races for me." Perhaps what we owe to the Maktoums was best summed up in *The Economist* in 1985 when Norman Macrae commented, "Because of three Bedouin princes, some misapplied American tax dodges, and a Mersey bookmaker's horse-dealing son (Sangster) the world's finest horses are once again training and running on English grass." The same year Sheikh Mohammed said, "We enjoy our horses. We don't bet. We run them all honestly and fairly and we thoroughly enjoy British racing."

He is also credited with a number of prophetic utterances: "One of life's great pleasures is doing what others think you cannot do," referring to the success of his Godolphin experiment in winning over 50 Group One races around the world in a decade. "Stride on and the world will make way for you." "In the race for excellence there is no finish line." "You don't fail when you fall. You fail when you refuse to get up again."

He has also said, "Horse-racing is one per cent of my life. One per cent. At most."

"Come on Prinny, make a name for yourself," his wife Princess Haya recalls her favourite moment in racing – a comment from the crowd when she was about to ride in an amateur race at Killarney in October 2006.

MAGNIER – John   b. 1948

Son-in-law to Vincent O'Brien, a tall handsome man with a touch of the "black Irish" about him – reputedly a throw-back to the Spanish seamen who survived both Drake and shipwreck off the Southern Irish coast in 1588.

A stallion master of international repute – not to be confused with a "stallion man" who merely looks after them – he managed the Coolmore Stud from 1975 and was the third partner, with Sangster and O'Brien, in the syndicate known in Lexington, Kentucky as "The Brethren", who raided the US yearling sales so successfully in the 1970s. In fact he was largely responsible for formulating the strategy of buying "mini-stallions" rather than animals for their prize money potential alone.

His wife Sue, Vincent O'Brien's daughter, owns a number of good horses in partnership with Michael Tabor – and the more recent ones all have a musical connotation. Maybe this is a race winning ingredient, for example: Bach (Chesham Stakes) Rossini (Prix Robert Papin) and Stravinsky (July Cup).

MAGUIRE – Adrian (Ire)   b. 1971

The 24 year old Irish steeplechase jockey who first came to prominence in 1992 when he won the Gold Cup on Cool Ground. This was after the Jockey Club had disqualified 12 horses he had ridden when incorrectly claiming 3 lbs. Then after a close fought race in 1993, when he completed his first century, he again narrowly failed to win the jockey's title in 1994, after being 25 ahead after Cheltenham, losing to Richard Dunwoody by five wins in the last week of the season. His agent's phone bill was £8000! As Dunwoody said, "I don't think there deserved to be a loser – only one result would have been fair and that is a draw." He fell foul of the stewards on a number of occasions for over-whipping. "He wants to win like a wolf wants its meat," according to Brough Scott, in a remark calculated to get several Montana cattle ranchers excited. In fact in the 10 month season he rode 916 times and sat on more horses for more trainers than anyone in the history of NH racing, sometimes riding at seven different tracks in a week.

He was retained by David Nicholson. The Duke, who said, quite simply, he is the best he had ever seen. Stan Mellor, the former champion jockey, compares him to Dunwoody by saying, "Adrian is a naturally good jockey; I think Richard is a more classical one. But Adrian has got what Peter Scudamore had – a great appetite for the game." His predatorial crouch seems to help his mounts to gallop and jump and his finish is such that a friend recently told him he could probably win on a rusty bicycle.

Maguire says, "It's more the driving than the riding that gets you tired, clocking up all those miles in the car." He also reckons that the highlight of his career was winning the King George VI Chase on Barton Bank at Kempton in 1993.

MAHER – Danny (US)   d.1916

He first won the jockey's championship in 1908, after which he was retained by Lord Rosebery for £4000, an immense sum in those days, together with another £2000 from the Australian, Mr A.W. Cox and a similar sum from Leopold

Rothschild to exercise third option. He was again champion in 1913. He rode nine Classic winners, including three Derbys on Rock Sand (1903) Cicero (1905) and Spearmint (1906) after coming over from America in 1900 with a big reputation – he was US champion in 1898 – riding for George Blackwell the trainer, and then for George Lambton as first jockey to Lord Derby. He liked to play a waiting game, but sometimes overdid it as when he failed to win the Goodwood Cup in 1910, when on the 20-1 on favourite Bayardo, the winner of 22 of his 24 races.

He was inclined to burn the candle at both ends, in spite of suffering from TB, probably the result of wasting, like so many other jockeys of his day. By 1914 his health had gone, and two years later he returned from wintering in South Africa to die at the age of 35, having squandered most of his money on an ill-advised New York hotel investment. A good example of his sardonic humour was when de Rothschild said after he had ridden a winner for him, "With all due deference to you, Maher, the best jockey I have seen in my life is Fordham." To which Maher replied, "So I have always heard, Sir."

MANNERS – John, 3rd Baron   d. 1927

Lord John "Hoppy" Manners served in the Grenadiers and was the archetypal laid-back Victorian soldier. A fine rider to hounds, he was Master of the Quorn when he decided to give steeplechasing a go, to which end he bought two proven Irish chasers. Within a season he had won the Grand Military Gold Cup on Lord Chancellor and the 1882 Grand National on Seaman, all the more remarkable as Seaman broke down at the last fence and was never to run again. Lord Manners than hung up his racing boots, and went back to hunting, having fulfilled every amateur's dream, and created a record in so doing.

MANNERS – John   d. 2009

John "Mad" Manners was aged 83 when he died from cancer. He trained a small string of point-to-pointers and hunter-chasers, including Cavalero (winner of the Foxhunters' (at both Cheltenham and Aintree) and Killeshin who Mad Manners bought for 1200gns from Ascot sales and came 7th in Lord Gylene's National and 6th in Earth Summit's the following year (1998). JMM was also known for his clashes with authority, as when he celebrated his first win by jumping over the rails and shouting loudly (£50 fine) or when he was banned for three years for failing to ensure that one of his point-to-pointers had a weight cloth.

MARGARSON – George

In 2006 speaking of the time when he was a jump jockey said, "I saw the arse end coming over and if I hadn't of got my head clear by inches that would have been it."

MARHAM – Gervase   d. 1637

Writer of a book called *Medicine for Horses* in 1616 gave the following advice: "They're fit for the saddle at four years of age, for the wars at six, for the races at eight, and for hunting or extreme matches at 10 or 11."

MARKS – Doug   d. 2007

Lambourn trainer, ex-jockey and comedian, with a number of owners from the entertainment world, such as Jimmy Tarbuck and Frankie Vaughan.

Apart from his wisecracks, his words of wisdom are many and memorable, as with his opinion of owners – the trainer's greatest problem in his view. "Owners are fine," he maintained, "no problem at all – until they win a race. Then, God help you. They reckon its easy from that moment on. They expect you to do it all the time, and they worry the life out of you if you don't." He said in 1975, "I have been everything in racing, except a horse." He certainly rode on the Flat and under Rules, taking out a trainer's licence in 1949, after winning both the 1000gns and Oaks in 1940 on the temperamental Godiva.

He also said, "I was a training nonentity until I was written about in *The* (*Sporting*) *Life*. Now I'm a famous nonentity."

QUEEN MARY – Wife of King George V

"Sad accident caused through the abominable conduct of brutal lunatic woman." The Queen describing suffragette Emily Wilding Davison, who threw herself under King George V's horse, Amner, in the Derby of 4th June 1913, injuring jockey Herbert Jones and causing her own death.

MASON – Jem   d. 1866

One of the great jump jockeys of all time, who first came to prominence in 1834 when he won the St Albans Steeplechase on The Poet by 20 lengths – carrying 4 stone deadweight as he only weighed 8 stone at the time – and after the horse refused at the first fence. This was a race run over various farmer's fields, often with strange configurations when a farmer refused right of way. In those days it was quite possible for a rider to choose his own line to the winning field, as long as he passed the flags on the right side. Certainly a horse might have to negotiate all sorts of going in the same race.

Mason also won the first Grand Liverpool (National) Steeplechase in 1839 on Lottery, who was so much better than his peers that he occasioned the start of handicap steeplechases. In 1841 Lottery was with the leaders at the water jump not far from home, when Mason pulled him up, realising the weight was too much for him. He was carrying 13 st 4 lb at the time having been penalised 18 lb for winning the Cheltenham Steeplechase. Apparently the horse wasn't at all keen on Mason, who often had to mount Lottery with his greatcoat on, so the horse could'nt see his colours, as he wasn't safe until he was in the saddle. Lottery eventually won his last race at Windsor in 1844 and it is said that after a period with Mr Hall's harriers at Neasden, he died in plough chains.

Two Mason anecdotes are worth recording. In a two horse match at Harrow, his horse Gaylad, was four times reduced to a walk and at the last, as neither horse could jump a stick, the onlookers pulled down the last fence and shoved Gaylad through so that he could just about walk past the post. Today a jockey who rode his horse to a standstill would be warned off for life. The second story shows a nicer side to the man. Tom Olliver, a three times winner of the National (once on the same Gaylad in 1842), of whom it was said, "He was born and bred hopelessly insolvent," was broke apart from owning a horse called Trust Me Not. He asked Jem Mason to buy the horse, but Jem replied, "Send the horse to me and I will win you a race." He sent Olliver £5 to pay the cost of transit, won the race and put Olliver on his feet again.

McCAIN – Donald "Ginger"   b. 1930

An ex-taxi driver, forever linked to Red Rum, the three times winner of the National in 1973/4 and 1977. He pestered Noel le Mare, a local Southport businessman, to buy him a horse he could train and that horse was Red Rum, by then a promising novice chaser. McCain's gallops were Southport's sands; maybe these helped him to a dramatic first National win over Crisp in record time. He reckoned that if a horse had ability, you could train it up the side of a mountain or down a mine shaft. His third win, ridden by Tommy Stack his former trainer, created a record that had not been achieved in 140 years.

Ginger said after his first National in 1973, "Liverpool has everything. To Hell with the prestige of winning at Cheltenham. I don't like the place." He also said, "Don't lets make the National a race for poofters and girls."

Southport Council in 1978 granted Red Rum the Official Freedom to Paddle, Walk or Trot on the beach where he trained and, at the height of his fame, his manure fetched 80p a bag.

He said to *The Racing Post* in 2006, "I don't understand how a man (Michael Dickinson) who can train the first five home in The Cheltenham Gold Cup can waste his time pissing about with flat horses in America." "I stick my tongue in my cheek and wind them up. When they ask you bloody silly questions you tell absolute crap and they take you seriously." (*Racing Post,* February 2006.)

His wife recalls: "He remembers going to the Waterloo cup when it drew bigger crowds than the Derby, although he very rarely remembered coming home." Ginger later retaliated by saying, "I've had two dogs in 22 years – my old dog died a couple of months ago and I miss her like crazy. I've had 1 wife and I think I might miss her when she goes, but I'm not sure yet."

McCOURT – Graham (Ire)   b. 1960

The Irish jockey said in 1996 shortly before retiring, "I came in on a winner now I'm going out on one."

McCOY – A.P. (Ire)   b. 1974

On reacting to news of Martin Pipe's retirement said in May 2006, "It's one of the few times on TV I actually felt like crying. It is one of the saddest things I've ever had to deal with in racing." Richard Dunwoody said of his co-rider Tony McCoy in March 2006, "People say they would get off their death bed to ride the Gold Cup. A.P. would get off his death bed to ride in a Taunton seller." In answer to the question why he's happy to have his life organised by others, said "I was born to ride horses not to do the dishes."

A national daily columnist said of him: "The Roy Keane of racing, an Irish jump jockey so single-minded in pursuit of winners it is a wonder some educated eejit has not referred him for addiction therapy." (March, 2006.)

McDONALD – Billy (Ire)   d. 2004

Californian bloodstock agent who was equally well known for notching up seven fiancees and for being shipwrecked on Alcatraz island in 1966, when trying to impress a local lady with his non-existant skills as a yachtsman. Unfortunately, the title of Birdman of Alcatraz had already been awarded elsewhere. He did find Alleged for Robert Sangster, who later won two Arcs (1977/8) and was syndicated for $13m. He became part of the Robert and Susan Sangster set, and while rich in wit and the ability to amuse, he was perennially broke. One of his more amusing gambits was to convince his latest girlfriend/fiancee that he owned Ballydoyle, or Coolmore, or the Nunnery (Sangster's Isle of Man house) or any other des. res. where he happened to be staying. His hosts usually played along. Charles Benson (*The Scout*) said in 1979, "Billy has been engaged seven times and had several near misses, including the most recent, and delightfully named, Dallas Sue – Billy has forgotten her surname."

Billy saw himself as a purveyor of champions to millionaires, and he was certainly a legend in his own lunchtime. Perhaps his most notable contribution to the annals of racing anecdote, was at the Earl of Derby's annual dinner held five days before the Epsom classic and always attended by the Senior Steward of the Jockey Club. In 1991 it was held at the Savoy and Billy was invited as one of the Sangster party. However he was very drunk before he arrived. Everything was fine until the Loyal Toast, when as cries of "The Queen" died away, Billy remained standing and raising his glass said, "I wanna take this opportunity while we're toasting the Queen to remember Bill Shoemaker" (the American jockey). 'Stoker' Hartington, the Senior Steward, nearly died of shock and as Robert dragged him down he muttered, "Whassamatter? Her Majesty wouldn't have minded. She likes him ... always has done." This small departure from custom later became known as Billy's Toast. As Billy was wont to say, "Nothing succeeds like excess."

M

McCRIRICK – John   b. 1940

An Old Harrovian, who filled various posts for course bookmakers before becoming a journalist. He worked on the *Sporting Life* from 1972-84. Then became At Large in *The Racing Post*; however it is his TV role in providing the latest course betting for Channel Four Racing, together with his tips, bookies jargon and outlandish dress, that has made him a household figure since 1983. In 1991 he was nominated one of the 50 Best Dressed Men in Britain, which could only have meant that the judge's panel was composed entirely of theatrical costumiers.

From his days as a bookie's assistant, he has produced some lovely one-liners: "A bank doesn't take bets and we don't take cheques," was one, and he describes his fellow hacks as the "most supine bunch of journalists in the world." In 1984 he said of Charles Benson (*The Scout*), "Quite the most nauseous spectacle was this Orson Wells figure ensconsed at the front of the Press Box, stuffing himself with lobster, swilling vintage champagne and waving condescendingly at the few rainsoaked unfortunates scurrying below whom he chose to believe were his friends." Benson of course was himself often equally scathing about his so-called friends. Fifty years on McCririck is the natural successor to Prince Monolulu – tipster extraordinary – the punter's friend.

In Septmeber 2005 he commented on Royal Ascot being held at York, "The Northern girl's chests were wonderful and the singsongs at the end of the days racing were truly emotional."

McGIVERN – Tommy (Ire)   b. 1957

Ex-jump jockey, who at Aintree one year was riding a no-hoper at the back of the field with Steve Smith Eccles when the latter started telling a joke. When he got to the punchline he found he was talking to thin air – Tommy was a faller. However S-E's horse fell at the next and as he was lying there, slightly winded, he was amazed to see Tommy come sprinting up. "Jeez," he said, "I thought I'd find you here. I knew you wouldn't leave me without finishing the story."

McGRATH – Jim

Ian Carnaby said of the man he felt was most likely to influence the destination of an attentive punter's final shilling, "There are times when his colleagues are made to feel like Dr Watson on a bad day."

MEACOCK – John

"His eccentricities, including giving his horses unpronounceable Persian names, transcended his lack of success and made him one of racing's greatest characters." racing anorak John Randall on the late trainer, whose horses included Vakil-ul-Mulka and Qalibashi.

MELLOR – Stan   b. 1937

The first jump jockey to ride 1000 winners in 1972, when joined by Richard Dunwoody in 1994 (he was joined by Peter Scudamore and John Francome in the interval) he said to the *Independent*, "The connection between all those who have got to 1000, considering what it takes, is that we must all be nuts." He retired in 1972 and became a trainer for the next 30 years with a yard in Lambourn, which he sold, but not before he had won two King Georges, a Whitbread and a Hennessy.

He also said of Fred Winter in the 1973 William Hill yearbook, "He didn't much want to be a jockey after he broke his back, but went on to be champion – four times. Then he was very dubious about becoming a trainer, but still saddled two Grand National winners in his first two years."

MERCER – Syd

The flat trainer tells a story which is a lesson to the uninformed punter. He had a very fast mare, called Wayside Singer, who he was putting in a sprint at Pontefract in 1974, with a colt named Young Vigorous, to whom she was due to give a couple of stone. However in a pre-race trial, giving the colt only a stone, the mare only beat the colt by a head, so Syd knew he was on to a cert. and withdrew the mare. As in the paddock, the horse's covering sheet only had a plain M on it, no one connected the animal with Syd Mercer and it started at 25-1. It only took eight seconds for Syd and the joint owner to back it to win £8000 and Young Vigorous flew in and broke the course record.

MILDMAY – Hon. Anthony (Later Lord Mildmay of Flete) d. 1950

He rode a horse called Davy Jones in the 1936 National, but forgot to knot his reins in the paddock before the race, an omission for which he was to pay dearly. Although only a 100-1 shot, with Golden Miller down at the first, and the favourite, Avenger, breaking his neck, Davy Jones was left in the lead. But at the second last, when 10 lengths ahead, the buckle broke as he slipped the reins through his fingers, and being unknotted, they parted, leaving Mildmay powerless to control the horse, who swerved and ran out at the last fence. In 1948 he was once again fancied to win the race on Cromwell, but once more disaster struck when he was up among the leaders. On landing after the third last, his neck muscles froze and his chin became locked against his chest, the result of breaking his neck in a fall earlier in the season. As he couldn't move his head, he couldn't see where he was going and eventually finished third. In 1950 he went missing after going for an early morning swim and was never seen again.

It was said of him, "There was never a harder rider, a better loser or a more popular winner."

MONOLULU – Prince Ras. (probably British) d. 1965

Peter McKay, better known as Prince Monolulu, was a well-known character on British racecourses after coming to this country at the turn of the century. He was also a highly visible one, with umbrella and baggy trousers, festooned with charms and ostrich feathers, as he sold racegoers his tips, crying, "I gotta horse... I gotta horse. There's five winners on a card." One might say he was a sartorial forerunner of John McCririck.

He really hit the headlines in 1920 when he publicly tipped Spion Kop to win the Derby; otherwise like all tipsters he had his good days and his bad days. His Book *I Gotta Horse* (1950) describes how he remembers punters losing their winnings either to cut-purses or the cosh, or gangs working scams with the bookmakers. Winners in those days were always marked men.

Max Miller, a comedian of the period, expanded on the tipster's theme with such quips as, "I backed him at 20-1...he came in at twenty past two!" "He's lying 4th, he's lying 5th... he's lying down!" "I backed him to win... I should have backed him to live." And, "They said the horse was a stayer... he should have stayed at home." I have heard a number of these wrongly attributed to Monolulu – if so they were hardly likely to separate the punter from the £1 in his pocket.

MONTROSE – Caroline Duchess of   d.1894

'Carrie Red' or 'Six Mile Bottom' as she was called, was 67 when she married her second husband, Mr Crawford, and came into a great racing stable on his death; her horses however ran in her *nom de course* of "Mr Manton." She won only one Classic, the 1000gns with St Marguerite in 1882, but laid the foundation for many more.

A strong personality, with a quick temper, she led her trainers a merry dance, and sometimes her parsons, since she endowed the Church of St Agnes in Newmarket. One Sunday, when the vicar included a prayer for fine weather – it being harvest time – at a time when she had a horse in the St Leger who acted on heavy going, she sent for him, saying "How dare you pray for fine weather in my church, when you know perfectly well it will ruin my horse's chance. I shall not allow you to preach here again." He retained the living for many years.

Once after selling her horse, Timothy to Capt. Machell, buying on behalf of another owner, who immediately landed the Gold Cup and the Alexandra Plate, she was heard to murmer "Two important races, and I haven't won a penny. They may go scot-free here, but One Above will surely punish them."

She also proposed marriage to the jockey Fred Archer – a novel way of retaining the services of the top rider of the day! In the end she offered him £6000 as a claimer (about £600,000) and eventually gave him a blank cheque; the sum was never disclosed.

MOORE – George

The owner of the sprinter Moorestyle was one of the first to realise that running a horse advertising his product – in his case kitchen furniture – could also bring dividends off the course. Mr Moore's knowledge of racing when he made his investment can be fairly assessed by his first question, which was where his horse would be "garaged". Unfortunately, this is not par for the course for owners as 95% of horses in training will show a loss. This means that more than half the owners win nothing at all!

MOORE – Ryan   b. 1983

The champion jockey said, "I can't believe people running horses for $25,000 haven't even bothered to do a good job of walking the course." And John Francome wondered why the Notnowcato's pilot was the only rider who deserted the far side of the course to find faster going and thus to win The Coral Eclipse, beating Authorised, partnered by Frankie Dettori 2007.

MOORE – Stan

"Stan Moore, the only trainer called after a London Underground station." Sir Clement Freud. in the *Racing Post*, December 2004.

MORLEY – Robert   d. 1992

This actor and owner was also a keen punter, and said "My father taught me that gamblers were much more desirable than sober citizens, for they were always on the brink of winning." In fact he preferred to be known by the codename allocated to him when he opened his first account with a bookmaker – "Tall Mast".

Years ago when he used to go dog-racing, he had a friend who told him you could tell which dogs were likely to win by the length of lead allowed them by the kennel staff. Dogs on a tight lead were the ones to watch. "All I can say," he said, "was that we followed the system for several weeks and lost a small fortune."

Never one to boast, he once said at Tattersalls sales, "I didn't realise I had such a valuable horse until I heard the auctioneer describe him."

He also claimed that if you disregarded the horses whose owners turned up in the paddock with wives and families and instead concentrated on the owner who brought with him a beautiful dolly-bird he was obviously seeking to impress – his was the horse who would be doing its best!

MORRIS – Mouse (Ire)   b. 1951

Trainer. "Being a jockey is the only job I know that you retire from and then have to start work."

MORRIS – Tony   d. 2010

"I've seen dozens who are better. Dubai Millennium wouldn't even get to knock at the door of the thoroughbred pantheon, less still gain admittance." In 2005, the writer took issue with Sheikh Muhammad's claim that Millennium was the best horse he'd ever seen.

Just after his hot St Leger favourite Meadow Court had been beaten in the 1965 race, Bing Crosby was asked for an autograph according to Tony, who was there reporting, Crosby rebuffed his keen fan with the immortal words – "Just piss off."

"A race on TV is a race on TV is a race on TV. They're all the same, can't convey atmosphere, can't stir the blood, can't move the soul. Racing was never meant to be watched through the lens of a camera, which can only provide a lousy substitute for the real thing." (*Racing Post*, 2005.)

MORRISON – Hughie

"If you give time to a big two year old you can end up with a good four year old rather than a bad two year old," said the patient trainer to the *Racing Post* in 2007.

MOTT – Bill (US)   b. 1953

"He's the best horse I've ever trained. He may be the best horse anybody's ever trained." On his US Champion horse Cigar and on his ideal jockey he said, "I like one who keeps a leg on each side and his mind in the middle."

MULLINS – Willie (Ire)   b. 1956

The Irish trainer is against the four day festival as is evidenced by the remark he made to *The Times* in February 2007: "I'd have to say we'd have one day of The Cheltenham Festival and three days leading up to it." Surprising as he has a tremendous record there, particularly with the champion bumper and he also won The Grand National with the 2005 favourite Hedge Hunter by 14 lengths. His father Paddy also trained Niclaus Silver to win The Grand National in 1961 before he had to sell him.

MUNRO – Alan   b. 1967

Flat racing jockey said of the exchanges that "They're a big negative. I could go out on a favourite, ride an honourable race, run into trouble, get beat and there's always someone out there who's had a lot of money on you to get beat."

MURLESS – Sir Noel   d. 1987

Clive Brittain, who worked for him for 23 years said he changed the whole system of training: "In Fred Darling's day high-spirited horses would be secured by three rack chains to keep them from moving about in their boxes. Sir Noel would only allow one. Old-time trainers would employ "twisting up" jockeys to really thrash a horse on the gallops. Murless also cut down on the ritualistic scrubbing and polishing of horses, which often resulted in sore skin." However he set great store by getting his horses as fit as possible at home and not on the course, which meant they were always trying. Lester Piggott, who came to Warren Place as a kid, recalled his first impression of Sir Noel, somewhat irreverently: "His hat was one of the oldest I had seen. And as he led his string out to exercise, I noticed his enormous feet and felt happy that I would never have to ride against him. I thought he'd only have to turn them outwards in the stirrups to make it impossible for anyone to pass him."

From 1948-1973 he took nine trainer's titles and achieved 19 Classic successes including three Derbys. He owed much of his success to Piggott, until 1966 when his manoeuvring and machinations to obtain rides elsewhere became too much for Sir Noel. It was their artistry that produced Crepello, whose brittle forelegs would almost certainly have resulted in his breakdown for any other combination. It was Piggott who gave his daughter Julie her first win in 1991 after she divorced Henry Cecil and starting training on her own account. She had known Lester since she was 10 and describes her old friend as "a very funny man." He later commented in 1996, "The business of training racehorses has gone the same way as prostitutes. Too many amateurs about."

M

MURPHY, Mick (Ire)

Ex-flat jockey living at Newmarket: "I've been in every stable bar the one in Bethlehem," the rookie trainer boasted whilst celebrating his debut winner Ballymartin Star's victory in a Tralee bumper in August 2005.

N

NAGLE – Florence   d. 1988

The racehorse trainer who, in 1966, forced The Jockey Club in The Court of Appeal to give licenses to women trainers. Lord Justice Denning said, "If Mrs Nagle is to carry on her trade without stooping to subterfuge, she has to have a training license." He was referring to the habit of women trainers at the time of either having a male friend or a stable lad to hold the license. The next year she took on The Kennel Club and achieved a double when they allowed women members as a result of her efforts. To breach two such all-male preserves was a remarkable feat.

She almost won The Derby in 1937 when her horse was narrowly beaten by Midday Sun, soon after which he was 'nobbled' and not much good thereafter.

NEVETT – Willie

Although champion jockey of the North for 25 years and winner of three wartime Derbys, he rode for many years in the shadow of Gordon Richards, to whom he was runner-up in the championship many times. When Willie first rode at Newmarket he is supposed to have overheard Gordon ask, "Who is this Northern jockey MacNevett?" "I'll MacNevett him," said Willie, and went out to ride three winners. This could well be an apocryphal tale as it wasn't really in Gordon's character. Both of them were natural lightweight jockeys, unlike poor Fred Archer to whom Gordon was often compared.

NEVISON – Dave

A professional gambler he said of the front-running tactics of jockey Joe Fanning, "Fanning must have some hypnotizing device tattooed on his arse as jockeys seem to allow this man to get away with it time after time." "I am not the snappiest dresser on the track but if someone comes up with a tip, I just look at their shoes. If they are wearing a £250 pair of Church's I might pay attention," the pro punter said to a national daily in June 2005.

NIARCHOS – Stavros (Greek)   d. 1996

The shipping magnate who joined the 1980s bidding bonanza at Keeneland at the same time as Sangster and the Gulf Arabs. His most newsworthy purchase was the Northern Dancer colt Nuryev for $1.3m, who later was first past the post in the 2000gns, only to be placed last due to Pacquet's reckless riding. Nevertheless, he was still syndicated at stud for $40m.

He later joined forces with Sangster and made a number of acquisitions through his syndicate, including Law Society who, racing in his colours and trained by Vincent O'Brien, won the Irish Derby in 1985. He also owned Miesque – by Nuryev – who collected the 1000gns in 1987 but was trained in France, as in fact were most of Niarchos' horses. He was also one of the 34 members of the syndicate who paid £10m for Shergar. It is interesting to think that the rustlers who made off with this prize from the Aga Khan's Ballmany stud in 1983 thought they had around £15m worth of stallion in the back of their wagon – in fact they had £500 worth of horsemeat! Shergar and any other top class stallion is worthless without his pedigree and the £70,000 fee for his services was based on legitimate reproduction. There was also no question of a ransom being paid, for to have done so would have put every other top stallion in danger, and there was not a member of his syndicate who did not have other substantial investments in the bloodstock business.

NICHOLSON – Herbert "Frenchie"   d.1984

So called as he was brought up and apprenticed in France, and was the modern day Svengali where creating jockeys was concerned. His legendary yard at Cheltenham was England's most exclusive riding academy, turning out among others Pat Eddery, Walter Swinburn, Paul Cook and Tony Murray, not to mention his son David, The Duke, one of yesterday's leading N.H. trainers (see under Nicholson – D.).

As a jump jockey in the 1940s he shared a title with Fred Rimell, and commenced training in 1946. He was a stickler for work and regularly mucked out four boxes himself before 7am; his motto was, "It's the little things that count."

NICHOLSON – David "The Duke"   d. 2006

He was known for fighting a seasonal duel with Martin Pipe, for the leading trainer's title over jumps, a title he won in the 1993/4 and the 1994/5 season with Adrian Maguire as his stable jockey; Martin Pipe, however, took the honours in the next 10 seasons – during which time the Duke died.

His father "Frenchie" sent him out on his first winner in 1955, and despite being exceptionally tall for a jockey – he was six foot in his tights and known to the French as "Le plus grand Jockey du Monde" – he rose to the top of his profession, even persuading the 10 yr old Mill House to win the 1967 Whitbread Gold Cup, after his confidence had been shattered by Arkle.

Most anecdote or quotations concerning the Duke highlight either his acerbic wit or his slight lack of humour, as when he captained the Jockey's cricket XI and on being told "Not out" after, as the bowler, he had loudly appealed for LBW, he marched over to John Buckingham the umpire, who was perched on a shooting stick with an injured leg, kicked the shooting stick from under him and said "Bollocks". Although he refused to speak to "Buck" for the rest of the match, he came up to him afterwards and asked him why he hadn't given the man out. When he was told the ball would have missed the leg stump he said, "Bloody good decision" and never referred to it again. The Duke was as competitive with his cricket as he was with riding and training, and this wasn't the only time he refused to allow the umpire to get the upper hand.

He summed up the Aintree starter Simon Morant by saying "He couldn't start a race for white mice." History doesn't relate what he said about Capt. Keith Brown! (See under Brown.)

Before he "defected" to Martin Pipe, Peter Scudamore was retained by the Duke in the early 1980s, and in 1986 at the Cheltenham Festival, they won the Triumph Hurdle and the National Hunt H'cap Chase. This was supposedly the meeting that a busload of Irishmen bound for Cheltenham, ended up in Devonshire because the driver followed the roads marked HR (Holiday Route) under the impression it stood for Horse Racing!

"They'll have to find some other bastard won't they?" on retiring in 1974, only to be reminded by the clerk of the scales that he had a mount in the next race. After his death Lord Vestey reminisced, "Cavalry Charge was sent off the odds on favourite but was beaten by a short head. David was booed into the unsaddling enclosure – Frenchie and I hid in the weighing room." Vestey had ridden a loser for him at Plumpton with unexpected consequences. As Nicky Henderson said, "He adored the sport, the horses, the people and the game itself."

NICHOLLS – Dandy

Ex-jockey, now trainer of sprinters, said just before he decided to quit the saddle, "I went outside, turned the sauna off, put the kettle on, made myself a mug of tea, got the scales and threw them into the field. Then I rang my trainer and my agent and told them that I wouldn't be riding that day or any other day." Father of Jockey Adrian and husband of ex-jockey Alex Greaves.

NICHOLS – Greg

When the Aussie ex-cricket Captain left the BHB in June 2006 he said "British racing is the best in the world. I get ostracised by my family for saying this because it is very un-Australian to accept that anything Britain does is superior."

NIXON – Sammy

"In my day we had Gully Gully, who dressed up in a black cloak as a wizard. He would have an apple in his mitts and suddenly it would disappear and come back cut in half with a tip in it." The 80 year old veteran bookie looks back fondly on his career. (*Inside Edge,* January 2005.)

NOSEDA, Jeremy   b. 1963

"If someone had told me when I started out training in England at the end of 1998 that I'd still be waiting to win my first English Classic, I think I'd have said, "Bloody hell, I don't want to be waiting that long." The 1960s icon was quoted saying this the day before winning the 2006 St Leger.

O

OAKLEY – Robin b. 1941

Former political editor of the BBC, as a contributor to *The Spectator*, he said, "Racing is the best fun you can have with your clothes on." He is also author of *Valley of the Racehorse – A Year in the Life of Lambourne* (Headline, 2000).

OAKSEY O.B.E – 4th Baron b. 1929

Born as John Lawrence, he was an amateur rider under rules for 20 years until he retired in 1975 on the advice of his doctor. He then became a well known *Racing Post* journalist and a much liked race commentator with ITV, the latter since 1970. However he wrote for the *Daily Telegraph* and *Horse and Hound* for 30 years until 1988, after which he received a written testimony from one of his readers: "Dear Bastard, You could not tip more rubbish if London Weekend bought you a forklift truck." Today he is mostly associated with the Injured Jockeys' Fund, based at Newmarket, of which he is now President, and a founding trustee since 1964.

His most notable riding successes were on Taxidermist in the 1958 Hennessy and Whitbread Gold Cups, and in the 1963 National, when he was second to Ayala on Carrickbeg. Like Devon Loch before him, he had the race won 50 yards from the line and then the seven year old ran out of steam and was beaten by 3/4 of a length. He is also the only person to have pulled up at Cheltenham when a fence in front, having convinced himself he had gone the wrong way, as he did on Pioneer Spirit in 1964. Ten years later he was second to Red Rum in the Scottish National and first in the Whitbread on Proud Tarquin, only to be disqualified and the race given to the Dikler – a decision he contests to this day.

Oaksey himself has produced a few neat observations on the sport: "In racing to insult a man's horse is worse than insulting his wife." "In racing there are fools, bloody fools and men who remount in a steeplechase." "The standard of permit-holders ranges through a large and competent majority, to those where neither the rules of racing, the science of training, nor for that matter the 10 commandments, play any significant part." "Fulke Walwyn was once kind enough to describe my style as 'a good enough example of the old English lavatory seat'."

"Arab involvement creating more jobs in racing and breeding, has generally been regarded as a good thing but it has also made it more difficult for the average person to buy quality blood stock." (When president of the Elite Racing Club 2004.)

O'BRIEN – Aidan (Ire)   b. 1969

The new Master of Ballydoyle was only 24 when he took over from Vincent O'Brien at the end of the 1994 Flat season, but is no relation to the Old Master. He only took out a licence in June 1993, when he took over from his wife, who as Anne Marie Crowley was the first woman to top the trainer's list in Ireland, but he came still close to beating Dermot Weld's record of 150 winners in 1994.

Having sent George Washington to stud and brought him back as a failure, Aidan said, "After covering 60 mares you would be a bit fresh, wouldn't you?" He was called in 2005 by *The Weekender*, "A grown up Milky Bar kid".

O

O'BRIEN – Vincent (Ire)   d. 2009

Legendary Irish trainer from Ballydoyle, Tipperary, who trained three Grand National winners on the trot between 1953 and 1955, Hatton's Grace who also won the Champion Hurdle three times (1949-51) and Vincent took the Gold Cup three times with Cottage Rake (1948-50) and a fourth time with Knock Hard in 1953.

The horse that put O'Brien on the map, however, was Cottage Rake. The young trainer was in the lavatory of a Dublin hotel when he overheard two vets discussing the horse whose sale had twice fallen through due to respiratory problems. "But at his age I don't think it will ever affect him." "I immediately told the only man I knew with any money to buy him." In 1947 he won the Irish Cesarewitch and the next year the first of his three Cheltenham Gold Cups. In 1949 he achieved a remarkable double by winning the first of his three Champion Hurdles as well with Hatton's Grace, an 18 Guinea purchase!

Although undisputedly the best jump trainer ever, by 1974 he had four Derby winners to his credit – including triple crown winner Nijinsky (1970), at which time he joined up with Robert Sangster (money) and John Magnier (Coolmore Stud) to form what was at that time the most influential triumvirate ever to hit the American bloodstock sales. Only three years later he won the Irish 1000gns and St Leger and the English Derby, The Eclipse and collected a hat-trick of Royal Ascot wins. In fact with only 18 winners, including Try My Best the top two year old in Europe, he took the English trainer's title. Between 1957 and 1984 he trained 16 English Classic winners alone, including six Derby winners ending with Golden Fleece in 1982 (to which can be added a further five Irish Derbys). He achieved a dominance over the Classics for 20 years in a way which is unique in modern Flat racing. It was in the line of Northern Dancer that he hit the genetic jackpot and with Lester Piggott that he established his hegemony on the Flat. He once said "A horse is like a car. He has only got a certain mileage. The difficulty is to discover how much it is."

However in 1986, with falling bloodstock prices, a virus in his yard, an infertile El Gran Senor, and a dead Golden Fleece (and no insurance money) he decided to go public. Vincent was Chairman, with Dr Michael Smurfit (Irish Racing Board) cattle king John Horgan, Sangster and Magnier as the main shareholders. However Classic Thoroughbreds, as it was called, by 1990 badly needed a Classic winner, and although Piggott in his first major "come-back" race provided them with one on Royal Academy in the Breeder's Cup Mile, he was only syndicated for his purchase price of $3.5m and the company was wound up in August 1991 with losses of $10.2m.

In 1973 Vincent had bought 50% of the nearby Coolmore Stud from Tim Vigors (see under Vigors), and it was his love of the land which prevented him from training in America or elsewhere, where the prize money was so much greater. He once said, looking back over his gallops, "I could never leave here – never," and he rarely travels without his brother Phonsie, who apart from almost winning the 1951 National on Royal Tan, is a superb judge of a racehorse. He also enjoys a reputation as a wit, raconteur and fisherman – often for bonefish on the Florida Keys with ex-President George Bush.

The Whispering Doctor, as he was known (a quietly spoken man, he was also given an Hon. LLD in 1983), was born with an uncanny rapport with thoroughbreds which enabled him to sense a spark of greatness in a young horse which could not be explained by conformation or looks. He was the Doctor Doolittle of the racing world, and his partnership with Piggott, professionally speaking, was like a great love affair – they were made for each other. In 1994, exactly 50 years after he had taken out his first trainer's licence, the Master of Ballydoyle finally retired at the age of 77, after winning a total of 44 European Classics. Piggott, who rode his first winner for him 40 years before, said: "He encouraged me to return to raceriding. I would not have thought about it otherwise." John Reid, another of his former stable jockeys, said "He was quite simply the best we will ever see."

Sangster put it another way: "He was a perfectionist and in many cases he achieved perfection." He died at the great age of 92.

O

O'GORMAN – Joe

After riding Panegyrist in a small race at Ayr in March 1989, when the horse at the age of 14, finally got his head in front after 38 unsuccessful attempts, was heard to comment, "Give him time – he could be useful."

O'LEARY – Michael (Ire)   b. 1961

Ryan Air owner, on winning The Cheltenham Gold Cup in 2006 with War of Attrition, said "I've died and gone to heaven."

OLIVER – Ken OBE   d. 1999

One of Scotland's greatest trainers, and one of racing's great characters, was the "Benign Bishop" who requested that The Carnival Is Over be played at his funeral service and that all drinks served afterwards at his wake should be large ones – they were! "Uncle Ken" not only produced five Scottish Grand National winners, but the perennial runner-up at Aintree, Wyndburgh, who would probably have won in 1959 (Oxo), since he was ridden by Tim Brookshaw with a broken stirrup iron from Bechers second time round. He was practicing interval training by cantering his horses up the Border hills in short spurts 30 years before its time, and inaugurated both the Kelso and Doncaster Bloodstock Sales. As an auctioneer he was guilty of one or two faux-pas as when anxious to secure another bid he turned to the under-bidder with "The bid is against you Madam." The man got up in disgust and left. On another occasion when his assistant asked him who the last lot was knocked down to, Ken said, "Over there, the fellow in the front row who looks like a baboon." He had forgotten to switch off his mike.

His first winning ride was on a one-eyed point-to-pointer called Delman. "I think we had one eye between us coming up to the first fence," he recalled. "Mine were tight shut." Latterly after a triple heart bypass he quipped, "One for blood and two for Tio Pepe."

O

OLLIVER – Tom   d. 1874

One of the nineteenth century's most colourful jumping characters, Tom was a brave and generous raven-haired gypsy who was hopeless with women and money and perpetually broke, which often landed him in a debtor's prison. On one of these confinements, the officers of a regiment he had coached in the art of cross-country riding, asked how they could help him. He replied "send me a damn good wall jumper". He won the National three times, was second three times and third once between 1842 and 1853.

His wit never deserted him as when a tedious owner asked about the staying chances of an extremely slow horse he opined "Honoured Sir, your horse can stay four miles, but takes a hell of a long time to do it". Of his rival Jem Mason, who had put him back on his feet by winning a race on Olliver's horse, Trust Me Not when Tom was otherwise detained, he said he would fight "Up to his knees in blood" for him. Tom added the extra L to his name since he felt it as well to have an extra £ at hand!

O'NEILL – John Joseph "Jonjo"   b. 1952

Although now a jump trainer at Gordon Richard's old yard at Penrith (Cumbria), his home since 1973, Jonjo is best remembered as the jockey who endeared himself to the public when, after partnering Dawn Run in her record-breaking Gold Cup win in 1986 – the first dual winner of both Cup and Champion Hurdle – it was announced he was undergoing treatment for cancer and would have to retire. Sadly Dawn Run shared his bad luck for, after winning 21 of her 35 starts, and prize money of more than £265k, she fell and broke her neck in the French Champion Hurdle in June of the same year, at Auteil.

Jonjo was champion jockey in 1977/78 and again in 1979/80, was rarely free of injury, but was nevertheless a strong and stylish rider. His other great wins were on Sea Pigeon (Champion Hurdle 1980) and Alverton (Gold Cup 1979).

O

In his early days he was once caught up in a hurricane in a novice chase at Newcastle. He was unseated: "I couldn't help it sir. I was blown off," he explained to his disbelieving trainer. He is also recorded as saying, "No sex before a race? That's a load of marbles. It doesn't apply to me or any other rider I know."

Jonjo, a Catholic, has doubtless been helped through his ordeals by keeping an open line to his Maker. He explains this as only an Irishman could: "I'm not very religious – but I'm a great believer in faith."

OSBALDESTON – Squire George   d. 1866

A great amateur race-rider, in 1831 he undertook to ride 200 miles in 10 hours for a £1000 wager, carrying 12 stone round a four mile course at Newmarket Heath (the now defunct Beacon course), changing horses every 10 minutes – a feat only beaten by Peter Scudamore in 1993, 162 years later. Although the Squire only used 29 horses against Scudamore's 50, he used 16 of them more than once and broke down one of them. The Squire's horses, like Scudamore's, were a mixture of racers, hacks and hunters, and one Tranby, was a highclass racehorse loaned to him by his friend John Gully, the prizefighter, and used no fewer than four times. Most of them had been tried out by the Squire during the preceding week.

He was disadvantaged by his age – 44, his weight – 11 stone 2 lb, and his need for sustenance during the contest – he stopped for three refreshment breaks of cold partridge and brandy and water, not to mention the fact that it was very heavy going – he rode during torrential rain, and that he fell off! When asked afterwards by a friend how he felt he said, "I am so hungry, I could eat an old woman." Additionally, he suffered from a bad back and had to wear a whalebone corset for support. The night before the race, in the Jockey Club Rooms, Osbaldeston took a side bet for £100 at 10-1 that he would finish in under nine hours; he did with 18 minutes in hand. This was not the only thing he did the day before the wager since according to one report he "had hunted his hounds in Northampton, and afterwards with the help of two hacks (presumably not the journalistic variety) he dined in Newmarket – 61 miles away!"

O

OSBORNE – Jamie   b. 1967

As a top N.H. trainer and ex-jockey (he was third in the 1993/4 season with 105 wins), and first jockey to one of the country's more powerful stables, Oliver Sherwood in Lambourn, it is interesting to find that 15 years ago he could earn around £100,000 a year in what has always been regarded as a poorly rewarded sport, certainly if compared with the Flat. As he currently is also single, still in his 30s and socially active when the next day's schedule allows, he is not nicknamed the "Corduroy Cavalier" for nothing!

Soon after he turned professional in 1988 he broke his back at Worcester and was off for six months – and considers himself lucky to walk again, let alone ride. He says that despite the fact that he was in breeches, boots and colours, a sister looked over his stretcher and said, "Oh, we fell off our pony did we?" Definitely a remark in the finest tradition of "Nanny knows best"! On the plus side, he can ride at 10 stone without much difficulty, so dieting and the sauna do not figure largely in his day. His main aim has been to win the big races, not to chase the title.

He says his agenda was to remain in one piece, upset as few owners and trainers as possible and keep on enjoying the game, much as he did in an incredible two hours at Cheltenham on the first day of the 1992 Festival, when he won the Supreme Novices, the Arkle and the Stayer's Hurdle in quick succession.

O'SULLEVAN – Peter CBE   b. 1918

Until his retirement the doyen of TV racing commentators and GOM of BBC's Grandstand, he also worked with Clive Graham (*The Scout*) for 24 of his 36 years with the *Daily Express* racing team, which came to an end in 1986. Before taking him on, Arthur Christianson, the Sports editor, laughingly said, alluding to his habits while working with the Press Association: "I am told that the terms will have to be sufficient to allow you to continue to stay at the Ritz in Paris." His speed of delivery and superb breath control prompted one journalist to say, "Had he been at Balaclava, he would have kept pace with the Charge of the Light Brigade in precise order, and described the rider's injuries before they hit the ground."

An owner too, his jumper Attivo won both the Triumph Hurdle and the Chester Cup and his champion sprinter Be Friendly won the Vernons Sprint Cup twice, the Hardwicke Stakes, and in 1968 the Prix de l'Abbaye with Geoff Lewis up. He was elected to the Jockey Club in 1987 despite his association with the media. How lucky for us that childhood ill health, originally diagnosed as an allergy to horses, was later proved wrong.

"I remember it clearly. The shop with its sawdust floor and the butcher with his straw hat." On recalling his first bet on The Grand National – two and a half p each way on 1928's hundred to one winner Tipperary Tim. (*The Independent* 2005.) "It's a photo... a six thousand pound photo I might add." Sir Peter talking about Attivo who got the verdict in the 1974 Chester Cup.

OWEN – Michael   b. 1979

The England striker said in January 2006, "If I was to appear on Mastermind, flat racing would have to be my specialist subject. It is also likely to be my career once I've stopped scoring goals" – which he was still doing in 2010!

OWEN – Capt. Roddy   d. 1912

As good an amateur steeplechase rider as George Lambton ever saw, he won the National in 1892 on Father O'Flynn at 20-1. The previous year he had ridden Cloister into second place but had objected to the winner, the Irish favourite Come Away. The Irish surrounded him, swearing they would have his blood, to which Roddy coolly declared, "Alright, but wait for the result, then I will fight every one of you – singly or the whole lot of you together." But as Come Away retained the race, he didn't have to.

O

When he was quartered at Aldershot, he was always away riding; so much so that his General – Sir Evelyn Wood, called him in to explain his absences. "Capt. Owen," he began, "I have been here for two months and I have not yet had the pleasure of making your acquaintance." "My loss, General, not yours," Roddy answered with a low bow. His C.O. laughed and gave him as much leave as he wanted. Four years later he died of cholera, while serving with Kitchener in Egypt.

P

PAGET – The Hon. Dorothy   d. 1960

One of racing's great eccentrics, her shy and retiring nature made her a recluse for the last 20 years of her life, but her huge inherited fortune – £1m at 21 – enabled her to race and bet on a vast scale both on the flat and over jumps; her bets were often for £20,000 – say £200,000 at today's money.

Her most famous racehorse was Golden Miiller, the steeplechaser whose greatness at his peak rivalled that of Arkle. She bought him as a four year old in 1931, paying £10,000 for him as a pair with Insurance, who won the Champion Hurdle in 1932 and 1933. Both were found by her trainer Basil Briscoe and unbelievably 'The Miller' won the Gold Cup five times on the trot (1932-36) In 1934 he was first ridden by Gerry Wilson, himself champion jockey seven times, who won the Grand National on him in record time, thus making him the first horse to complete the double. The Hon Dorothy then proceeded to give her trainer, jockey and head lad, admittedly among other gifts, a 3ft statuette of the horse – in chocolate! It is doubtful whether Piggott would have been amused. However she also erred the other way with her staff, for instance at Xmas when instead of putting 6d in the mince pies she filled them with cheques.

In 1935 The Miiller was an almost unheard of 2-1 favourite for the National and there was talk of a bookmakers conspiracy to prevent him winning. So when the horse dug his toes in at the Ditch and shot Gerry over his shoulder accusations were rife. Wilson believed it was a flare put down by a newsreel company which momentarily blinded the horse. However Miss Paget blamed Briscoe, who asked her to remove her horses from his yard. The Miller was eventually retired in 1939 – the winner of 28 races. Her legendary betting stakes were often based on somewhat unscientific methods; one was to decide the amount staked by investing the phone number of anyone ringing her up on the morning of the race – in pounds. In those days a call from one of her London friends would have resulted in a bet of thousands, but if they lived in the country probably tens of thousands. It is said that as she slept most days and worked all night her bookmaker allowed her to place her bets in the evening of the day they had run. Such faith in her honesty can only have been supported by her losing bets! According to her jockey, Scobie Breasley, who she always referred to as "that wretched Breasley" – probably because as an Aussie he always looked miserable in the English climate, in the early hours of one morning she once consumed 30 cold lamb cutlets. Once during the last war, her chauffeur-driven car broke down, making her late for a meeting. She vowed this would never happen again and in future a spare car followed her whenever she went to the races. Obviously petrol rationing didn't come into it.

On the flat she won the 1943 Derby with Straight Deal, and became leading owner that year. The daughter of Lord Queensborough was always conspicuous on the course by her bulky figure, lank dark hair and shabby clothes, usually an ankle length coat, shapeless felt hat, and Glastonbury boots. Apart from her extraordinary appearance, she will be remembered for her enormous appetite, bad manners, and unadvertised kindnesses – such as her visits to Wormwood Scrubs Prison. She was truly one of the Turf's great characters.

PAKENHAM – Anthony   b. 1952

Owner of Sir Percy, who had just won a cheap enough Goodwood maiden (later to win the 2006 Derby), explaining why he'd just turned down huge offers for his horse: "What would you do with the money? Spend it all buying lots more horses and never find one half as good as the one you've sold."

P

PALMER – Chris

Towcester racecourse chief executive said in September 2005, when he announced they would be charging a fiver to get in from October, "In some ways, letting in everyone free was an admission that we were a naff track with poor facilities."

PAYNE – George   d. 1878

A famous Victorian Turfite, who devoted his life and fortune to racing, hunting and cards, whose father was shot dead in a dual. Sent down from Christ Church College, Oxford, he lost £33,000 at the age of 20 over Jerry's St Leger win (1824), after which he retired to bed "to avoid giving wiser men the pain of looking at a fool." He later stood to win £50,000 on Savernake, when losing to Lord Lyon in the Derby of 1866. His only Classic victory as an owner was the 1000gns with Clementina in 1847 ridden by Flatman. He was a great friend of Admiral Rous, who thoroughly disapproved of his enormous wagers.

PEACOCK – Matt   d. 1951

Extremely dour Yorkshire trainer from Middleham, best-known for producing Dante to win the last Newmarket Derby in 1945 (after this it was run at Epsom, as it was pre-War), for Sir Eric Ohlsson. After being unbeaten as a two year old, sadly the horse had an eye problem which lost him the 2000gns, and eventually, after much uncertainty and rumour, caused him to be scratched from the St Leger. Matt's usual farewell after leaving a Southern meeting was "Goodbye! Now I'm off back to England." He also believed in getting his horses onto the racecourse as quickly as possible. "Gallop 'em for brass. They gallop for nowt at home and that is no bloody good to anybody."

PEARCE – Lydia

Owner of The Sprinter Stargem said in 2005 "She is a six furlong horse with a five furlong brain."

PERSSE – H.S. d. 1960

Trainer of the great Tetrarch, said in 1940, "Good trainers, like good wives, are born not made. Without natural flair it's better to keep away from racing stables and run a garage, for no amount of teaching will transform a horseman into a horse trainer."

He also said, "Small ears maybe alright on a Hollywood star but not on a racehorse." He went on to add that he'd never yet trained a horse with short prick ears and a pig eye that was not a rogue.

PETRE – Capt. Bobby d.1996

Winner of the first post-war Grand National in 1946 on 25-1 outsider Lovely Cottage when still an amateur. But within two years his racing career was finished; firstly, when exercising his horse, he broke a leg jumping off the sea wall at Bognor Regis, resulting in an amputation and then, after taking up training, he had his licence withdrawn when it was established that samples taken from a horse he had pulled up at Plumpton two months earlier, Bray Star, showed that a stimulant had been administered.

Petre continued to hunt, but it wasn't until 1985 that he was allowed back onto a racecourse (Aintree), when he and all surviving National winners were handed a trophy from the Princess Royal.

PESLIER – Olivier (Fra)   b. 1973

Prepared for the race "By putting a bottle of champagne in the fridge. Now I'm going to drink it," the French jockey said having ridden the winner of The Ascot Gold Cup in 2005. He also won the 1998 Derby on High Rise and was champion jockey four times.

PIGGOTT – Lester   b.1936

"The Long Fellow" dramatically, after a $4^{1/2}$ year absence, came back in October 1990 at the age of 54 to win the Breeder's Cup mile at Belmont on Royal Academy for Vincent O'Brien. Pat Eddery, when told of Lester's comeback plan, gave a disbelieving laugh and said, "He must be mad – good old Lester!" The next year he rode 49 winners in the UK and over 100 worldwide. He was apprenticed to his father Keith at the age of 12 – when he had one winner; still only 15 he won the Eclipse and the Wokingham Stakes, and in 1954 he gained the first of his 9 Derby wins on Never Say Die at 33-1. In 1984 his 28th Classic victory on Commanche Run in the St Leger broke the longest standing record in the sport – set by Frank Buckle 157 years before. He has taken 11 Jockey's titles and first retired at the end of the 1985 season with 4349 wins on British soil.

Thankfully stories surrounding Piggott are legion. Capt. Nicholas Beaumont, Clerk of the Course at Ascot, remembers the time when there was a commotion in the paddock caused by Lester trying to mount a grey from one side, with a very worried little apprentice trying to get up on the other. It was actually the youngster's ride but there were two greys in the race and Piggott could only remember his mount's colour. Lester's legendary meanness have bred one or two good ones; such as the stable lad leading him in after a big win saying, "Would there be a quid in it for me, Mr Piggott?" "Sorry I didn't hear you, I'm deaf in that ear," replied Lester. The lad, not to be put off so easily, ran round the other side and growing bolder said, "Will you be giving me £2 for the win, Mr Piggott?" "Try the £1 ear again, son," muttered Piggott. His deafness incidentally was not put on, being a childhood defect. Northern trainer Mick Easterby boasts of being the only trainer who got away without giving Lester a present by pleading poverty, as a farmer, when his horse Valerian had won at Pontefract. Apparently Lester countered with, "Can't you manage a bag of spuds?" Again after Crepello's Derby, Sir Victor Sassoon gave Piggott a flashy Lincoln Continental. Lester immediately invited Fulke Johnston Houghton's mother Helen, who was like a second mother to him, for a spin. However her enjoyment was somewhat diminished when he stopped for petrol and tapped her for a loan! Trainer David Barker obviously believed this. When asked in 2006 what he most remembered about him said "He once rode for my uncle and the horse dumped him going to the start. Lester sent my uncle the cleaning bill for his breeches."

Jeffrey Bernard was in Newmarket once interviewing Lester for the *Sunday Times*, after which Lester offered Jeffrey a lift to Newbury races in his aeroplane. A week later he got a bill for £35 – in due course this was followed by a reminder. Duly incensed, JB told one of the starting stall handlers who in turn told Piggott that Jeffrey was very annoyed about it. Apparently, Lester laughed so much he hardly made it out of the stalls. Most of the stories about Lester's meanness are really about him winding people up; perhaps he wasn't really mean, just very careful! He also lacked false modesty as when he was talking to the Queen after winning for her at Ascot, and when she said, "You made it look so easy Lester," he replied, "It *was* easy Ma'am." A couple of illustrations of Lester's dry sense of humour are to a furious trainer, who after he was beaten by a neck, said "That's it Lester, you'll never ride for me again." Lester replied, "Oh well, I'd better hang up my boots then, hadn't I?" And after being sacked by Vincent O'Brien. the next time he beat one of his horses by a short head, Lester brushed past a deeply unhappy Vincent in the unsaddling enclosure and grinned, "Will you be needing me again?"

Piggott, the supreme racerider, was a menace at riding work, when he usually ignored the trainer's instructions, belted along as fast as he could, and wanted the ride on anything that overtook him. He did this at Ballydoyle once, when instead of bringing on The Minstrel steadily, with the Classics in view, he brought him in blowing like a whale, commenting nonchalantly, "Something must have frightened him out there." O'Brien was furious and banned him from riding work for a month. However, after The Minstrel had won the 1977 Derby, he said "Had Lester not been riding I doubt if the horse would have won."

His height meant that he had to develop a unique riding style by raising his knees 6" above the withers and transferring his weight forward. This thrust his bottom absurdly high, and once when asked why he did it, it elicited the famous reply, "Well I've got to put it somewhere!" His dry wit is not always sufficiently appreciated as when, at a grand reception at the French Embassy in Washington, he turned to Johnson Houghton, as they were descending the wide staircase and whispered, "Shall we hold hands?"

After Nijinsky's Derby (1970) Piggott said, "He is without doubt the greatest horse I have ever ridden." However, after his defeats in the Arc and the Champion, Lester changed his mind and said, "Overall I'd have to say Sir Ivor (1968 Derby) was the best." Nijinsky was still syndicated as a stallion for what was then a record $5.44m.

Piggott has been accused of Machiavellian tactics to 'jock off' riders of well fancied horses, often when he himself was booked to ride another. The late Jeremy Tree, the Beckhampton trainer, said "You never knew whether Lester would definitely ride your horse until you saw him on it in the paddock." But Geoff Lewis points out "Lester was a businessman – it's no good being the best loser in the game.... I was too soft (referring to his allowing Lester to snap up 15 of Frank Durr's rides when the latter was injured) and it cost me the championship after being 20 in front of Lester at the time." However Piggott's callous attitude at times was not so forgiveable. After getting Commanche Run's owner to give him the St Leger ride in preference to the stable jockey, the American Darrel McHargue, Darrel chose to stay at home playing tennis, rather than travel to Doncaster. When the rain bucketed down on the morning of the race Lester was asked if it would spoil the horse's chance. "No," Lester replied, "but it might spoil McHargue's tennis." His blatant opportunism certainly cost him his contracts with Murless and Sangster. Lester's partnership as stable jockey with Henry Cecil struck oil straight away with the success of Fairy Footsteps at Newmarket in the 1000 gns (1981) and when the Daily Star's caption read "Fairy Footsteps winning the 1000 gns at Newbury." Lester chuckled, "That filly must be f.....g good. She started at Newbury and still won!" However it was Henry Cecil who inadvertently brought about Lester's downfall with the taxman.

Before the start of the 1982 Flat season, Cecil sent his owners a letter setting out the 'private' arrangements agreed with Piggott over and above his normal fees and percentages. These 'perks' would include shares in stallions he had ridden in a big race win and it was well-known that they were not officially declared. However one of the owners, a bloodstock agent named Walters, had a court case against Tattersalls in which Cecil was asked, but refused, to intervene. To get his own back, Walters circulated the letter, which by chance he had kept, to the Press and *The People* published it in February 1985 to give the I.R. the impetus it needed to mount a full scale inquiry into the whole cash payment system. Unfortunately for Piggott, VAT is only paid on recorded income, so when the Revenue started to unearth other payments he had the Customs and Excise on his back as well. It is ironic that while the prosecutor's name was Hidden – Lester's assets very clearly were not! However during the trial his humour did not desert him, when he turned to Cecil and said, "Do me a favour, Henry. While I'm away, don't write any more letters." The (probably apocryphal) story over what prompted the Revenue to act was Lester sending them a cheque on one of his undisclosed bank accounts. He eventually did a year at Highpoint open prison which he passed off as "A f.....g waste of time."

A suitable Piggott quote to end on is perhaps the one recorded by Simon Barnes of *The Times* just before his last race at Nottingham in 1985, when someone at the press conference asked, "Is there anything you haven't done as a jockey that you hope to do as a trainer?" Lester, after 30 years of near starvation replied, "Eat" – Barnes went on to describe Lester's breakfast as a cough and a copy of *Sporting Life*.

His own achievements are engraved on a special panel in the National Horseracing Museum at Newmarket, and of all his tributes there is one that sums it all up. Jimmy Lindley said "Lester was racing's genius. He was the best; nobody will ever follow in his footsteps. The Americans have a saying that a cavalry officer would ride a horse until it dropped dead and then an Apache would come along and get it to go another 20 miles. That's how it has been with Lester."

Tony Morris said of him after he'd won the Derby on Teenoso, "He was like the supreme artist plying his craft from the saddle, his genius as sublime as that of a Rembrandt or a Beethoven, and his accomplishment on the same plain." "He could even think like a horse." Jump jockey Graham Bradley said of his childhood hero. "That's one thing about not wanting to talk very much – I get time to read about racing, and to listen and to think," Piggot revealed in a 1970 interview with Kenneth Harris.

"Wasting's not much fun but maybe it's just as bad being a fat man." As quoted in a 1967 interview.

PIPE – Martin   b. 1945

The Somerset jump trainer who won a record 230 races in the 1990/91 season broke Arthur Stevenson's record of 2644 winners during the 1999/2000 season but in half the time! However he has had his share of failures – notably with King's Kestrel, bought as a yearling for £250,000 and sent to him by Somerset cricket skipper Roy Kerslake. His habit of pulling up half way through a race contributed to his total inability to win one; when last heard of he was being trained as a show jumper. Another failure was when one of his horses escaped from his yard and was making off down the road, hotly pursued by Pipe, when he suddenly realised his watch had come off. Martin is a very practical fellow and as the horse was only worth £500 and the watch £2500 he stopped chasing the horse to retrieve the watch, only to find that a car had already run over it and squashed it flat.

Pipe's mass-production of winners – numerically he is the most successful trainer of jumpers in racing history – has been largely the result of his advanced training methods and his horses' superior fitness, particularly at the beginning of the season, which often allowed them to indulge in front-running tactics. However his success gave rise to all sorts of gossip about doping and other malpractices. One West Country trainer said to Peter Scudamore quite seriously, "I know what he'd be doing; he'd be taking the blood out of the good ones and putting it into the bad ones!" The *Daily Star* even sent in one of their reporters to get a job as a stable girl.

Himself the son of a successful bookmaker, he once said " The bookmaker always wins in the end you know. That's why I'm here and he isn't." He also said that nowadays the bookies don't give you a chance and anyway he was far too busy to bet himself. One time he did gamble was when he took on the ex-Table Tennis champion Chester Barnes as his assistant – a gamble that has paid off despite Chester's unorthodox background. Another was when fancying his chances at the ping-pong table, he bet Chester he would beat him, and did.

Having saddled the Champion Hurdle winner, Make a Stand, at the 1997 Festival, he had to make good a promise to his son to buy him a £45,000 car. Luckily he also retained a 50% share in the horse, which he had originally bought for £8000, so he still showed a profit at the end of the day. He has still to win the Cheltenham Gold Cup. "I don't want to be here – I'd rather be at the sales buying Contraband." The horse later won the Arkle trophy at Cheltenham 2005. "That's another daft jockey I've got. He knew he was in for a bollocking if it went wrong, but he rode a great race!" The jockey was Tom Malone, who ignored Pipe's orders and went on to win on Cantgeton in October 2005.

"I don't think I've been on the cold trainer's list before, but I have to say in all honesty it's not a particularly nice place to be." (He just won a race with Lough Derg to break his losing streak of 47 runners at the end of 2005.)

He showed unexpectedly raw emotion on the death of Valiramix when he said, "He was an especially lovely horse and we kept his box empty for about six weeks. Whenever you walked past you felt his death all over again." (*The Guardian* October 2006.)

P

PITMAN – Mrs Jenny   b. 1946

The celebrated N.H. trainer, now retired after winning two Nationals, and who took out her licence in 1975, is not a good example of the gentler sex as some of her errant stable lads will testify. This was borne out by her affirmation, when the *Daily Mirror* dared to suggest that Burrough Hill Lad's recurrent leg trouble would prohibit him running again. "If I get hold of the man who wrote that rubbish, there is every chance of him being castrated."

Known to the Press as the 'Turban Lady', in deference to her preferred headgear, she has said "If you want to get rich, Flat racing is your scene. But if you want to be happy, steeplechasing is the thing." The outspoken Jenny has been known to stray onto what are normally regarded as male preserves: "No sex before a race? That's a load of cobblers. No one who knows jockeys could imagine them saying 'Not tonight darling. I'm riding in the National tomorrow.'" Jenny has always been concerned about weight: "If he were mine I wouldn't run a horse in the National with more than 12 stone." And then again, "If you want to understand weight… try running for a bus with your hands full of shopping. Then think about doing that for four and a half miles."

She still remembers applying for her licence at the Jockey Club, and thinking it rude when the stewards on the other side of the polished table whispered in her presence. When asked why she fell out with the ghost writer of her novels, Peter Burden, she remarked, "I don't buy books of the top shelf and my book ain't a top shelf book." (*Racing Post*, 2006.)

PITMAN – Richard   b. 1956

Ex-husband of the redoubtable Jenny, he originally rode for Fred Winter for whom he won the 1974 Champion Hurdle on Lanzarote. But he is best remembered for two races he narrowly failed to win – on Pendil in The Dikler's Gold Cup in 1973 and on Crisp in Red Rum's first National the same year.

He said about Crisp's National to *The Guardian* in December 2005: "I made a basic error and one which is unforgivable as a leading rider. I picked my whip up in my hand after the last fence when I should have sat still to keep the tired chaser balanced." As a race commentator with the BBC he was once stopped by a security guard at Belfast Airport who said, "What about your hat, Mr Pitman?" The beaming commentator obligingly lifted it and said, "Is there a rabbit, or is there a rabbit?" "Jasus! Mr Pitman," he replied, "There isn't even a hair!" He took over his wife's yard at Lambourn before he himself retired as a trainer in 2009. "Come back when you're not pregnant!" Useful advice from his Bajan waterskiing instructor to a portly R.P.

PONSONBY – Henry

He recalled one of his syndicate members saying "If you lose – you're concrete. If you win you can have Belinda for the night." Recalling a colourful member from the East End of London who arrived at the races with his glamorous blonde companion on his arm, as reported in *News Weekend* in 2005.

PORTER – John   d. 1922

One of the great trainers of the Victorian era, who between 1868 and 1900 had 23 Classic successes, including seven Derby winners. The unbeaten Ormonde was the greatest of these and was only really extended once – in the Derby with Fred Archer up – later beating the previous year's Derby winner Melton in the Hardwicke Stakes. Incredibly he won over only six furlongs on his last appearance at Newmarket in 1887. At his owner's (the Duke of Westminster) Jubilee garden party in London, Ormonde, having walked across Westminster Bridge from Waterloo, behaved impeccably – his only social gaffe being to eat the carnations presented by the Queen of Belgium.

There were three crack colts in 1886, but Ormonde was better than either Minting or The Bard, both of whom in a normal year would have been in the record books.

As it was Porter took the Triple Crown with Ormonde (and with Common in '91 and Flying Fox in '99). 1882 however was truly the fillies' year, since not only did Shotover win the 2000 gns and Derby, Porter also saddled Geheimness, the Oaks winner, while St Marguerite, a chestnut filly by Hermit as was Shotover, won the 1000gns for 'Mr Manton' (Caroline Duchess of Montrose) and Lord Falmouth's Dutch Oven took the St Leger.

Porter's other truly outstanding animal was La Fleche (by St Simon) bought by the immensely rich Baron Maurice de Hirsch, a friend of the Prince of Wales, whose racing manager, Lord Marcus Beresford, no doubt advised him to purchase the filly at a (then) staggering 5500 gns. She won the filly's Triple Crown in 1892 and should have won the Derby had her jockey, the erratic George Barrett, not ridden her so badly, leaving her 10 lengths to make up at Tattenham corner, which she failed to do by only 3/4 of a length.

He always said he "could train a good horse by the side of the road. It's the bad beggar that requires all the attention."

PORTLAND – The 6th Duke of   d.1943

His main claim to fame was as the owner of St Simon, which he became when Matt Dawson, his trainer, bought him for 1600gns at the sale of Prince Batthyany's estate despite a ruse by Dawson's brother John, the Prince's trainer, to daub one of his hocks to give the impression of a blister, in the hope he wouldn't find a buyer. His owner's death rendered all his engagements void, including the 2000gns, but he won the Epsom (now the Coronation) Cup, the Gold Cup and the Goodwood Cup, beating the 1883 St Leger winner, Ossian, by 20 lengths. He retired to stud the unbeaten winner of 9 races, and Matt Dawson said of him, "I have trained only one good horse in my lifetime – St Simon." He was champion sire nine times and produced 10 Classic winners.

The Duke in 1889 won £73,000 and gave the lot to charity; compare that with 1897 – only eight years later, when with more horses in training, he won one race – worth £490.

PRESCOTT – Sir Mark   b. 1945

In 2005 the trainer declared, "If you said to me would you rather win The Waterloo Cup (Greyhounds) or train a horse to win the Derby, you know, I'd rather win the cup." "We were beaten by a better horse and a nicer trainer." His comment on Pam Sly whose filly Speciosa had just seen off his horse in the 1000gns.

PRICE – Capt. H Ryan   d. 1986

He made his name as a jump trainer after the war, winning the National (Kilmore 1962) Gold Cup (What a Myth 1969) and three Champion Hurdles, but by 1971 he was concentrating on the Flat at Findon, after handing over his jumpers to erstwhile jockey Josh Gifford. He won the Oaks with Ginevra (1972) and the St Leger with Bruni (1975).

In 1967 controversy reigned after Hill House won the Schweppes Gold Trophy at Newbury with Josh Gifford up. A dope test showed a large amount of cortizone and the enquiry which lasted for 171 days eventually concluded the horse manufactured some of his own. Hill House ran 23 more times, often refusing to start at all, and never won again.

Brian Taylor, his stable jockey, remembered once seeing a betting slip of the Captain's, where he had a lot on at 25-1 – but each way. "But I thought you said he'd win?" said his assistant, which didn't phase the Captain a bit. "That's just in case the jockey makes a balls up," he said looking straight at Taylor. This didn't stop him telling the *Sunday Express* on another occasion, "I've never betted in my life. Never. Why I succeed is because I try with every single horse." Perhaps the thought was father of the deed as he again said in 1974 – "All the skulduggery over the last 50 years has been sponsored by the bookies." He also said, "Most of my quick decisions have been good ones. After all, I met my wife on Sunday and married her on Thursday."

P

PULLEN – Frank   d. 1991

Jump trainer and notable patcher-up of horses with bad legs, once allowed John Oaksey to ride a good old chaser which had won several selling races. On asking if he managed to buy him back alright, Oaksey received the scornful reply, "Buy him back? When I took the bandages off, they were fainting all round the ring!"

R

RANK – J.V.   d.1952

Heir to a flour mill fortune, whose interests later merged to become Rank, Hovis, Macdougall. His ambition was to win the Derby, Grand National and Waterloo Cup (coursing). Between 1935-38 he was second in all three – but two winners of the National slipped through his grasp. He was dissuaded by a friend from buying Reynoldstown (1935 and 1936) simply because he was black, and he died before his Early Mist (1953) won in the colours of his new owner – Mr J. Griffin. His Derby second was Scottish Union, who was also second in the 2000 Guineas, but did win the St Leger in 1938.

However he owned one of the great wartime chasers in Prince Regent, who because of the war could not race outside Ireland, where he was already a legend – winning the Irish National in 1942 carrying 12st 7lb – before coming over to Cheltenham in 1946 to win the Gold Cup. However now eleven, and carrying the same weight, he just failed to win the National on the run-in, losing to the lightly-weighted Lovely Cottage.

RAJPIPLA – Maharajah of   d. 1951

The owner of the controversial 1934 Derby winner Windsor Lad; controversial since the crowd thought that Rae Johnstone on Colombo, had pulled the horse, which was hardly likely as he later admitted he had been offered £10,000 to do so.

A few days before The Derby was to be won he was persuaded to see a fortune teller. She said, "You're going to win a big race – I think it's going to be The Derby." To which he replied, "You're telling me!" She was right because Windsor Lad won the Derby for him in 1934. However Charlie Smirke, the winning jockey, was himself boxed in, when he narrowly failed to win the Eclipse on Windsor Lad, and so gave the Maharajah cause once again to believe that a horse had been pulled. Within 10 days he sold the horse to Martin Benson, the bookmaker, who immediately put Smirke up again and proceeded to win the St. Leger. As a 4yr old Windsor Lad this time won the Eclipse and also the Coronation Cup – a rather expensive and faulty piece of moral judgement on the part of the Maharajah.

"TEASIE WEASIE" – Raymond OBE   d. 1992

Born Raymond Bessone, the flamboyant hair-dresser who, after winning the National in 1966 with Ayala, was refused admission to the Royal Enclosure at Ascot in 1968. However he was let in the next year and proceeded to startle both racegoers and horses with the colour of his morning suits – from Orange to Nipple Pink – until he was asked to reconsider his attire in 1983; surprisingly he did so.

He won the National again in 1976 with Rag Trade and pursued a number of manly sports, perhaps in an effort to counteract his effeminate image, including big-game hunting, where he upset his Eaton Place neighbours by parading his trophies on the balcony railings of his flat.

RICHARDS – Sir Gordon   d. 1986

Record breaking jockey – winner of 4870 races, champion jockey 26 times, the last at the age of 49 – and later trainer. Loyalty meant everything to Richards; in 1946 he refused a huge retainer of £7000 to ride for the Aga Khan in order to remain with Fred Darling until his retirement, and later rejected an offer of £100,000 to film his life story.

After his first win in 1921, he was asked by Martin Hartigan's travelling head lad why he had taken the horse round the outside: "Well, sir," he said, "you said he wanted it farther so I went farther (sic)."

Although not known for his classic successes, he won the fillies Triple Crown on Sun Chariot in 1942 and the same year the 2000gns on Big Game, both owned King George VI. When Tudor Minstrel was fourth in the Derby the public thought that Richards practically pulled his head off. One late-night caller had the nerve to tell him that he had found a horse's head and bridle on Tattenham Hill! Brownie Carslake, the jockey, attributed his success to one word – balance. Such was the strength in his legs that he could keep an animal balanced even with a loose rein in a desperate finish.

His training career, which he gave up in 1970, was something of an anti-climax. As he said himself, "I was a coaxing trainer, not like the genius who taught me (Darling). He would walk down the yard at night with his little stick under his arm and all the horses would stand to attention." Scobie Breasley said he never had a cross word all the time he rode for Sir Gordon – but there again he never gave him any riding instructions either. Apparently Graham Rock didn't agree with him when he said in 1978, "When Gordon Richards thinks one of his jockeys has lost a race he should have won, he is about as reticent as a Hyde Park orator."

In 1933, the year he broke Fred Archer's 1885 record with 259 wins, he rode 12 consecutive winners in the October, a world record. He won the last race at Nottingham, the next day he went through the card at Chepstow, and the following one he took the first five only to only to finish third in the last race on the 3-1 on favourite when he didn't think he could possibly be beaten. However he only won the Derby once – on Pinza in 1953 – after 28 attempts! Of Fred Archer he said "Don't forget that at 8 stone I had far more opportunities than Archer at 8st. 8lb. His achievement in 1885 was the greatest feat a jockey will ever achieve."

A fitting epitaph was provided by Noel Murless who said, "In my life I have only had 4 'greats' – Abernant, Petite Etoile, Crepello and Sir Gordon Richards".

R

RICHMOND AND GORDON – 5th Duke of   d. 1904

Although it was the Third Duke, when Colonel of the Sussex Militia, who allowed his brother officers to race on the crest of the South Downs, where he trained his own racers, it was not until 1829 that the Fifth Duke, in concert with Lord George Bentinck, established Goodwood Races in the Summer Racing Calendar. In 1839 his son, when Lord March, rode Guava to win the March stakes, and in the 1842 meeting he rode five winners, incredibly, since he was an amateur, four on the last day.

Charles' II's French mistress, Louise de Kerrouailt, created Duchess of Portsmouth and thought by many to be a spy for Louis XIV, was the mother of the First Duke, as indeed the King was his father. Several decades later The Earl of March, who by then owned Goodwood, talking to *The Daily Mail* said, "We have far too many chavs I'm afraid. I won't be asking visitors to wear morning coats but I would like to see the ladies in nice summer frocks with linen suits and Panama hats for the gentlemen." The Fifth Duke died when he was very nearly 100 years old.

RICKABY – Fred

"Rick" (d. 2010 aged 93), Frederick Lester (d. 1918 in the Great War) and William "Bill" (d. 2010) – Rick was Jockey to George Lambton for many years and was, according to Fred Archer, absolutely fearless. As a boy he was riding in a match for Lord Durham against Tom Cannon, who was a great match rider. Durham asked, "Are you afraid of Tom Cannon?" Rick replied, "No my lord, but he always beats me by a head."

He once rode a very promising two year old of Lord Randolph Churchill's into second place, but when asked by the owner afterwards how he ran Rickaby took a good look at the questioner and replied, "What the hell is that to do with you?" Lord Randolph was furious and told his trainer not to put him up again, whereupon Sir Frederick Johnstone who overheard him, said, "Of course with that old hat and coat of yours he mistook you for a tout."

One morning, on the Heath, a batch of horses came thundering by, and he was asked by a watching owner if that was what they called a half speed. "Yes," said Rick, "but it would take them a long time to find the other half."

Rick won three Classics, but his son young Fred was an even better rider than his father and by 1912 was first jockey to George Lambton. He won the Oaks and 1000gns four times by 1917, then joined the Tank Squadron and was killed in one of the last actions of the war, refusing to come home earlier when he had the chance to do so. However his son Bill Rickaby also had three Classic successes before retiring in 1968 to take up a racing appointment in Hong Kong. His aunt Iris is Lester Piggott's mother.

If you add the fact that it was a Rickaby that trained the 1855 Derby winner Wild Dayrell, you can safely say that the Rickabys are one of the great racing families of the last 150 years.

RILEY-SMITH – W.   d. 1954

Brewer (Smiths of Tadcaster) and owner, one of whose best horses was Scottish Archer, which he once rode himself in a bumper for which he had to make enormous efforts to reduce weight. He described these as follows: "The early martyrs were supposed to go through great privations but they were childs play with what I went through. I was dropped at York twice a week and walked home to Tadcaster, which gave me varicose veins. About three times a week for six weeks I got a tremendous sweat up by getting into the mash tub at the brewery. My meals were the sort Ghandi would have had when he got jaundice. I gave up wine, women and never sang a note. Came the great day, I went into the weighing room, where trainers pointed at my stomach and burst into fits of laughter. Feeling like a new-born babe, I still weighed out at 12st. 12lb and had to carry 10lb overweight!"

R

RIMELL – Fred   d.1981

Started life as an N.H jockey, was champion jockey before he became engaged to Mercy who was only 16 at the time, apparently they both liked to hunt. Fred was equally keen on racing, cricket and tennis. He was also a wonderful raconteur. However after breaking his neck a second time he gave up riding to become a trainer. He trained four Grand National winners at Kinnersley including Niclaus Silver, bought a few months previously in Ireland, and Comedy of Errors. When he died, Mercy, took over the yard, sent out over 230 winners including Gay Brief thus giving the yard a third Chamion Hurdle win. She retired at 70!

His most memorable quote was not reported until March 1994 in a daily newspaper when he said to Jim Old, who was still an amateur jockey at the time, "If Jesus Christ rode his flaming donkey like you just rode that horse then he deserved to be crucified".

ROMANS – Dale (US)

Trainer who reacted fairly calmly to his horse's (Roses in May) poor draw in the 2005 Dubai World Cup, when he said, "You have to dance with the lady you came with."

ROBINSON – Sir David   d. 1985

Although he won his first and last Classic in 1955 (2000gns – Our Babu) it wasn't until he sold his TV rental business in 1967 that he expanded his racing interests to become Britain's largest owner with 120 horses in training.

He was so retiring that he refused to make the Gimcrack Dinner speech in 1968 (although he did the following year). An extremely popular owner, he was never elected to the Jockey Club, who no doubt considered him a "box-wallah", but he probably didn't mind that much. His memorial is Robinson College, Cambridge; the funding for this and his other charitable gifts by 1985 reputedly amounted to £26.5m, for which he received a knighthood.

Ill health forced him to break up his racing interests by 1978, but he will be remembered for such good Classic horses as My Swallow, Tudor Music and Green God.

ROBINSON – Philip   b. 1961

The jockey made the following excuse as to why Rakti was spooked before his Royal Ascot defeat by Valixir in the 2005 Queen Anne stakes: "Some woman leaning over the rails started to click-click-click and it just set him alight."

When he was talking about the enigmatic Rakti in June 2005 he said, "He's good but he knows he's good… it's like a game of chess with him the whole time. He might do anything and if you make the wrong move, you'll upset him and that's it for the day."

ROBSON – Sir Bobby

Football manager explained his winner finding technique to *The Mail on Sunday* in 2005: "A woman in our group backed a horse called Half Free because she considered herself half free because she had a on-off relationship. It romped home at 33-1 and since then I've always looked at the names of horses for clues."

ROSEBERY – 6th Earl of   d.1974

Inherited Mentmore Stud in 1929 and spent the next 40 years as an active member of the Jockey Club, winning two Derbys with Blue Peter (1939) and Ocean Swell (1944) and three other Classics. Harry Rosebery did not hide his Jewish ancestry.

R

To a would-be buyer of one of his fillies, he chuckled, "You don't expect to get a bargain from me do you? After all, look at my pedigree – by a Scottish sire out of a Jewish dam!"

His naming of horses became a hobby; amongst his better efforts were Monty (after the Field Marshall) by Bellicose out of Exhibitionist; Caruso by Sing Sing out of Donna; Bun Fight by Combat out of Must Eat and for the double – Jolly Roger by Blue Peter out of Saucy Wench!

When he died, he was remembered as much for such remarks as, "The public don't count," and when he mislaid his binoculars at the first meeting in 1969 where members of the N.H. Committee were admitted to the Jockey Club stand, "Comes of having all these damned jumpers about" – as for the much needed reforms he brought in when Senior Steward. However, since he was one of the most intolerant men to have set foot on the Turf, few mourned his passing.

He also said in 1945 when President of The Thoroughbred Breeders Association, when discussing artificial insemination, "Suppose bottles of Hyperion or Fairway extract were disseminated all over the world – with hundreds of mares in foal to these two horses, in the course of a year the inbreeding would cause the breed to deteriorate beyond all imagination."

ROUS – Admiral Henry   d. 1877

The third and last of the great Jockey Club dictators after Bunbury and Bentinck. He turned the rough and ready racing of the 19th Century into the organised sport it is today. His greatest achievements were the introduction of rules for handicapping and administration as written in his Law and Practice of Horse Racing.

His reputation in the Navy was made when he steered the rudderless frigate "Pique" home from Labrador in 20 days in 1835. By 1845 he was ready to give up politics – he was MP for Westminster for five years – to devote himself entirely to the Turf. Although he admitted "...the game is up (if you) suppress betting by legal enactment", nothing enraged him more than to hear of colossal wins. He once wanted to expel a man from the Jockey Club who had won more than £50k on a single race. But it was as handicapper to the Jockey Club he would want to be remembered, a post he held from 1855. But even here he knew very well that if it was impossible to stop some animals winning it was equally impossible for others to get first home even under a featherweight. "I'll eat my hat if that horse wins," was one of his favourite remarks, which according to his friend George Payne, should have made a fortune for his hatter. One of his more eccentric habits was to hide behind The Bushes on the Rowley mile at Newmarket and suddenly jump out to egg on a jockey who was making a nonsense of his handicap. He maintained the public handicapper should be, like Caesar's wife, above suspicion; he was called "The great master of weights". Once, having dealt with one of the big races, he exclaimed, "There, now none of them can win." On another occasion when he discovered a jockey weighing in at 6 lb overweight – "Brusher" Wells the biggest man ever to ride at 8st. 7lb. – he cuffed him on the back of the head, roaring, "Get out! I'm ashamed of you." He also left the Jockey Club with rules to ensure its survival as an upper class and all-male institution. So much so, that it was exactly 100 years after his death that the first women members were elected.

"I always suspect that the improvement of the breed of horses means to get the best horse and to win the most money." Cynicism about breeding ruled in his thoughts.

S

SANDERS – Seb   b. 1971

Quoted by trainer Clive Brittain after Seb Sanders saddle slipped while partnering Extreme Beauty to victory at Yarmouth in July 2005: "I can't tell you how good the filly was, it's the part the wife will have to massage tonight that I'm worried about."

SANGSTER – Robert   d. 1994

The following story gives a good insight into how the young heir to Vernon's Football Pools had to be a winner at all costs. His first horse was a handicapper called Chalk Stream, which ran in the colours of his first wife Christine. Under the clever stewardship of Wirrell trainer Eric Cousins, the horse first won the Liverpool Autumn Cup and was considered a good thing for the 1961 Gt. Jubilee Handicap at Kempton. However as the horse could behave very mulishly at the start, Robert arranged with Eric, who was positioned high up in the stands, to signal to him down on the rails, only if the animal broke well, so that he could still get Major Upex of Heathorns to accept his £100 bet, which at 8-1 would be worth about £8000 today to the winner. He did and won, as Robert laughingly admits.

But in 1963 Eric almost ceased to be Robert's trainer, when his filly Brief Star, just got up on the line to beat Salan, also trained by Cousins, in the Ayr Gold Cup. Having left Eric in no doubt what would happen if Salan won, Robert turned to him and said "Of course you know I was only kidding, don't you?"

In 1971 two things happened which were to change Sangster's life, and with it the breeding of British bloodstock. He watched Green God win the Vernon's Sprint Cup to establish himself as top sprinter of the year. It was then explained to him how the horse had been syndicated the night before to go to stud for £60,000 win or lose – and how the sums worked for his new owners. The same day he was introduced to John Magnier, the Irish Stallion Master, who owned Coolmore Stud and who had set up the deal for the new syndicate. However, it was not until two years later that, in the company of Vincent O'Brien, the legendary Irish trainer, they first attended the yearling sales at Keeneland, Kentucky with $500,000 to spend. By 1975 the trio had concluded that their breeding policy would be to buy 'baby stallions' as yearlings and that they would concentrate on the line of Northern Dancer, the prepotent Canadian sire, who had already produced the great Nijinsky. That year's purchases ($2m) included a chestnut son of the Dancer, soon to be called The Minstrel, the eventual winner of the 1977 Derby.

However in 1979, the Maktoums entered the buyer's market and the Tipperary Syndicate had to raise their game to stay in. That year one of the 22 colts they bought for $13.5m. was by Northern Dancer, cost around $1m, and, as Storm Bird, later made them a record-breaking $28m. Although he hadn't run right in his only race as a 3 yr old after a disgruntled stable lad had hacked off his mane and tail, he had beaten To-Agori-Mou, the 2000gns winner, as a 2 year old, in the 1980 Dewhurst. As Sangster said at a press conference at the time "A top racehorse, or a top stallion, is an international commodity. He can be moved instantly to where he is most valued. Better still, he never answers back."

By 1985 even the Arabs were appalled at the escalating yearling prices and that Spring the Brethren – Robert, Vincent and John – were invited to a Summit in the Desert (Dubai) to discuss a possible collaboration in the sales ring, an event which heralded the bloodstock crash of 1986. Reflecting on the last four decades Robert said "For me its not been the glamour; its the most fantastic adrenalin kick, and if it goes on like this I won't make 60." But he did!

SLY – Pam   b. 1942

The trainer whose filly Speciosa had just won the 1000gns in 2006 said, "I hope this gives all the little people hope. Don't give up – you can do it."

Speaking about the same filly in August 2005: "We've got her on a magnesium based product which they apparently give to mental patients, but she's still a witch in her box."

ST. GERMANS – 9th Earl of   d.1988

Known as the "Bookie Peer" after opening up a turf commission agency in 1950 which led to him being a witness in the Francasal betting coup case, involving the switching of two French horses at Bath. He described how one of the conspirators had approached him to misrepresent himself as a Member of the Jockey Club to the Chief Constable of Bath to get him to deal with the small matter of cutting the "blower" line to the racecourse as a simple case of malicious damage. Failing this he was to offer the C.C.'s wife a fur coat! After declining this interesting opportunity, Nicky – Lord Eliot as he was then – phoned Scotland Yard.

A sometime owner and trainer, he listed his recreations in Who's Who as "huntin' the slipper, shootin' a line and fishin' for compliments."

St.GEORGE – Charles   d. 1991

The millionaire Lloyds Insurance broker and Chairman of the loss-making Oakley Vaughan Agencies, where he attracted a number of sporting personalities before going into receivership in 1988, the first Lloyd's firm to have done so in its long history. He did a yankie bet every Saturday, according to Jeffrey Bernard, who also said he was the kindest and most generous man he had ever met. When Jeffrey was in the Middlesex Hospital he was visited by Charles, who, as he left, slipped £200 under the pillow saying, "You'll need some money for toothpaste."

After winning the 1972 Oaks with Ginevra, he was one of the syndicate which bought Rhinegold, who was just pipped to the post by Roberto and Piggott (ironically later to become one of his losing Lloyds' Names) in the 1973 Derby, but went on to win the Arc. His horse Saumarez also won the Arc in 1990, but only after he had sold it. Nonetheless he won 56 Group races, 11 of them with Ardross, and had some notable winning bets.

When visiting his good friend, Lester, in a hospital near Longchamps, he arrived just as Piggott was about to pop a pain-killing suppository into his mouth. "Non, non Monsieur, said the nurse, pointing to his bottom. "Too late," Lester grinned, "I've swallowed two already."

In 1991 after watching Piggott riding Michelozzo's (1989 St Leger) half brother, Michelotti, to victory at York, he remarked, "One day I'll come back here in a wheel-chair and Lester will still be riding." A few months later he was dead.

SASSOON – Sir Victor   d. 1961

Owner/breeder of several outstanding horses, culminating in Crepello, the winner of the 1957 2000gns and Derby. Sir Victor was 75 when Crepello won the Dewhurst, but he always had suspect tendons and, throughout his career, raced with Newmarket cloth sewn on each foreleg. His trainer Murless, had to retire him before the St Leger, but Piggott maintained for many years that he was the best horse he had ever ridden.

In 1923 Sassoon came over from India, where his family were bankers and merchants, to take over the racing interests of Mr. Goculdas, a Bombay cotton merchant who had fallen into financial difficulties. He also came into over 100 horses in India where his nom de course was Mr Eve, a name he later gave to his

Newmarket stud. He proceeded to spend a fortune on yearlings (he inherited £15 million) but he didn't achieve his first English Classic success until 1937 when Exhibitionist won the 1000 gns and the Oaks, although he had won five Irish Classics by this time. Apart from Crepello, he won three other Derbys between 1953 and 1960.

Although he owned a bloodstock dynasty and enjoyed a lifestyle not dissimilar to the Indian Princes he had known as a young man, it is said that when he stayed at the Ritz, he insisted on laundering his own underwear. As a pillar of the Turf for 30 years, it is strange he was never elected to the Jockey Club; perhaps his Baghdadi Jewish background did not conform closely enough to Admiral Rous' rules of membership.

SAVILLE – Peter   b. 1944

Former B.H.B chairman talking to *The Racing Post* in 2005 about the betting exchanges said, "My instincts tell me that those who condoned the introduction of exchanges have created a dangerous cocktail that has already and will continue to bring racing into disrepute."

SCOTT – Brough MBE   b. 1942

Old Radleian jump-jockey with 100 winners to his credit before he retired in 1971, he has been racing correspondent for the Sunday Times since 1974, and was chief racing presenter for ITV before joining Channel 4 Racing.

Brough has made many quotable comments on the sport: "...the raffish excitement that something might have what the Irish call 'a little improvement about him,' is part of racing's attraction." "...the sport is a business, but above all a business to be enjoyed." "It's not just performance that counts – it's people." "Racing can't not have a crowd problem. Part of the fun is carousing." Most commentators are guilty of one or two stirring banalities, and *Private Eye* attributed this one (falsely according to Brough) to our hero: "Here comes the unmistakable shape of Lester Piggott – er – or is it Joe Mercer?"

But on Piggott's sentencing for tax evasion in 1987 he was more philosophical: "Now we've locked him up. That's sad, for while its proven how much he took, no-one will ever assess how much he gave."

He has also accused the Jockey Club of only being interested in the breed and discipline, which is no doubt why one of its members, Lord Cadogan, speaking to Brough in 1987, felt justified in saying "Oh! I think things have moved a long way. I mean my grandfather would never have dreamed of talking to someone like you."

He said in 2006, "Millions of pounds have been wasted in trying to market this game, but nothing so promotes it than the spectacle of top class horses coming back for more." Reacting to the news of Robin Cook's death in 2005 he said, "The first time I met him was at the second-last at Chepstow on Welsh Grand National day some 20 years ago. You don't really go there unless you really love the game."

SCOUT – The

Hereditary nom de plume of the *Daily Express* race reader and tipster. When Cyril Luckham retired in 1950, Clive Graham, ably assisted by Peter O'Sullevan, took up the challenge until he died in 1974. John Oaksey paid him the following tribute: "All men may not be equal on the Turf, but Clive Graham came nearer than any man I have known to living his life as if it were true. Lords or layabouts, bookies or billionaires, tycoons or tic tac men, stewards or spivs; the status mattered not the least to him. What mattered was the man."

Charles Benson, already 18 years on the paper's racing staff, took over his title, until he took early redundancy in 1986, and his exploits deserve a separate entry (see under Benson, C.).

SCROPES, Richard

Richard of Danby Hall in Yorkshire has as his racing colours "azure a bend or" (blue with a gold belt) and remembers that the first Duke of Westminster wrote to his grandfather for permission to name his 1880 Derby winner Bend Or, no doubt mindful of the historic trial in the Heralds Court in 1385 when his ancestors The Grosvenors failed to claim these colours for their arms as The Scropes proved their right to them as the "ablest tournyers in all the country", a title won by Sir William Scrope in an early Plantagenet tournament. The House of Scrope goes back to the Norman conquest, if not to Edward The Confessor.

SCUDAMORE MBE – Peter   b. 1958

Eight times National Hunt Champion Jockey, just before he retired in 1993, the iron man of steeplechasing beat an 162 year old record set by the legendary Yorkshire sportsman Squire Osbaldeston – in Scu's case not for a £1000 wager but to raise £50,000 for charity. The Squire used 29 horses, some more than once, to complete 200 miles in eight hours and 42 minutes, riding round the now defunct four mile Beacon course at Newmarket. Scudamore used 50 horses and superior tactics to cover the same distance with minutes to spare.

Peter's 1678 wins was a record, but despite his two Champion Hurdles (Celtic Shot 1988 and Granville Again 1993), he never won a Gold Cup or the National in 15 seasons. However in June 1989 Scu went to Cheltenham to ride in three heats against Bill Shoemaker the legendary US jockey, who at 57 was making a farewell world tour after a career of 8802 wins. The challenge was at 10st 7lb, riding hurdlers on the flat; Scu squeeked home 2-1 up.

He once played in a charity six a-side cricket match under the captaincy of Imran Khan, along with Johnny Gold, owner of Tramp, the London nightclub, Errol Brown of the pop group Hot Chocolate, and Denis Waterman the actor. Imran complained after they were beaten, that the team played abyssmally, to which Denis replied, "You can't ride horses, run nightclubs or act, so don't expect us to play cricket!"

Shortly after collecting his MBE, he was invited to attend a special party at Buckingham Palace, his third visit, for the Princess Royal's 40th, Prince Andrew's 30th and Princess Margaret's 60th Birthdays. As he and his wife Marilyn entered the ballroom, the Queen turned to Prince Philip and said, "Oh look, he's back again."

He said of fellow retired champion jump jockey Richard Dunwoody to the *Daily Mail* in March 2005, "He has acted like a lost soul since he had to give up riding."

SEFTON – 7th Earl of   d.1972

An active member of the Jockey Club who helped to modernize racing at Newmarket, and who was an owner of some good horses including the Coronation Stakes winner St Lucia. However, the public knew him as the owner of Aintree; occupation enough for a gentleman, at least in his view as evidenced by his reply once to the question, "What do I do? You might just as well ask a hottentot who his tailor is." Unfortunately, his sale of the Grand National course to the Topham family was not generally appreciated, and the fact that the nation nearly lost the home of steeplechasing's Blue Riband, was largely laid at his door.

SHARIF, Omar   b.1932

"I don't like to travel far to my racing – if you lose, a two hour return journey is torture," said the renowned actor, owner and gambler.

SIEVIER – Robert Standish   d.1939

Born in a cab, he was destined to become an adventurer, but Bob Sievier's main claim to fame was owning and training the amazing filly Sceptre, a full sister to Ormonde, bought for a record 10,000 gns in 1900 as a yearling. He was an inveterate gambler, winning and losing fortunes; in fact, when she was three, the debts he ran up in Monte Carlo in the spring forced him to put her in the Linconshire before she was ready, which, after backing her to win 40k, she lost by a head. However she then proceeded to win four out of the five Classics, losing only the Derby, and this due to appalling riding on the part of her jockey, Bert Randall, who allowed her to get left at the start.

In 1904 Sievier was forced to bring an action for slander against Sir James Duke, who had accused him of cheating at cards. He lost the case on a technicality, and shortly afterwards was "warned off" by the Jockey Club (rescinded in 1907), with no evidence whatsoever of having breached the Rules of Racing, although a lot of muck-raking had accompanied the court case. Unfortunately, his enemies among the Establishment chose to use this as a pretext for ousting this 'blackguard' from their midst. He got back at some of them by founding *The Winning Post*, a scurrilous paper largely aimed at libelling or blackmailing his enemies. As a result he appeared in court on several occasions and on one of them counsel asked him, "Are you not a gambler, pure and simple?" "I may be pure," Sievier replied, "but simple – never!"

It was rumoured he won £250,000 from the bookmakers before the Great War – around £10m in today's money; but by 1924 he was broke again. However, he was still capable of the grand gesture. When the Aga Khan cut him dead before the Cesarewitch, he was so infuriated he put everything he had on the Aga's filly Charley's Mount at 100-1, who came home unbacked by any of her connections. Seeing the Aga in the paddock before the next race, he shouted, "Hi, you!" And when he saw he had everyone's attention he bowed low and roared, "Thanks for the tip, Your Highness, I've just won enough to buy you a bloody banjo!"

SIMPSON – Barry

Racing manager to Sir Robert Ogden, said in June 2005, "La Chunga is named after a night club in Cannes. We always knew she was a very fast filly, and La Chunga is full of very fast fillys!"

SIMPSON – Rod   b. 1945

The trainer said, "I've been astounded how open doors have been – after all I've been away for a while. I never realised until now I was such a popular bastard!"

SLOAN – J.F. 'Tod' (US)   d. 1933

Came to England in 1897 and proceded to revolutionise both our riding style and tactics. According to John Hislop, "His short stirrup leathers and reins, low crouch and habit of making the running from start to finish, was at first viewed by the racing world in much the same spirit as Victorian society received Darwin's theory." They called his style "monkey on a stick", but Steve Donoghue and Danny Maher adopted it to English conditions with great success. Tod, however was a man of moods, and on one occasion lay down in the paddock, saying to George Lambton, the trainer, "I'm tired to death, I can't ride anymore." Then he saw the beautiful little two year old filly he was meant to ride; leapt to his feet and won the race easily. Fred Rickaby said of him, "If I were an owner I should not run a horse unless Sloan rode it."

Tod was abnormally short in the leg, hence the childhood name of Toad, which was later contracted to Tod. His name of course is immortalised in cockney rhyming slang with "on your tod" (Sloan) – hence "alone". He was discovered by the notorious American gambler George 'Pittsburgh Phil' Smith and he was always linked to syndicated gambling which his flashy life style did little to dispel. In fact after four seasons he was told not to bother to reapply for his licence, but not before he had won 254 races with an incredible 31.7% success rate.

He claimed to have $1m in the bank at one stage, but his nightly card sesssions with wild American gamblers soon relieved him of that, and he was eventually deported in 1915 for a gaming offence. He ended up as a barman in Los Angeles, where he died in the charity ward of the city hospital.

SMIRKE – Charlie   d. 1995

The cocky Charlie was retained by the late Aga Khan for most of his riding life. Unfortunately his relationship with Frank Butters, the Aga's strict trainer, was less than cordial, so that when he had more than one horse running, Smirke was often put up on the less fancied animal. This happened in 1936 when Gordon Richards was given the Derby ride on Taj Akbar, while Charlie had to content himself with the Guineas runner-up – Mahmoud. Charlie of course had the last laugh when Mahmoud won in record time; a record which was only beaten, by Lammtarra in 1995, although perhaps a trifle suspect as there was no electronic timekeeping in those days.

Butter's dislike was evidenced by a reported wartime conversation on the Heath, when Smirke was fighting in Sicily: "Gallop-watcher: Have you heard the news Mr Butters ? Charlie Smirke has been awarded the VC. Butters: What for? Watcher: For stopping a German tank. Butters: I'm not surprised, when he was riding for me he would stop anything." Apparently Alec Head, the Aga's next trainer, viewed him with equal loathing. As fellow jockey Edgar Britt said, "If Charlie's riding had been on a par with his gamesmanship he would have been the greatest jockey ever." Even so he numbered four Derbys among 11 Classic wins.

Known both for the quickness of his tongue as well as his fists – he trained as a boxer – his cockney wisecrack when he won the Derby on Tulyar in 1952, gave us the headline in the next day's papers, "What did I Tul-yar?" He has also been described as the first 'celebrity jockey' since his face was as familiar in West End night-spots as on the racecourse. Accompanied by his girlfriend Ella, he would regale his owners with amusing, if implausible, stories. Eventually someone would say, "Go on pull the other one, Charlie," whereupon an indignant Charlie would say, "It's true- honest! Gawd strike Ella if it ain't." Ella, a deeply religious girl, would go white as a sheet.

SMITH ECCLES – Steve   b.1955

In 1991 he became the ninth post-war jump jockey to ride 800 winners; unfortunately he had only added 61 to his tally when he retired three seasons later. As he said at the time, "I didn't give it up – it gave me up!"

However, he has provided us with some memorable anecdote, often in the company of his great mate, John Francome, with whom he shared the same wicked sense of humour. Paul Haigh of *Pacemaker* magazine tells how once when he was listening respectfully to some criticism from the stewards with his hands cupped behind his back, Francome who was standing behind him, suddenly unzipped his fly and slipped his member into the cradle. The stewards panel may still be mystified as to why their weighty words of admonition merely reduced Messrs Smith Eccles, Francome and Bill Smith to convulsions. Two days before he finished third in the 1986 Grand National, he claims he was hi-jacked in his own car, while he was asleep in the back as a result of being thrown out of the house after a row with his then girlfriend. On waking up to find it in motion on the Motorway with someone strange at the wheel, he shouted at the equally surprised driver, who stopped the car and ran off. Riding at Moonee Valley (Melbourne) he impressed the media, after winning the first two races, by bringing his horse to the front just as they were approaching the last in the steeplchase. The true story was as he went out on the last circuit he turned to Scu and said, "Why are all these Aussies in such a hurry? We've got another circuit to go." "No we haven't," said Scu. "Bloody Hell," Steve replied, and set off in hot pursuit of the leaders.

On another occasion, the dictates of losing weight led him into a somewhat embarassing situation, after he turned to the 'pee-pill' as a last resort. What he didn't realise was that there was a delayed action effect followed by a significant reduction in flow-rate. The net result was that he had to sprint down to the first fence at Fontwell to relieve himself, which became a five minute affair and caused a three minute delay in starting the race. As the race was being covered by SIS, the bored cameraman spotted the hapless S-E and beamed him live into the nation's betting shops with his breeches round his ankles.

The Aintree meeting for the National was something of a celebration for Southern jockeys who often stayed up most of the night drinking and playing cards. Steve recalls one occasion when the Duke (Nicholson) arrived to pick up his riders at 7am for riding out when one of them, John Burke, appeared still wearing his dinner jacket.

His most obscure objection story was at a meeting at Wexford in 1987 when a jockey called Pat O'Donnel was riding a fancied runner in a 10 horse race. Pat finished last but objected to the other nine runners for taking the wrong course. The stewards were obliged to study the video patrol film only to discover that the first nine had all gone the wrong side of a marker at the turn into the straight. The objection was sustained and Pat was given the race after the other nine had all been disqualified. Another time when the stewards held a bizarre enquiry was in Australia when a trainer was faced with the problem of getting a horse of some ability, who was inclined to dwell at the start, to leave the starting stalls in a five furlong dash. His plan eventually was to position his foreman (head lad) behind some bushes at the start, so that when he saw the starter pull the lever he could dash out of the scrub and crack his long stockwhip on the horse's rump. This he did with pinpoint accuracy; the animal leapt out of the stalls, led all the way and won easily. The trainer was given a small fine which was more than compensated for by his substantial wagers.

Shortly before Steve retired he said, "These days I may be the exception to the rule – a rare reveller among a breed of Perrier-sipping, calorie-watching, eight hours a night pros. I don't say they are wrong and I am right, but I do sometimes wish I had a bit more company." "Women jockeys are a pain. Jumping's a man's game. They are not built like us. Most of them are as strong as half a Disprin," declared the jockey in 1998, clearly not a supporter of the feminist movement.

SOUMILLON – Christophe (Bill)

The Belgian jockey discussing favours with *The Racing Post* September 2006 said, "When I ride in England, English jockeys don't stop me but they don't do me any favours either. It would be the same if an American jockey came to ride in France."

"Most French people after years of conveniently forgetting Soumillon is Belgian, are now reminding everyone of his nationality." A French based reader of *The Racing Post* said this after Soumillon's bizarre 'kiss my bum' gestures following his 2006 King George VI win on Hurricane Run.

SPENCER – Jamie   b. 1991

Flat jockey married to 'The Pouting Heiress' Emma, presenter for Channel 4, prior to visiting Zambia for Aid for Africa charity said to *The Times* in July 2006, "It will do me good to see what really matters in life. We get so wrapped up in ourselves as jockeys. Often I've left a racecourse after getting beat on two favourites and thought the world had come to an end." Tom Segal said to *The Weekender* in July 2006, when asked about him, "I call him the handkerchief because he's always in a pocket."

STEVENS – George   d. 1871

A frail jump jockey, riding at under nine stone, who nonetheless is the only man to have ridden five Grand National winners – three from 1856-64 and the last two on The Colonel in 1869 and 1870. In 1869, his mentor, the great George Olliver, said "... the last half mile is a long way from home. Be cautious and go not too soon; the post is the place to win at." George rode a waiting race and won by three lengths. Sadly he was killed at only 38, when his hat blew off, causing his normally staid cob to whip round and fling the best jump jockey in England head-first against a stone.

STONEHAM, Desmond

The French racing expert made the following declaration to *The Racing Post* in July 2006: "Racing in France struggles to attract sponsors, largely because racing is often not considered a sport, but merely an offshoot of the gambling industry by many potential benefactors."

STOUTE – Michael (Bbd)   b. 1945

He came to Britain in 1964 from Barbados and began training in 1972. However it wasn't until 1981 he achieved real fame and at the same time became leading trainer as a result of handling the Aga Khan's prodigiously talented Shergar, to win the Derby and the Irish Sweeps Derby. In the latter with three furlongs to go Shergar, with Piggott in the saddle, was coasting. As Peter O'Sullevan enthused, "He's only in an exercise canter." His four length margin was achieved without any apparent effort and Lester was looking around on either side as if for someone to talk to.

According to Julian Wilson, his cricket fell well below classic standard as when playing for his own XI against his stable lads, he marched to the wicket at 36 for 5, waving his bat at Wilson the other end with a business-like: "Okay, let's stop the rot" – only to be bowled first ball by a full toss.

His reply when asked why he decided not to enter Hawker's News in the 1994 Derby after winning the Lingfield Trial, was "To save Sheikh Mohamed a few quid on his entry fee." When his appeal was rejected against a swingeing fine in 2006, he said "I'll tell what I will say – I have nothing to say."

SWAN – Charlie (Ire)   b. 1968

Irish champion jump jockey who, for some reason, still rates one of the highlights of his career, finishing fifth on Last of the Brownies in the National. You would have thought when he first won the Irish National on Ebony Jane in 1993, it was a more memorable occasion.

In 1992 he figured in a bizarre incident when at Victoria (Australia) he took the wrong course while in the lead on the favourite, thereby costing punters AUS$300,000 (£140,000). His five week suspension was ultimately reduced to one, which allowed him to be fairly philosophical: "I like Australia and Australians," he said. "I hope to come back to make up for the mistake."

The same year, when he rode his 93rd winner, he broke Martin Moloney's Irish record, which had stood for 42 years. In April 2003, when he announced his retirement, a punter exclaimed somewhat wryly, "Swan – you should have retired yesterday."

T

TAAFFE – Tommy   d. 1967

"When I won my first bumper my first son was born. We named him Pat and jokingly said now we've found the new Tom Taaffe we've just got to find the next Arkle," is what the Irish trainer apparently said to TV viewers after Kicking King won The Cheltenham Gold Cup in 2005. He followed this up by saying, "He absolutely pissed it... it was the horse who gave me the idea of coming here."

TATTERSALL – Richard   d.1795

The founder of the firm of Tattersalls, known all over the world as an auction house for the sale of bloodstock. By 1766 Richard, a Yorkshireman, had amassed sufficient capital to build premises on a plot he leased from Earl Grosvenor at Hyde Park Corner, for the sale of horses. These sales were held twice weekly and soon 'The Corner' became a fashionable rendez-vous for London society, where carriages, dogs and hounds were also auctioned. A special room was even set aside for members of the Jockey Club. Towards the end of the century sales were also conducted outside the Jockey Club Rooms at Newmarket, until they moved to their present site, Park Paddocks in 1870. Just before this the London firm moved to Knightsbridge Green, where sales were regularly held until the outbreak of war in 1939. Their Monday sales were immortalised by H.M. Bateman in his cartoon 'The man who bid half a guinea at Tattersalls'.

However Richard was not only known for his sales rooms. In 1779 he bought a five year old horse, bred by Sir Charles Bunbury by Herod, who while unbeaten himself, became the champion 18th century sire. This horse was Highflyer – leading sire from 1785 to 1798 (with the exception of 1797). During this period his progeny won 974 races to a total value of £140,000, or about £50m at today's values. At stud he proved the ideal sire for mares by Eclipse. By way of a tribute, Tattersall had the following inscribed on his memorial stone: "Here lieth the perfect and beautiful symmetry of the much lamented Highflyer, by whom and his wonderful offspring the celebrated Tattersall acquired a noble fortune, but was not ashamed to acknowledge it".

TAYLOR – Alec   d. 1943

Trained at Manton, the classic establishment owned by Robert Sangster, as had his father and grandfather before him, and then his two sons. Between 1905-1927 he sent out the winners of 1003 races in this country and was leading trainer on 12 occasions – seven on the trot from 1917-23. He was not known as The Wizard of Manton for nothing.

In 1908 he trained Bayardo, one of the outstanding horses during the first half of the century never to win the Derby – probably due to interference during the race. However he won 22 out of his 25 starts including the St. Leger, and although his stud career was a short one, since he died at 11 years, he founded a dynasty through his grandson Hyperion, the 1933 Derby winner, who headed the sires list five times. Alec believed in very light work for two year olds and luckily his owners were rich enough to indulge him, but their patience was rewarded as his policy produced 21 Classic winners, including three Derby winners – two of which, Gay Crusader (1917) and Gainsborough (1918) won the Triple Crown.

He retired in 1927, a dignified and reserved batchelor of the old school, who always preferred to carry his own bag rather than take a taxi. This frugality presumably bore fruit, since when he died he left £600,000 which today would be worth over £10 million!

T

TAYLOR – Edward Plunkett (Can)

During the last war, Churchill appointed him to head the British Munitions Supply Council in North America, and afterwards he built up an empire in oil and metals, and with it a fortune which he later used to revive racing in Canada. While Chairman of the Ontario Jockey Club he eliminated most of the minor tracks and improved the better ones; probably no-one has done more for racing in his own country than EP. He maintained a separate racing establishment from his wife and at times competed against her. Once when his horse finished a short head in front of hers he received a cable from friends in England with the cryptic message, "Stop beating your wife." His laconic reply was, "At least I do it in public!"

However it wasn't until 1961 that the man became a legend. That year at Windfields, his Ontario stud farm, he bred Northern Dancer, a brilliant racer (1964 Preakness & Kentucky Derby in record time) and stallion, who became the most influential sire of English Classics winners since the war. The list is infinite, but his own crops include Nijinsky (1970 Triple Crown), The Minstrel (1977 English and Irish Derbys)and El Gran Senor (1984 2000gns and Irish Derby). At the height of the bloodstock boom in 1984, Windfields took home $17.7m for 14 of his yearlings at Keeneland.

EP's Stallion Master was Joe Thomas and it was he who made one or two highly quotable remarks as at the 1986 Keeneland Sales: "See those Nijinskys going through the ring at around $200,000? It cost $250k to go to the sonofabitch. Somebodys gonna be unpleased." Unfortunately the crash of 1986 meant that early in 1989 EP's son Charles had to close the stud as soon as Northern Dancer retired – but he kept one barn and a paddock open until the great stallion died in 1990. His last son went to Japan in 1989 for $2.8m. – a fitting memorial, but too late to save the farm.

TESIO – Federico (Ita)   d. 1953

When future generations ask, "Who was the greatest breeder, the outstanding sire, the best racehorse of the first half of the century?", the answer will probably be: "Tesio, Nearco, Ribot" – so said John Hislop, himself the breeder of the great Brigadier Gerard, of Senator Tesio, the Wizard of Dormello, which was the name of his stud by Lake Maggiore.

He bred, amongst others, Nearco (1935) was grandsire of Northern Dancer (bred at Windfields 1961, W. Taylor's Canadian stud), the most prepotent sire since the war, as well as siring Dante (1945 Derby) Nimbus (1949 2000gns and Derby) and Sayajirao (1947 Irish Derby and St Leger). Ribot, who raced in the colours of his partner the Marchesa Incisa della Rochetta, retired unbeaten after 16 races, including the Arc twice (1955/6) and the King George VI. His offspring, sired in Newmarket, Italy and Kentucky, are also a living testimony to the genius of his breeder.

Tesio won the Italian Derby 20 times between 1911 and 1953, the year of his death, and his findings on the laws governing heredity and inheritance in horses are still required reading for would-be breeders. He said "The thoroughbred exists, because its selection has depended not on experts, technicians or zoologists, but on a piece of wood : the winning post of the Epsom Derby. If you base your criteria on anything else, you will get something else, not the thoroughbred."

He used to name all his horses after artists – but his two greatest, Nearco and Ribot, are somewhat ironically named after two of the most obscure painters you could think of!

THOMAS, Peter

"For the cost of the day at Sandown Park you could probably record a whole month of Countdown, with Richard Whiteley's blazer allowance included." On discussing whether Channel 4 will remain committed to televising racing. (*Racing Post*, March 2005.)

T

THOMPSON – Derek   b. 1950

"It's win or bust. The jockey could win with a double handful." Thommo discusses the chances of Hayley Turner on her red car ride, Wunderbra, to which the show host quipped "The horse has his knockers." Hayley won at 5/2.

THORNE – John   d. 1982

Jump jockey who died after a fall in a point to point at Mollington, near Oxford, aged only 55. The year before he was runner-up in the National, riding his own Spartan Missile, even though he once said, "I always wanted to swim the Channel and ride in the National, but I was too fat for the National and too thin for the Channel."

THORNTON – Alicia   b. 1782

In 1804 at York, there took place a match which must have given considerable entertainment to the crowd of 100,000 who turned up to watch it on the Knavesmire. It was between Alicia, the sexy 22 year old live-in lover of Colonel Tom Thornton (53 years) and her love-lorn brother in law, a certain Capt. Flint and was for a purse of 1000gns and sidebets of another 500. The Colonel's horse, Vinagrillio, went lame inside the last mile of the four mile contest and Flint cantered home alone. The jealous Colonel refused to settle, and at the next racemeeting Flint horsewhipped him, for which he was thrown into jail. Whereupon Alicia, tiring of both of them, enhanced her reputation by next challenging Frank Buckle, the reigning champion, to a match over two miles, which she won, stunningly clad in purple and riding sidesaddle. Even receiving four stone this was a remarkable achievement, since Buckle had just won the 1805 Oaks and had 27 Classic races to his credit – a record in fact and one which was destined to stand until Lester Piggott surpassed it in 1984 when he won the St Leger on Commanche Run.

Quite a girl, La Thornton was once described as being "as fascinating as Anne Page," actress and then heroine of The Merry Wives of Windsor, "but hardly of such pretty virginities."

TREE – Jeremy   b. 1925

An ex-Life Guardsman and merchant banker who became one of the luckier Flat trainers, since two of his Classics successes were due to disqualifications. The first was the 1980 2000gns with Khalid Abdullah's Known Fact, by courtesy of Pacquet's reckless riding on Nuryev, and the second was the 1985 Arc when the Prince's Rainbow Quest was given the race after Sagace was disqualified for interference.

He did of course get three other Classics winners first past the post, and had three notable wins on the trot in the William Hill Sprint with Sharpo in 1980-82.

TURNER – William Jr (US)

"I grew up with Winky Cocks." An innocent remark made by the American trainer who used to hang around with Winky, son of hall of fame jumps trainer, W. Burling Cocks.

TWISTON-DAVIES – Nigel   b. 1957

"In the paddock we might talk about how pretty the girl next door is, but that's about it, because if I ever try to give him instructions he'll ask me just how many winners I rode." On his relationship with stable jockey Carl Llewellyn. March 2005, Llewellyn paid tribute to his guv'nor in The Cheltenham Festival: "I know for a fact he's got some pretty awful horses to win a race."

V

VAN CUTSEM – Bernard   d. 1975

As a trainer he gradually established the reputation as one of the shrewdest men in the game. While he was not known for his Classics successes – only saddling one English winner, High Top in the 1972 2000gns – he achieved prominence with the mare Park Top, when she won both the Coronation Cup and the King George VI as a five year old. He originally bought her with an American owner in mind, as a yearling in 1965. As he had been given a blank cheque and she went for only 500gns, he felt he couldn't place her with his new patron; instead he offered her to his old friend Andrew Devonshire. The Duke was not amused as he had owned her dam, who he reckoned was fairly useless, but he took her in the end. She didn't race as a two year old, and he nearly sold her at four years, but he was persuaded to keep her in training for another season, and with what result, since she also ran second in the Arc.

Van Cutsem was also trainer of some notable two year olds, such as Sharpen Up and Crowned Prince, winner of both the Champagne and the Dewhurst Stakes. His wife, Mimi, a du Pont, was happily a major share-holder in the syndicate which paid a record price for the animal.

VITTADINI – Dr Carlo (Ita)   d. 2007

A wealthy aristocrat from Milan, who will always be remembered for his horse Grundy, who apart from winning the English and Irish Derbys of 1975, defeated Bustino by half a length in one of the hardest and most moving flat races of all time – the King George & Queen Elizabeth Diamond Stakes at Ascot in the July. Dahlia, the winner for the previous two years, was five lengths away third, and her record for the race was smashed by 3.45 seconds. As the flaxen maned colt battled home under Pat Eddery, his trainer Peter Walwyn could be heard shouting "Come on my son!" and Grundy did just that. He was bred by Tim Holland-Martin and early on showed he had a certain presence, which was just as well as when bloodstock agent, Keith Freeman paid 11,000 gns for him on behalf of his Italian owner, he told Holland-Martin, "I don't know why I have bought that colt, I am not sure of his sire (Great Nephew), I don't like dams who just stay (Word from Lundy), and I hate his colour (chestnut), yet there is something very exciting about him." Holland-Martin himself said after the Derby, "You can marry Einstein to an actress, but to develop the perfect brain in the special body you have got to have the right upbringing." It certainly took all of Walwyn's patience at home and Pat Eddery's on the track to harness his brilliant natural speed to enough restraint to stay one and a half miles. All credit to Grundy himself, since in the preceding March he was kicked in the face only three inches below his left eye, which might have put a lesser horse out of training.

The good doctor has impeccable English, immense charm, a light hearted approach to life, and a daughter, Carla, who has twice won the Diamond Stakes at Ascot.

W

WALWYN – Fulke CVO   d.1991

The outstanding Lambourn trainer of hurdlers and chasers (five times champion) – particularly those of the Queen Mother – and prior to that of N.H. and flat racers for Hon. Dorothy Paget. He first achieved fame in 1936, when he rode Major Noel Furlong's Reynoldstown to the horse's second Grand National victory. Three years later he fractured his skull and had to retire from raceriding. His successes in the big races are still the stuff that trainer's dreams are made of with one National winner (1964), four Gold Cup winners, two Champion Hurdles, six Hennessys and seven Whitbreads, the last when he was 73 with the Queen Mum's Special Cargo.

The eccentric Hon. Dorothy Paget, 'DP', the owner of Golden Miller – five times Gold Cup winner, for whom Fulke won 365 races – was one of the turf's great characters. As DP lived at night, like Winston Churchill, she used to telephone her trainer at all hours. That is until the lovely Diana, Fulke's first wife, put her foot down and insisted on no calls after 10 o'clock. Fulke thought his 1962 Cheltenham Gold Cup winner, Mandarin, was the best and gutsiest horse he trained. However it took him two years to teach him to jump and two bottles of stout a day ! The same year, with Fred Winter in the saddle, he went on to win the French Grand National with a broken bit and a broken down tendon – gutsy indeed.

WALWYN – Peter   b. 1933

The Lambourn trainer is a younger cousin of Fulke, and son of the man who, after winning the Grand Military in 1920, managed to convince the Army that they should have a School of Equitation, at Weedon, of which he became the first instructor. His father also founded the British Show Jumping Association and frequently took his son to Cheltenham races while still a schoolboy. After this Peter's future career was never really in doubt.

In 1965 he and his wife 'Bonk' bought Seven Barrows from the Candys. Around the yard he is often referred to as Basil (of Fawlty Towers fame) and the following story only helps to reinforce this soubriquet. His hack had thrown him on the gallops two days running to his ever increasing fury – the third day it threw him again. Peter picked himself up and shouted, "I've had enough of you. Your b...y balls are coming off in the morning!" It wasn't until 1974 he won his first Classic (the Oaks with Polygamy) and with it his first Trainer's title. But in 1975 he really hit the headlines with a horse called Grundy. Not only did he win the 2000gns, and the English and Irish Derbys, he captured the King George VI by beating the four year old Bustino and the previous record by a staggering 2.36 seconds. According to Julian Wilson this was the Race of the Century.

Sometimes called 'Big Pete', he was explaining this to a French owner, who informed him that in France 'Grand Pete' means Big Fart! According to Jeffrey Bernard his annual thrashes on Lurcher Show days were never to be forgotten. Peter used to describe the gargantuan spreads attended by about 200 people as "nice when a few friends pop in for a drink." Equally every year on Derby Day he takes a posse of young people to Epsom to walk the course and partake of the fun of the fair. One year he ran into his assistant coming out of a clairvoyant's tent. She said, "She told me I'm going on a long journey." "You are," Pete replied, "you're taking our runners to Catterick tomorrow."

W

WATKINSON – Ian   b. 1948

Another jump jockey who rode in the 1970s and 1980s who had his own way of dealing with the overweight problem. This involved wearing 'cheating' boots on the scales before changing them back to his riding boots outside the weighing room. However at Stratford one day, the clerk of scales spotted the ruse and decided to autograph the sole of each boot, saying he would inspect them when the race was over. The crestfallen Watkinson had to put racecards in his soles, but they still almost cut his feet off. Once when riding a horse known to refuse at the start, he gambled on the same thing happening and, having cheated the scales with both boots and saddle to make 10s 7lb, he went to the start at 11-2, assuming he wouldn't have to weigh in if he won didn't complete the course (he'd have faced a suspension if he had). To his surprise the horse took off like a rocket and might well have been placed if he hadn't pulled him up, as if lame, and walked him over the line. This enabled him to shout "pulled up" as he passed the scales, and avoid running the risk of being asked to weigh in, which once a day all riders who have completed the course are asked to do. The next day the clerk collared him in the carpark and pointing to the *Sporting Life* said, "You told me you pulled up – it's got you down here as finishing fifth." "I shouldn't worry about that," Ian said, "they give these press jobs to anyone nowadays."

Ian was known as the Iron Man for his stoic attitude to his copious injuries. Once at Sedgefield, the St John's Ambulance men decided not to wait for the ambulance, and having loaded him onto the stretcher, made off at a brisk trot. This was uncomfortable enough but then the tail-end Charlie tripped, depositing Ian on the ground for the second time; this time face down. His resultant broken nose turned out to be quite the most serious of his injuries. Once at Wetherby he was so keen to ride Tingle Creek, the great front-running chaser, that he kept the ride after dislocating his knee in an earlier race, and – after being lifted into the saddle – made all after the first fence to win; a very painful experience. This was only topped on the occasion when he decided to ride Night Nurse in a big race at Ascot only three days after his second cartilage operation, which usually means at least a four week lay-off. He won on painkillers and then insisted on riding in a later race – he got thrown! He even tried to fulfil his engagements at the 1978 Cheltenham Festival with a broken pelvis. As it happens his rides were fairly mouthwatering, with Alverton (Gold Cup 1979) in the Arkle Chase (which he won) and Sea Pigeon in the Champion Hurdle (he came second, but won it in 1980 and 1981). Ian conned the doctor, but couldn't get out of bed the next morning and spent the next 16 days in hospital.

Eventually at Towcester, the fearless Watty had one fall too many, and after he regained consciousness, three days later, he had to retire.

WAVERTREE – Col. Lord (William Hall-Walker)   d.1933

A true eccentric who enjoyed master-minding a coup, having a row with his jockey and trainer, and winning classic races – probably in that order. He also depended on the stars to dictate every event in his life, including his racing strategy, which led him to sell Prince Palatine before he won the St Leger and two Ascot Gold Cups for his new owner. However he did win four Classics, including the St Leger with Night Hawk in 1913, besides breeding the 1909 Derby winner Minoru, who was leased to the King at the time.

After virtually giving up racing in 1915, after more disagreements with his trainer, Robinson, he gifted his Kildare stud at Tully to the nation, to become our National Stud (now the Irish National Stud). This was also foretold by the stars and left him with only one or two horses, acquired on the cheap, and the time and incentive to plan his coups. In 1923 one of these, Baydon, suddenly disappeared from his trainer's yard, apparently having been trained at Clarehaven in the interval, but as a hunter, before turning up at Ayr in clandestine manner the day before the Gold Cup. With no overnight declaration, there was no accurate list of runners until 45 mins before the race and as trainer Fergusson was unable to offer any explanation as to the horse's whereabouts, he was thought to be a non-runner. However on the day an obscure jockey called Stanton was engaged and won by two lengths at 100-6 to bring off a substantial gamble for his connections. John Hislop, who was assistant to Victor Gilpin at Clarehaven at the time, tells this story and confirms it was typical of Wavertree's quirky nature.

WEATHERBY – James

Appointed secretary to the Jockey Club and Keeper of the Match Book in 1770, since when a member of the family has held the position, coupled with that of Chairman of Weatherby and Sons, until the death of Simon Weatherby in 1983. Weatherbys are the administrative arm of the sport – one might say racing's civil service, without which the Jockey Club couldn't govern. Like civil servants they are discreet, loyal, shun publicity and are allergic to change. However they have played an estimable part in the development and control of the sport, employing about 180 people at the firm's base at Wellingborough, with a computer which fights a losing battle to cope with the multiplicity of tasks they undertake, and as a result suffers from terminal overload. Many owners and trainers have had a run-in with Weatherbys, but getting angry with them is both frowned upon by the Jockey Club and mostly unproductive. Born in the age of the horse-drawn carriage, like the club it represents, Weatherbys have not yet quite come to terms with the modern age.

WELLS – John 'Brusher'   d.1873

Died at the age of 39 due to 'wasting', the scourge of Victorian jockeys, which was to claim the life of Fred Archer a decade later, and Tom French before him, aged only 29. Tall for a jockey, he was also nicknamed 'Tiny', but this didn't stop him twice becoming champion in 1853/54 at which time he could still do six stone!

He won eight Classics, including three Derbys for Sir Joseph Hawley; Beadsman (1858) and Musjid in 1859 when it was said, "Not one jockey out of 50 who cared a straw for his life would have dashed through the mob of horses that shut him in as he did." When he won the third time on Blue Gown in 1868 the baronet gave him the entire stakes of £6800. His retainer however was said to be only £100. Custance said he was the "tallest and biggest I ever saw ride at 8st 7lb," although he was 6lb overweight when he won the 1867 Champagne Stakes, also on Blue Gown. He was a bit of a dandy and was seen just before the 1869 St Leger, which he won for Hawley, exercising the eventual winner, Pero Gomez, wearing an Alpine hat, a suit made from the Gordon tartan, and a pair of red morocco slippers.

WERNHER – Sir Harold (d. 1973) and Lady Zia

Former owners of Luton Hoo, in Bedfordshire where the Queen spent her honeymoon (Lady Zia was her godmother), and where latterly a good part of 'Four Weddings and a Funeral' was filmed.

Sir Harold, a member of the Jockey Club, will be remembered for Brown Jack, who after winning the Champion Hurdle in 1928, was switched to the Flat, largely at the insistance of Steve Donoghue who rode him for the next seven seasons, winning the Queen Alexandra Stakes at Royal Ascot no fewer than six times.

Lady Zia owned Meld, winner of the fillies' Triple Crown in 1955 and the Coronation Stakes, where Scobie Breasley, who rode the runner-up, said he had never seen such acceleration in a filly. Before she died at stud at the ripe old age of 31, she produced Charlottown, winner of the 1966 Derby, ridden by Scobie Breasley. Scobie and his wife were subsequently summoned to lunch at Luton Hoo, but instead of the "bloody great cheque" they were expecting, Her Ladyship handed over a gravyboat – silver plated at that. As Scobie said, "What a let-down. I suppose people as rich as that have little sense of what is of value to others."

WESTMINSTER – Anne, Duchess of   d. 2003

As her name is permanently linked with that of Arkle – one of the three greatest chasers since the war – it is often forgotten that she won another Gold Cup with Ten Up (1975) and the National with Last Suspect (1985). Arkle, trained by Tom Dreaper, was the Irish champion, and triple Gold Cup winner with Pat Taafe up, from 1964 to 1966, twice at the expense of the English champion Mill House, who he only lost to once in four meetings – the Hennessy Gold Cup, when he slipped on landing at the final ditch. However he took the Hennessy in 1964/5 when he added the Whitbread and the King George VI chase to his tally. It was in this race the next year that he broke a pedal bone and had to be retired to the Duchess's farm in Co. Kildare. His injury was all the more unfortunate since the

Duchess had already said, "I will never let my Arkle run in the National because I adore him, because he is one of the family and because he is much too precious to me."

Such was his domination that the handicapper increased the weights if Arkle was absent. His greatness was in some part due to a low heartbeat and his greyhound style of overlapping his forelegs with his hind legs which gave him both acceleration and finishing speed. He never fell on the course, and Timeform in 1966 rated him the "greatest chaser ever."

WESTMINSTER – 1st Duke of   d.1899

Reputedly the richest man in Britain, he owned and bred the great Ormonde, only the 4th winner of the Triple Crown in 1886, when he was ridden by Fred Archer. Apparently at the end of the 1886 season, he insisted on riding Ormonde at exercise, much against John Porter's wishes although he was an exceptional horsemen, after which he said it was "...the most disagreable experience I ever went through, his hind legs were so powerful that I thought I was going to be shot over his head with every stride. I knew perfectly well I had no control over the beast at all."

Before the start of the 1899 2000gns, Flying Fox caused innumerable false starts, so much so that the Duke had given him up. He eventually passed the post an easy winner, at which the Duke let out a piercing "View Holloa!" No member of the Jockey Club had ever committed such an outrage before.

WHITNEY – J.H. 'Jock' (US)   d.1982

From the time he and his sister inherited their mother's stud in 1944 he became a patron of British racing and as his cousin 'C.V.' had already inherited a powerful stable from his father, and in 1940 imported the English Derby winner

(1936) Mahmoud (see under Aga Khan) to become leading US sire in 1946, with more than 70 Stakes winners, they jointly raced a number of top stars in the States.

His most famous horse over here was undoubtedly Easter Hero, who won the Gold Cup for him in 1929 and again the following year. He might have made the sequence three, but his new owner, Capt. Lowenstein, a millionaire Belgian financier, insisted he be trained for the 1928 National, to the exclusion of the Gold Cup. After leading the field and treating the Aintree fences with disdain, he landed right on top of the Canal Turn fence and stayed there. In the melee, the tubed Tipperary Tim ran out the winner at 100-1, in much the same way Foinavon did thirty-nine years later. Shortly afterwards Lowenstein vanished out of his private plane over the Channel and Easter Hero became the property of Jock Whitney, who gave him to Jack Anthony to prepare for the 1929 season. After winning the Cup by 20 lengths, he again ran in the National, carrying top weight of 12st 7lb, and was only just beaten with the plate on his nearside fore broken and hanging loose. Along with Prince Regent and Crisp, he will go down in history as the best horse never to win a Grand National.

WHYTE – John

One of racing's first entrepreneurs, who opened the Notting Hill Hippodrome in 1837 – the first 'modern' chase course – when Lottery, the first National winner, won a chase on the first day's racing.

It was built on 200 acres of meadowland parallel to the Portobello Road, boasted three tracks, including a 2.5 mile chase course, and 75 boxes near the present Underground station. Unfortunately, the venture was a failure and the land was sold for building development in 1841; however by the 1850s the developers had run out of cash and the unfinished state of many of the houses led to the area's nicknames – the Goodwin Sands and Coffin Row.

WILSON – Emma-Jayne   b. 1983

Champion Canadian apprentice (aka Bug), although born in England, after chalking up over 250 winners said, "Sexism isn't a factor in Canada. People don't look at me as a female rider and I'm as hard and strong as anybody else in the weighing room."

WILSON – Gerry   d.1969

Having won the National on Golden Miller in 1934 he was jocked off after the next year's race for being too honest. After an epic dual with Thomond II, to win the Gold Cup for the fourth time (twice with Wilson up) The Miller at 2-1 was the hottest National favourite ever, and Gerry was offered a bribe to stop him, whereupon he immediately informed owner, trainer and stewards. On the day the horse was never going well after such a hard race at Cheltenham, and one before Valentine's tried to refuse, was driven on bucketing and twisting, and ejected the luckless Wilson from the saddle. Although the film camera supported his story, speculation pursued Gerry to his dying day, and although he wasn't sacked immediately, he was axed in the autumn when Golden Miller ran out with him at Newbury. The Miller was obviously soured off by Aintree's huge fences, since he refused at his next two Nationals, but ran well elsewhere winning his fifth Gold Cup in 1936. Previously the racegoers were described by the *Sunday Times* as "a more filthy and disgusting crew than we have yet had the misfortune to encounter," and of the horses, "save Hokey Pokey, there was nothing that could hobble or climb, much more leap over a hedge." Presumably they hadn't seen Lottery!

WILLIAM III 1689-1702

William of Orange was a keen betting man, winning races at Newmarket with a number of horses. His trainer/manager, the deeply unattractive Tregonwell Frampton, used his royal appointment to advance racing until his death in 1727. His post to all four monarchs was Keeper of the Running Horses. Eccentric of dress and hating women, he lacked all moral scruples; so much so that it was said that "Sin came upon the Turf with the advent of Frampton." However he introduced method and rules into racing and did much to improve training techniques.

A race was certainly staged at Beverly in 1690 and was soon established with cockfights to entertain the punters as well as the racing. This mixed fare soon became a feature at other fixtures. However the King's true passion was hunting and his death was caused by a fall while riding in the park near Hampton Court. His horse stumbled on a molehill – the King broke his collarbone and died shortly afterwards. A Jacobite toast at the time was, "To the little gentleman in black velvet." They were of course referring to the mole!

His reign saw the import of the Byerly Turk around 1690, one of the three great Eastern sires to whom all pedigrees can be traced. The second, the Darley Arabian, was sent home from Aleppo in 1704. By 1731 the last, the Godolphin Barb or Arabian, had been bought by Lord Godolphin from Mr Edward Coke – some say drawing a Paris water cart.

WILDENSTEIN – Daniel (Fr)   d. 2001

An international art dealer who has been a successful owner over here since winning the July Cup in 1975. However he has achieved as much notoriety as fame for his regular dismissals of jockeys and trainers. To have been sacked by Wildenstein carries the same kind of cachet as went with being jailed in Sweden, some years ago, for driving over the alcohol limit. He has dispensed with the services of Pat Eddery, Peter Walwyn, Lester Piggott, Henry Cecil and Walter Swinburn.

Although his star filly Allez France (1974 Arc) never showed her true form over here, he had three Classic winners in 1976 when he was leading owner. After removing all his horses to France in 1985, to sighs of relief all round at Cecil's yard, it was somewhat ironic that only two months later Eddery should win the Arc on Rainbow Quest on the disqualification of Wildenstein's Sagace.

When asked by *Pacemaker* magazine in March 2005 whether he knew a lot about breeding he said, "I've studied every book there is on breeding and, when I was growing up, my bible was Bobinski table of families."

While hardly known on the American tracks, he does owe something to the native American, since all his 1976 Classic winners were named after Red Indians or their tribes – viz. Running Water, Pawneese and Crow. Unlike most leading European owners, he has not been elected to the Jockey Club.

WILLOUGHBY de BROKE – John, 20th Baron   d. 1986

His title was awarded after the Battle of Bosworth in 1485 by Henry VII. A long-serving and outspoken member of the Jockey Club since 1941 and twice Senior Steward, he will be remembered for blackballing Christopher Soames in 1967 which led to the ending of the blackballing system in the election of new members. His presence in the audience at the Victoria Palace was acknowledged by the Crazy Gang hailing him as 'Lord Willoughby de Skint' in deference to his continual lack of success as a punter; he gambled away many thousands. His friends thought he was in fact 'broke' as he spent his last months in a very inexpensive nursing home, living mainly off sausages and corned beef. Although he bred and owned numerous winners in training with Harvey Leader and Gavin Pritchard Gordon, there were none of any real merit. Despite all this he left over a million.

Aly Khan said his wife, Rachel, had very pretty breasts; according to Woodrow Wyatt he should have known, as he saw quite a lot of them. He was fond of telling the story of an ex-black marketeer and would-be owner who, in 1945, got in touch with a certain Epsom trainer and enquired what the training fee was. He was told it was 5gns a week and 10% of any winnings, to which he countered with 4gns a week and his horse's share of the stable manure. Back came a very prompt reply, "Sir, if I have to train your horse for as little as 4gns a week, you can rest assured, on his feed, he won't be producing any manure."

He occasionally came up with another old chestnut: An owner asked his trainer at the end of the season, "Is there anything I should know about the animal when I take him home?" "Yes," he replied, "don't whatever you do let him out in a field without a halter – he's almost impossible to catch." But he still had the advantage of him. "Why on earth not?" said the puzzled owner. "He's not worth catching," replied the trainer.

WILSON – Julian   b. 1940

Old Harrovian racing commentator for BBC TV of whom one listener wrote, "Why does Julian Wilson have to say 'orf' in the review of a race? Orf is a disease which affects sheep." Also described by another punter as 'Mr Craven A'. He is a fan of Swindon Town FC. He writes racing books and has worked for the Mirror Group of Newspapers in various capacities which has allowed him to sound off on a number of topics, on which he has been less than enthusiastic – like Sunday Racing. He also breeds racehorses on a small scale and acts as racing manager for a few friends, some of whom rather unkindly report that his ears were developed specifically to act as air-brakes when going down the Cresta Run at speeds of up to 80 mph!

His high point as an owner was when Tumbledownwind won the Gimcrack in 1977 – which allowed him to have a go at the Levy Board at the Gimcrack dinner. Actually he admires the modern Jockey Club "They talk to you now, don't they? In the old days journalists were afraid to criticise them for fear of being warned off"(or even 'orf').

He said about South African racing in *The Racing Post* (March 2005), "Domestically the sport appears increasingly divisive, blinkered and threatened by public apathy."

WINTER – Fred CBE   b. 1926

Champion jump jockey four times, winning three Champion Hurdles, two Nationals and two Gold Cups. 1962 was his best year when he won the Cup on Mandarin and the National on Kilmore, not to mention riding Mandarin to victory in Le Grand Steeple de Paris with "no brakes and no steering" after his rubber bit broke at the third of 21 fences. Retiring in 1964 he applied for a job as assistant starter and was turned down – which paved the way to his becoming eight times leading trainer.

Fred's acid comments to jockeys and lads riding work for him were famous: to Jimmy Duggan after his horse had refused, depositing him the other side of the hurdle, he said, "You never stop improving do you?" As Winston Churchill once said to his son-in-law, Christopher Soames, when he was conferring with Winter in the paddock at Sandown, "I shouldn't bother to tell Winter what do. You are talking to a Master of his craft." Ryan Price echoed his words in 1980 (*The Racehorse*) when he said, "Fred? Well he's simply a genius. Funny because I never thought he'd make a good trainer." Nor apparently did Fred if he only wanted to be a starter!

WINSTANLEY, Mark

On a steward's enquiry that took place at Taunton into the improved display of a runner there, he is quoted as saying: "Thankfully, the carrot crunchers who steward the Zummerzet gaff had the gumption to enquire why L. Vaquero had shown more improvement than a Greek female athlete after a supermarket sweep around Boots." (*Weekender*, December 2004.)

WOGAN – Terry (Ire)   b.1938

Apart from being an enthusiastic follower of the sport from his early boyhood in Ireland, he achieved fame, some say notoriety, with Wogan's Winner, the daily selection given to 'a grateful nation' via Radio Two's Breakfast Show in the early

1980s – with an unspecified amount of help from Tony Fairburn, Director of the Racing Information Bureau.

Terry recalls in their book *To Horse! To Horse!* the Irish priest who announced to his awakening congregation, "this is the last Sabbath before Ascot," and then so far forgot himself during the Lord's Prayer as to say, "Thy will be done on Earth as it was at Epsom."

Terry himself saw the unfairness of racing when his horse, Wogan's Wager (he was part of a syndicate) strolled in a comfortable last in his first race; only to record four wins out of five after he had sold his share – the first two wins at 25-1 and 10-1!

He also tells the story of Fast Buck Billy, the professional punter, who at Churchill Down (US) abandoned form and logic after a losing sequence which cost him $250k, preferring instead to follow a dream which told him to back every horse whose name was associated with hats. The next day his friend, who was in on the plan, was mildly impressed to see him win $50k on Bowler in the first race. Billy then proceeded to recover his previous day's losses with wins on Sombrero at 10-1, and Gay Beret in the third; he went ahead with Stetson in the fourth. After Cap That captured the fifth and Mon Chapeau the sixth, his friend said, "What's next?" "Nuttin,'" said Fast Buck, "none of the names tie in with hats." The last race was won by Yamulka at 66-1 – a pity no-one told him its the little skull cap worn by orthodox jews.

Wogan's Winner actually showed a profit three seasons running and in the last of these the William Hill Organisation tells a remarkable story about a man who walked in, tipped £20,000 out of a suitcase, and asked for it to be put on Wogan's Winner. The bewildered manager asked him what the selection was "I dunno," the punter replied, "but I expect the BBC will tell you." They did and and it won at 5-2, which netted the man £45k after tax. The next day when he collected his winnings he left £25k to go on that day's selection – again without knowing its name. That won also at 2-1 making him another £45k; somewhat encouraged by this time, he placed £40k at 9-2 on what turned out to be Wogan's third winner in a row, taking our intrepid punter to well over £250k in total winnings. Hills never discovered his name and never saw him again. Nor did the Racing Bulletin Team ever get the statutory 'Wish you were here' postcard from whatever tropical island his winnings took him to!

Some years ago the Sheikh of Abu Dhabi was making a State visit to Britain and was invited to the Royal Box for an afternoon's racing at Windsor. John Rickman, who was covering the racing for ITV, thought the viewers might like to learn of the Sheikh's selection for the day's big race. The Sheikh approved of the idea and Wogan was appointed as go-between to convey his choice to JR who in turn would broadcast it to an expectant nation. The Sheikh's eagle eye eventually settled on a particularly unprepossessing speciman, who Gentleman John quickly confirmed as a 25-1 shot. On returning from his mission, our Terence was informed that the Sheikh would like to have a bet and would he arrange it. To say Wogan was in a state of panic would be to put it mildly; how could he get on even a 1000th part of the Ruler's daily oil royalties? Then he thought of the Tote and relaxed a bit – they could obviously cope with whatever he wanted to invest. After some voluble instructions in arabic, the Sheikh nodded towards a large gentleman in white robes, who turned out to be the Keeper of The Oily Purse. The purse itself was eventually produced from the innermost folds of the flowing garment and from its depths this huge man extracted a crisp new 10 shilling note (or 50p) which he handed over with great solemnity. The horse duly finished last and Wogan has the ten bob note to this day; being a gambling man himself he never put on the bet.

WOOTTON – Frank (Aus)   d.1940

The boy wonder and Champion Jockey in 1909 at the age of 15 – Fred Archer was 17 – took three more championships before he turned 20! When he was still only 16, and weighing 7st 4lb, he beat Danny Maher on the Derby winner Lemberg, getting up on Swynford in the St Leger. The effort completely exhausted him and that night he was heard shouting in his sleep, "I won't let you up Danny. You shan't get up."

His weight soon began to give him problems, and although he was a brilliant horseman with an uncanny ability to sum up other horse's capabilities, his career on the Flat only lasted seven years. He actually rode seven winners at Royal Ascot in 1912. After serving in Mesopotamia in the Great War, during which he won the Baghdad Grand National, he turned to riding under rules after the war and topped the NH table in 1921 to become the only man ever to head both lists.

WRAGG – Harry   d.1985

Leading rider in 1941 he won three Derbys – between 1928 and 1942, and 10 other Classics. He also won the Eclipse five times. He then trained at Newmarket for 26 years from 1947, winning all the English and Irish Classics, bar two (the Irish St Leger and the English Oaks).

He was known as 'The Head Waiter' because of his highly successful waiting tactics, a nick-name he owed to an anonymous punter who was heard to say "… that bugger could be head waiter at the Cafe Royal." Arguably his best quote was, "If a racehorse could talk, one of the first things he would tell his jockey would be 'If you don't know where the bloody winning post is, I'm sure I don't'."

Harry was also a brilliant opportunist and outwitted Gordon Richards on one occasion, when an obsequious starter, seeing that Gordon's horse was acting up, called out, "Are you ready Mr Richards?" Quick as a flash, Wragg called back, "Yes sir I'm ready." The tapes went up and Harry shot off to win the race comfortably.

Y

YORK – Frederick Duke of 1763–1827

One of George III's deeply unattractive sons, who nevertheless won the Derby twice – once in 1816 with Prince Leopold (running in the name of Mr Lake the Duke's Master of Horse) and again in 1822 with Moses. He was such an inveterate gambler, that when he died, to discharge his mountain of debt, the Government is said to have ceded Cape Breton to his creditors.

Z

ZETLAND – 2nd Earl of   d. 1873

Lord Lieutenant of Ireland, his fame on the racecourse is chiefly the result of owning Voltiguer, the 1850 Derby winner. However shortly before the race he was asked to pay nomination forfeits of £400 to guarantee a run. With true aristocratic disdain, since he didn't bet himself, he withdrew the horse to the consternation of his estate workers and tenants, who had bet their all on the horse alongside many other punters. Eventually they got his brother-in-law, Mr Williamson, to intercede for them and he changed his mind. Voltiguer won at 16-1, making we are told £200 for his coachman, worth about £30,000 in today's money. The next year at York, the same horse won one of the most famous matches in British racing history, against The Flying Dutchman.